# Praise for *Argo CD: Up and Running*

This book from two leading Argo experts is clear and to the point. You'll be up to speed quickly and well on your way to being an advanced Argo practitioner.

*—Michael Crenshaw, staff SWE and lead Argo CD maintainer, Intuit*

If you want a guide that masterfully demystifies the Argo CD and GitOps world, look no further. Whether you're just beginning or fine-tuning a production setup, the authors distill years of practical experience condensed into this book that will serve as a trusted reference long after the first read.

*—Lipi Deepaakshi Patnaik, senior software developer, Zeta Suite*

I wish I had this book when I first started learning Argo CD—it would have made implementation so much easier.

*—Werner Dijkerman, Kubernetes and DevOps engineer, Awesome Cloud*

Andrew and Christian discuss several applicable examples in-depth at an enjoyable reading pace—a practical reference!

*—Nadir Doctor, architect*

This book is a must-read for anyone adopting GitOps with Kubernetes and Argo CD. It provides the practical guidance needed to effectively get started with Argo CD and scale it for use in multi-cluster environments.

*—Manuel Dewald, lead software architect at Codesphere and coauthor of* Operating OpenShift

Working with Andy and Christian, you naturally learn by osmosis. I'm thrilled they've captured their deep knowledge of real-world GitOps patterns and advanced Argo CD in this book, allowing anyone to benefit from their proven experience and be inspired by their passion.

*—Natale Vinto, director of developer advocacy, Red Hat*

In my experience, GitOps and Argo CD are widely deployed but commonly misunderstood. Andrew and Christian are working hard to change this, covering both the theory and the execution. This book is my go-to reference for everything from deploying applications to operationalizing Argo CD.

*—Daniel Bryant, platform engineer and PMM, Syntasso*

The authors have done an outstanding job curating a thoughtful and thorough journey through Argo CD. Whether you're deploying your first application or scaling GitOps in an enterprise setting, this book equips you with the tools and mindset you need to succeed. A standout resource in this ecosystem.

*—Samyak Ahuja, software engineer, Uber*

# Argo CD: Up and Running

## *A Hands-On Guide to GitOps and Kubernetes*

*Andrew Block and Christian Hernandez*

**Argo CD: Up and Running**
by Andrew Block and Christian Hernandez

Copyright © 2025 Andrew Block and Christian Hernandez. All rights reserved.

Published by O'Reilly Media, Inc., 1005 Gravenstein Highway North, Sebastopol, CA 95472.

O'Reilly books may be purchased for educational, business, or sales promotional use. Online editions are also available for most titles (*http://oreilly.com*). For more information, contact our corporate/institutional sales department: 800-998-9938 or *corporate@oreilly.com*.

**Acquisitions Editor:** Megan Laddusaw
**Development Editor:** Jill Leonard
**Production Editor:** Kristen Brown
**Copyeditor:** nSight, Inc.
**Proofreader:** Emily Wydeven
**Indexer:** Sue Klefstad
**Cover Designer:** Susan Thompson
**Cover Illustrator:** Karen Montgomery
**Interior Designer:** David Futato
**Interior Illustrator:** Kate Dullea

June 2025: First Edition

**Revision History for the First Edition**
2025-06-16: First Release

See *http://oreilly.com/catalog/errata.csp?isbn=9781098142001* for release details.

The O'Reilly logo is a registered trademark of O'Reilly Media, Inc. *Argo CD: Up and Running*, the cover image, and related trade dress are trademarks of O'Reilly Media, Inc.

The views expressed in this work are those of the authors and do not represent the publisher's views. While the publisher and the authors have used good faith efforts to ensure that the information and instructions contained in this work are accurate, the publisher and the authors disclaim all responsibility for errors or omissions, including without limitation responsibility for damages resulting from the use of or reliance on this work. Use of the information and instructions contained in this work is at your own risk. If any code samples or other technology this work contains or describes is subject to open source licenses or the intellectual property rights of others, it is your responsibility to ensure that your use thereof complies with such licenses and/or rights.

This work is part of a collaboration between O'Reilly and Akuity. See our statement of editorial independence (*https://oreil.ly/editorial-independence*).

978-1-098-14200-1

[LSI]

# Table of Contents

# Preface

Cloud native technologies, regardless of where they reside (on the public cloud or in a private datacenter) continue to proliferate. For those running containerized applications, Kubernetes has become the de facto solution for running and managing these applications at scale and, as a result, several different architectural patterns have emerged over time. GitOps is one such pattern that describes a set of processes for managing infrastructure and applications within source code stored within a Git repository. While GitOps is not exclusive to Kubernetes, it has strong ties to Kubernetes, as the practices and principles have become the cornerstone for managing the platform.

While GitOps provides a framework that defines how to align infrastructure as code (IaC) concepts for managing resources using content stored within source code management tools, there is still a need for a tool that can realize these goals and the declarative nature of the content. In the world of Kubernetes, Argo CD has become one of the most popular tools for implementing GitOps paradigms. Given its broad adoption within the Kubernetes community for use by both infrastructure and application teams, having an understanding of how it can be used effectively is essential.

## Who Should Read This Book

This book is primarily written for Kubernetes administrators and developers who want to utilize GitOps practices to improve the user experience around cloud native technologies, along with those looking to operationalize Argo CD using the full set of features provided by the tool. However, since many development teams are also leveraging Argo CD to deploy and manage their own applications, these teams will also find most of the content applicable for their use as well. Upon the completion of this book, you will be better equipped to implement Argo CD within your organization in a manner that supports production use.

Whether you just started your Argo CD journey or are a seasoned power user, we wrote this book to be applicable for all levels of experience. By including key topics and a set of relatable examples, this book will become a reference that you can use from day one and beyond.

## Why We Wrote This Book

Argo CD is one of the most popular toolsets in the Cloud Native Computing Foundation (CNCF) and is quickly becoming the de facto standard in GitOps implementation. Even with its popularity, best practices and getting-started guides are sparse and scattered throughout the ecosystem. We wrote this book as a central place for those looking into operationalizing Argo CD without having to scour the internet for the information. Both of us have spent a large amount of time in the open source community, as well as various enterprise organizations, assisting in the implementation of Argo CD in their own environment. We've collected our shared experiences and seek to be able to share them broadly so that others, like yourself, can become successful in your Argo CD journey.

## Navigating This Book

The adoption of cloud native concepts is a journey. The following is a glimpse of what you can expect as you make your way through this book:

- Chapters 1–3 cover everything that you need for beginning to be productive working with Argo CD, including the goals the project seeks to achieve, the installation methods, and common methods for interacting with the platform.
- Chapters 4–5 place an emphasis on one of the most important topics within Argo CD: Applications. As the primary vehicle for managing resources in Kubernetes using GitOps, an in-depth overview of Applications will be provided, including the tools that can be used to define Kubernetes manifests, the content source for these manifests, and how and when they are applied to Kubernetes clusters.
- Chapters 6–9 cover a number of topics that focus on the management of Argo CD, including authentication and authorization, cluster management, multi-tenancy and security.
- Chapters 10–11 go beyond the basics, including advanced Application design and deployment patterns and extending the base functionality of Argo CD to take GitOps to new heights.
- Chapters 12–13 discuss some of the key areas that are applicable for using Argo CD within large organizations, including how both the tool as well as GitOps in general can be incorporated into continuous integration/continuous delivery (CI/CD) workflows, as well as how to operationalize the platform at scale.

- Chapter 14 might appear to be the end of our journey with Argo CD. However, it is just beginning, as this concluding chapter provides a number of resources for how to keep the conversation going with other members of the Argo CD community, as well as areas for further exploration.

## What This Book Will Not Cover

This book will focus on how to get up and running with Argo CD in a Kubernetes environment. This book will not go over how to install Kubernetes nor how to manage the lifecycle of a Kubernetes cluster. Furthermore, there are many ways to do the same thing. We will be focusing a lot on Helm in this book; however, that is not to say that using other methods aren't valid. It is impossible to go over every valid option. There are also many tools/projects that do similar things. Beyond Argo CD, usage of a particular tool over another doesn't mean we are endorsing that tool or that we would use that particular tool all the time in every scenario. A lot of the time, we chose the tool for the sake of brevity. We will try and call out all these exceptions as we go over them.

## Prerequisites

Before getting started, we will go through some of the prerequisites you might need in order to follow along in this book. We assume that you have access to an operational Kubernetes cluster; we will describe how to run an environment on your local machine using kind. However, we recommend that you test these out on a test system (and for that, we recommend kind).

### kind

Although the steps outlined in this book should "just work" with most Kubernetes implementations, the exercises will make use of kind, a tool for running local Kubernetes clusters within container "nodes." You can get started with kind by visiting *https://kind.sigs.k8s.io*.

The kind website includes instructions on how to install the `kind` binary and any of the other prerequisites. Several providers are available, which map to popular container runtimes, including Docker, Podman, or nerdctl (containerd), which enables its use among a greater set of end users.

### Helm

We use Helm routinely throughout the course of this book, so it will be necessary to have the Helm binary available in your `$PATH`. You can visit Helm for installation guidelines (*https://oreil.ly/Iy8UF*).

## Kubernetes Client

Since we will be interacting with Kubernetes clusters, it will be important to have the kubectl client available. You can follow the instructions on the official Kubernetes documentation site (*https://oreil.ly/kfRhX*).

## Argo CD CLI Client

Argo CD comes with the `argocd` CLI client that interacts with the Argo CD API server. You can follow the instructions found on the Argo CD website (*https://oreil.ly/KiJLu*) for installation of this client.

## YAML/JSON Processing

To make things easier, we use a lot of `jq` and `yq` to modify/update JSON/YAML in place. You can find information about these tools by visiting their respective websites: jq (*https://oreil.ly/RIguC*) and yq (*https://oreil.ly/huq-E*).

If you're using Linux or a Mac, you might be able to find these utilities using their respective package manager (for example; you can run `brew install jq` on a Mac).

## Companion Git Repository

Throughout this book, you will work through a series of exercises and examples as you expand your knowledge of Argo CD. These resources are available within a Git repository (*https://oreil.ly/argoCD_UR_repo*).

Since Git is the source code management (SCM) tool for not only interacting with the companion repository but also GitOps as a whole as well as Argo CD, it is important that you also have Git installed locally on your machine. Information related to Git, including the supported installation options and platforms can be found on the Git website (*https://git-scm.com*).

# Conventions Used in This Book

The following typographical conventions are used in this book:

*Italic*
: Indicates new terms, URLs, email addresses, filenames, and file extensions.

`Constant width`
: Used for program listings, as well as within paragraphs to refer to program elements such as variable or function names, databases, data types, environment variables, statements, and keywords.

**`Constant width bold`**
: Shows commands or other text that should be typed literally by the user.

*`Constant width italic`*
: Shows text that should be replaced with user-supplied values or by values determined by context.

This element signifies a tip or suggestion.

This element signifies a general note.

This element indicates a warning or caution.

## Using Code Examples

Supplemental material (code examples, exercises, etc.) is available for download at *https://oreil.ly/argoCD_UR_repo*.

If you have a technical question or a problem using the code examples, please send email to *support@oreilly.com*.

This book is here to help you get your job done. In general, if example code is offered with this book, you may use it in your programs and documentation. You do not need to contact us for permission unless you're reproducing a significant portion of the code. For example, writing a program that uses several chunks of code from this book does not require permission. Selling or distributing examples from O'Reilly books does require permission. Answering a question by citing this book and quoting example code does not require permission. Incorporating a significant amount of example code from this book into your product's documentation does require permission.

We appreciate, but generally do not require, attribution. An attribution usually includes the title, author, publisher, and ISBN. For example: "*Argo CD: Up and Running* by Andrew Block and Christian Hernandez (O'Reilly). Copyright 2025 Andrew Block and Christian Hernandez, 978-1-098-14200-1."

If you feel your use of code examples falls outside fair use or the permission given above, feel free to contact us at *permissions@oreilly.com*.

## O'Reilly Online Learning

For more than 40 years, *O'Reilly Media* has provided technology and business training, knowledge, and insight to help companies succeed.

Our unique network of experts and innovators share their knowledge and expertise through books, articles, and our online learning platform. O'Reilly's online learning platform gives you on-demand access to live training courses, in-depth learning paths, interactive coding environments, and a vast collection of text and video from O'Reilly and 200+ other publishers. For more information, visit *https://oreilly.com*.

## How to Contact Us

Please address comments and questions concerning this book to the publisher:

O'Reilly Media, Inc.
1005 Gravenstein Highway North
Sebastopol, CA 95472
800-889-8969 (in the United States or Canada)
707-827-7019 (international or local)
707-829-0104 (fax)
*support@oreilly.com*
*https://oreilly.com/about/contact.html*

We have a web page for this book, where we list errata, examples, and any additional information. You can access this page at *https://oreil.ly/argoCD_UR*.

For news and information about our books and courses, visit *https://oreilly.com*.

Find us on LinkedIn: *https://linkedin.com/company/oreilly-media*.

Watch us on YouTube: *https://youtube.com/oreillymedia*.

# Acknowledgments

*Andy Block:*

They say that it takes a village to raise a child, and this sentiment is certainly true for both the GitOps and Argo CD communities. It would not be possible to produce a publication, such as this book on Argo CD, without the continued support of the open source community. In particular, I would like to thank Dan Garfield, who has helped shed light into what it takes to build a business that is focused primarily on GitOps. In addition, I wanted to also thank Michael Crenshaw. whose unbelievably deep knowledge of Argo CD has helped me time after time better understand all of the minute details of the project. These insights directly translated into the ongoing support that I am able to provide to community members along with material within this book.

Of course, I could not forget my colleagues at Red Hat who have helped and supported my endeavors within the GitOps space. From Raffaele Spazzoli and our endless conversations on Helm, Kustomize, and various GitOps patterns to Gerald Nunn and our thoughts and designs for what it takes to properly architect and operate GitOps as a platform service within some of the most regulated organizations in the world. And, to the entire OpenShift GitOps team. Thank you for making me feel like an extended member of your team, where our ongoing collaboration has enabled our customers to apply GitOps principles at scale, using some of the most secure and trusted software available.

Finally, Argo CD is just one of many GitOps tools in the industry. There will never be a single GitOps tool, and we are all better because of that fact. A big thank you goes out to those in the GitOps community, including Scott Rigby, Alexis Richardson, and Stacey Potter. Your continued partnership and collaboration is truly appreciated!

*Christian Hernandez:*

The path to being a subject matter expert in a particular technology—to the point where you write a book—isn't a path you take alone. There have been many people in my career who have helped me get where I am. I would like to take this opportunity to give many thanks to those people.

My time at Red Hat was paramount to my development, and I couldn't have done it without the mentorship and leadership I received from Scott Cranton, Chris Morgan, and Erik Jacobs. Your willingness to let me grow was pivotal in my success. I cannot express my gratitude enough for everything. Also, to my "OG OpenShift TigerTeam" coworkers. We were lucky enough to work together during the best time of my career. Being able to work with experts in the field propelled me to be the best I can be. Also, a very special thanks to Chris Short, who always pushed me to be the "Kelsey Hightower of GitOps."

Lastly, I would like to thank Hong Wang, Jesse Suen, and Alexander Matyushentsev. Creating the Argo Project was a bold and brave thing to do (even if you all didn't know it at the time). Growing with the Argo Project has been a privilege; and now working with you all directly has elevated me to a level of expertise that I wouldn't have imagined. I am proud to be a part of your journey, and I wouldn't be here without what you three have created.

*Both:*

We are deeply grateful to the tech reviewers for their meticulous attention to detail and technical expertise, which greatly enhanced the accuracy and quality of this book. We would like to thank the following:

- Vladislav Bilay
- Manuel Dewald
- Werner Dijkerman
- Nadir Doctor
- Predrag Knežević
- Jess Males
- Benjamin Muschko
- Gerald Nunn
- Lipi Deepaakshi Patnaik
- Rick Rackow

Your invaluable feedback helped us refine complex concepts, ensuring clarity and precision for readers. The insights and suggestions you provided were instrumental in strengthening the technical depth and real-world applicability of the content. We sincerely appreciate the time and effort you dedicated to reviewing, catching errors, and offering thoughtful recommendations. This book is stronger because of your contributions, and we are truly thankful for your commitment to making it the best resource possible.

CHAPTER 1

# Introduction to Argo CD

Kubernetes caused a disruption within the tech industry. Its role as the cornerstone of the entire cloud native ecosystem cannot be overstated. The Cloud Native Computing Foundation (CNCF) was started with Kubernetes as its foundation, and as a result, many open source tools were developed around premises of leveraging the immutable and declarative nature of Kubernetes. As popularity and adoption grew for Kubernetes, so did the cloud native ecosystem as a whole. The need for different use cases led to the development of Kubernetes-native projects and tools (along with various startups) that were needed to further springboard the ever-growing adoption of Kubernetes and cloud native architecture.

One of the many challenges that came with Kubernetes adoption was the issue of "cluster sprawl." Cluster sprawl (not very much different from VM sprawl back when virtualization hit the scene) became apparent and the idea of "clusters as cattle" became popular, replacing the old idea of a "central cluster for everything" that was popularized by virtualization platforms. The need to be able to manage the lifecycle of many clusters at scale became something that was paramount to the success of Kubernetes and cloud native deployments. This is something that early adopters of Kubernetes ran into while they were operationalizing their cloud native architecture.

Throughout this chapter, we will dive into these themes and also walk through what Argo CD is and the role it plays in the Kubernetes and cloud native ecosystem.

## What Is Argo CD?

When Kubernetes came onto the scene in 2014, it quickly became the way to manage containerized workloads at scale. Kubernetes' declarative nature made it easy for end users and enterprises to explicitly describe the end state of their application deployments—while leaving the work up to Kubernetes. This new way of working came a long way from the more traditional imperative methods that had existed for years. Still, many users found themselves using Kubernetes in an imperative fashion. End users and enterprises were still managing Kubernetes configurations (i.e., YAML) manually or via event-based triggers and scripts. For example, users replaced their `ssh` commands with `kubectl` commands, and applied these Kubernetes configurations manually, leaving them largely untracked.

Argo CD is one of the many tools that came out of the need to manage application deployments across multiple Kubernetes clusters spanning various environments. Furthermore, it became important to not just manage these deployments, but also keep them tracked and versioned. Intuit was an early adopter of Kubernetes and knew all too well the issues with adopting such a fast-moving technology. This led Intuit to make a strategic move to become more of a technology company, and it doubled down on this strategic move by acquiring Applatix (*https://oreil.ly/hPi57*) in 2018. This acquisition provided the foundation needed to create the Argo Project. The Argo Project became the home to various DevOps-based toolsets, and their capabilities helped quickly onboard developers into Kubernetes, microservices, and cloud native architecture as a whole.

One of the main hurdles in adopting Kubernetes was the user/developer experience. Kubernetes is a powerful platform, but it was really built with the expectation that you are familiar with a lot of system operation experience. The principal of the Argo Project was to build toolsets from the ground up with not only GitOps in mind, but also a developer experience mindset at the forefront—which is where Argo CD comes into play.

Argo CD is one of the tools that lives in the Argo Project. It was written with GitOps and developer experience in mind; it is designed to deliver changes/updates to a Kubernetes cluster or to many clusters at massive scale. Argo CD detects and prevents drift within Kubernetes clusters by working with YAML, stored in a Git repository and using native functionality found in Kubernetes. While Argo CD is known for its ability to implement GitOps, it also has been used as a generic DevOps tool for those who are using Kubernetes to deploy and manage workflows in a non-GitOps environment. This flexibility has led Argo CD to be one of the most popular toolsets in the CNCF ecosystem.

Argo CD works with Helm and Kustomize to further provide flexibility and render the YAML produced by those tools before applying them to the Kubernetes cluster. We will look at Helm and Kustomize more closely in Chapters 3 and 4.

## Why Argo CD?

There are many reasons why DevOps professionals have adopted Argo CD. Part of the mass adoption of Kubernetes meant that many of the imperative, event-driven ways of deploying applications weren't taking advantage of the benefits of the declarative approach Kubernetes had built in.

### Unifying Application Definitions

Argo CD took the different pieces that made up an application running on Kubernetes and turned them into a unified, deployable unit of work. Typically, an application deployment is made up of individual Kubernetes objects (for example a deployment, a service, and a namespace), and they each were managed individually—coupled loosely together. Argo CD brought these related objects into an atomic unit of work known as an Argo CD *Application*. Here, an end user can have these Application definitions, configurations, and environments managed in a declarative and version-controlled way. Application deployments and lifecycle management could now be automated, auditable, and easy to understand. Argo CD Application specifics will be covered in Chapters 4 and 5.

### Configuration Drift

Configuration drift has been an issue in application deployments for as long as we have been delivering applications. Still, this issue has been plaguing us for quite some time, and many tools have been developed to combat this issue. Infrastructure as code (IaC) tools aimed to solve a lot of these issues, but it wasn't until immutable infrastructure (Kubernetes hand in hand with containers) came about that allowed us to truly solve this issue of configuration drift. Argo CD takes advantage of the reconciliation loop of Kubernetes and keeps deployments from drifting from their source of truth—whereas event-driven processes tend to have to wait for an event to trigger a reconciliation. Many DevOps professionals rely on Argo CD in order to prevent configuration drift at scale. Bringing clusters under the control of Argo CD gives DevOps professionals a sense of trust that the environment is as it should be.

### Rollback and Disaster Recovery

Argo CD can be used to expedite the rollback/disaster recovery process. Since Argo CD keeps your cluster in sync with its source of truth, you only need to revert your source of truth (usually in Git) to a working state. Argo CD will then work to set your cluster back to its desired state. Similarly, disaster recovery works the same way. DevOps professionals use Argo CD to recover by simply installing Argo CD and pointing to a specific target state in Git (whatever version that may be), and Argo CD handles the rest.

## The GitOps Movement

It seems that GitOps has quickly become the tech industry's latest and greatest buzzword and marketing's favorite term to throw around. But when searching for the term *GitOps*, you will likely come across a lot of concepts that seem to be unrelated to one another. You are also likely to find a lot of concepts that you are familiar with. So, is GitOps something that application developers/software engineers use? Or is it designed more for infrastructure teams or system administrators to use in managing their environments? Maybe it is just a spin or a new term for DevOps, or continuous integration/continuous deployment (CI/CD).

In actuality, GitOps takes different approaches to automation, application delivery, infrastructure management, and security and brings them under a single management umbrella.

The topic of GitOps almost always naturally starts with a discussion around DevOps, a term on which GitOps is clearly based. The DevOps movement was born out of the need to automate application delivery. It allows the teams that wrote, delivered, and supported the software to work together to support a common goal. DevOps isn't necessarily a department but rather a culture in your organization. So how does GitOps relate to DevOps? That's simple: GitOps *is* DevOps. GitOps is the natural progression of DevOps, and it implements the best of what DevOps practitioners were already doing—they just didn't know it yet.

### Origins of GitOps

Weaveworks (*https://github.com/weaveworks*) is credited with the creation of the GitOps name. The story can be summarized that back in 2017, Weaveworks was operating as a software-as-a-service (SaaS) company that hosted its customer's applications on its platform using Kubernetes. There was once an incident where a mistaken configuration change (a case of "fat-fingering a config") took down its entire platform, but the DevOps engineers were able to bring back the system in a relatively short time. When asked how they did it so quickly, they described their process and procedures, which Weaveworks CEO and cofounder Alexis Richardson, called *GitOps*.

### OpenGitOps Principles

In October 2021, the GitOps Working Group released the OpenGitOps Principles (*https://oreil.ly/UTE3V*), a set of principles for managing software systems. With this release, the working group aimed to define what GitOps actually is and not let it succumb to being just another buzzword. The current version, version 1.0, has four principles.

### Principle 1: Declarative

The first OpenGitOps principle states:

> A system managed by GitOps must have its desired state expressed declaratively.

The reference to the *desired state* means that you represent the way you want the system to work in an "end state," which will be the final state achieved by changes made by the GitOps environment. This is the difference between imperative and declarative; as you'll recall, Kubernetes operates in a declarative manner.

### Principle 2: Versioned and Immutable

The second OpenGitOps principle states:

> Desired state is stored in a way that enforces immutability, versioning, and retains a complete version history.

The canonical example of the "versioned and immutable" principle is Git, which is why GitOps picked up this term for its name. The functionality of Git makes it versioned and immutable because each change is tracked in a new version without altering previous versions. The idea is that you can revert back to a previous version while preserving an audit of all the changes that have been made.

### Principle 3: Pulled Automatically

The third principle states:

> Software agents automatically pull the desired state declarations from the source.

This principle is where GitOps starts to differentiate itself from a traditional event-driven CI/CD process.

Although triggering changes and updates via webhooks or other events is a valid way to automate builds, it's not (by itself) GitOps. GitOps software agents (or *GitOps controllers*) check the desired state by pulling and checking declarations from Git at regular intervals, which means *polling* as well as pulling. In GitOps, there is no webhook that needs to be hit. Instead, there is a reconciliation loop. This leads us into the final principle.

### Principle 4: Continuously Reconciled

The final principle is another place where GitOps differentiates itself from event-based workflows. It states:

> Software agents continuously observe the actual system state and attempt to apply the desired state.

This principle directly mirrors the functions of the Kubernetes controllers, but GitOps applies it to a whole application or infrastructure stack instead of just one object. We've seen that the desired state is pulled from configuration information that is versioned and stored in an immutable storage system. If there is a difference between the desired and running states, they are reconciled by changing the running state. This is happening continuously at a regular interval. "Continuous" here is understood in the industry to mean that reconciliation continues to happen at a chosen interval of time. Reconciliation doesn't have to be instantaneous.

## Comparison of GitOps Tools in the Ecosystem

The need to have all your systems in sync has existed for quite some time. This is where the paradigm of "infrastructure as code" came about, along with many tools, such as Terraform, Ansible, Puppet, and Chef (among others). Kubernetes was no different. As it gained traction, the need to be able to manage deployments at scale (and keep them in sync) was as big as ever. From that need sprung two major, cloud native GitOps controllers: Flux and Argo CD.

### Flux

Flux (*https://fluxcd.io*) originated from the engineers at Weaveworks. The tool was developed as a means to "keep the lights on" for Weaveworks' managed services. This tool was refined and then released as an open source project in the CNCF. Its current iteration, Flux v2, is built upon the idea of *toolkits*. It includes individual Golang libraries that use the Unix philosophy of "do only one thing, but do it well." Technically speaking, Flux v2 is just software that is built using the toolkit, and it is possible to build your own software around these toolkits.

### Argo CD

Argo CD, as explained earlier, was developed inside of Intuit. The goal of Argo CD was to quickly on-ramp Intuit developers to their Kubernetes-based platform. It can be seen as an early attempt at *platform engineering*, and Argo CD can be seen as Intuit's internal developer platform (IDP). The idea was to abstract away all the nuances of deploying and managing applications onto Kubernetes. Argo CD wasn't the first tool that was developed at Intuit, because other complementary (DevOps-focused) tools were also needed. Together, they were packaged as the Argo Project (described in more detail later in this chapter) and donated to the CNCF.

## Comparison of Flux and Argo CD

A deep comparison of these two tools is beyond the scope of this book. The main differences are really in the philosophical approach of how to manage a Kubernetes platform. Notably, Argo CD only wants to work on raw YAML, and it wants to mimic the functionality of `kubectl` as much as possible.

Take, for example, how each tool handles Helm. Flux uses the Helm Golang library to deploy Helm charts, whereas Argo CD renders the raw YAML (using the `helm template` command) in order to apply it to the Kubernetes cluster. So, how does that impact Argo CD users? It means that running `helm ls` will not return anything against a Kubernetes environment managed by Argo CD, whereas one managed by Flux will. The trade-off is that in an Argo CD-managed environment, diffing (the process of seeing what's different in the running state versus the desired state) is possible with a Helm chart deployment, whereas in a Flux system, you cannot see the diffs.

Another big difference is that, although you can get a UI via Weave GitOps, there is no native UI for Flux because Flux is strictly a CLI/API-based tool. Argo CD is built as a "complete" product, which includes a rich UI, RBAC system, and other multi-tenant tooling.

Deciding which tool to use has many factors, and that level of nuance is outside the scope of this book. From here forward, we'll go on the assumption that you have chosen Argo CD as your GitOps tool of choice. After all, why else would you be reading this book!

# The Argo Ecosystem

Normally, when people say or think *Argo*, most folks who are already well familiar with the cloud native ecosystem automatically think *Argo CD*. However, Argo CD is just one of the subprojects that are part of the overarching Argo Project. The Argo Project is a suite of DevOps tools aimed at making the lives of SREs and developers easier and at quickly onboarding those who aren't familiar with Kubernetes. In fact, many are surprised to learn that Argo Workflows is the most popular of the toolsets within the projects (based on the number of GitHub stars). The tools within the Argo Project are:

*Argo Workflows*
: A cloud native workflow engine that is popular with the AI/ML community and recently has seen an increase in users adopting Workflows for CI

*Argo CD*
: A recent hot topic in the cloud native world; Argo CD takes a GitOps approach to managing and deploying applications on Kubernetes at scale

*Argo Rollouts*
: An advanced progressive delivery controller that works hand in hand with Argo CD (it can also be used by itself, independent of Argo CD) to help end users perform Canary and blue-green deployments using their own Ingress/ServiceMesh controllers

*Argo Events*
: A generic event bus with dependency management

There is also Argo Labs (*https://github.com/argoproj-labs*), an area within the Argo Project that acts as an "incubation" area for tools that are related to the Argo Project ecosystem. For example, Argo CD ApplicationSet (now included with Argo CD), started out in Argo Labs before being included as a general availability (GA) enhancement to Argo CD.

## Summary

This chapter summarizes the challenges and solutions within the Kubernetes and cloud native ecosystem, highlighting the rapid adoption of Kubernetes and the resulting need for efficient cluster management. A key issue that emerged with Kubernetes was "cluster sprawl," requiring better management tools for handling multiple clusters at scale. Argo CD, a tool developed under the Argo Project, addresses these challenges by enabling GitOps for managing and deploying applications across Kubernetes clusters. Argo CD integrates with Kubernetes' declarative nature to track and version application deployments, preventing configuration drift and supporting rollback and disaster recovery processes. The chapter also discusses GitOps principles, its evolution from DevOps, and the benefits of using Argo CD compared to other tools like Flux. Finally, the chapter introduces the broader Argo ecosystem, which includes tools like Argo Workflows, Argo Rollouts, and Argo Events that together offer a comprehensive suite for DevOps and Kubernetes management. With this foundation, you should now have the context and the *why* as we dive into implementation-specific configurations for the rest of this book.

CHAPTER 2

# Installing Argo CD

Like most cloud native applications, Argo CD features a microservices architecture that comprises multiple components and technologies. Each Argo CD component, working together, helps support a fault-tolerant and robust system that helps enable the full set of features and capabilities. Understanding how all of these services work together in concert provides a greater awareness of the architecture, their significance, and how they are incorporated into the overall system as a whole. This chapter introduces the architecture and design of Argo CD along with detailing the various ways that it can be installed in a Kubernetes environment.

## Argo CD Architecture

Since Argo CD is a GitOps-based solution designed for Kubernetes, the architecture emphasizes the use of as many Kubernetes primitives as possible, which will be described in detail in this chapter. As introduced in Chapter 1, Argo CD sources content stored in repositories and realizes those configurations within a Kubernetes cluster. But what does that look like, and what are the components involved?

### Kubernetes Controller Pattern

One of the key benefits of using Argo CD, aside from the capability to define Kubernetes resources within source repositories and apply them automatically to a cluster, is that Argo CD can be configured to enforce those configurations to stay in place, even if they are modified. This is known as *drift management*. Argo CD accomplishes this by implementing a Kubernetes concept called a controller, which executes a nonterminating control loop for managing and monitoring the desired state of at least one resource. Based on a defined configuration, the controller will ensure that the current state matches the desired state.

For example, *Deployments* are a common method for registering workloads into Kubernetes, and as part of the creation of a Deployment resource, a ReplicaSet is also created, which will ensure that a specified number of pods are always running. Kubernetes accomplishes this through one of the built-in Kubernetes controllers, the ReplicaSet controller, which monitors all pods that have been created for a given ReplicaSet and ensures that the actual state of the resource(s) in the cluster matches the expected and defined state. If the actual state does not match the expected state, the controller will reconcile the difference until the current state matches the defined state.

Chapter 5 will cover divergence and diffing.

This controller pattern applies to not only the resources that end users manage but is also foundational for Argo CD itself. The properties that drive the core configurations of Argo CD are stored within ConfigMaps and Secrets, which include:

- Baseline Argo CD server details
- Connectivity details to external source repositories
- Security

However, as one can imagine when designing a system for which there may be a complex set of properties, there is a limitation of the types of properties that can be stored within the simple key/value constructs provided by not only these Kubernetes resources, but also any of the API's resources that are included with a standard Kubernetes installation.

Argo CD is not alone when it comes to solutions for adding new ways of managing resources within a Kubernetes environment. This need led to the creation of custom resources, which are implemented through Custom Resource Definitions (CRDs) and enable an end user to register a new resource type within Kubernetes. By defining a new resource type, not only can the properties of this resource be defined (so that consumers can become aware of and comply with the acceptable fields and their rules), but a new API endpoint in the Kubernetes API server is also registered to facilitate the management of these resources.

A concept similar to a Kubernetes controller, known as an operator, builds upon the primitives of a Kubernetes controller for managing the current and desired state of resources in a Kubernetes cluster and applies them to CRDs. Given that custom resources typically have domain-specific values and meaning associated with them, an operator is built with this domain-level knowledge of how to interpret those values and ensure that the state of resources within Kubernetes matches those defined values.

Argo CD makes use of several custom resources, and their properties are the primary vehicle to enable end users to manage their Kubernetes resources using GitOps-based principles. The use of Kubernetes controllers and custom resources is fundamental to the overall Argo CD architecture.

## Argo CD Architecture Overview

Given that Argo CD implements a microservices-based architecture, there is no single Argo CD component, but instead multiple distributed systems that act in a coordinated fashion. Figure 2-1 depicts the overall Argo CD architecture, including the relationship between each of the services and resources.

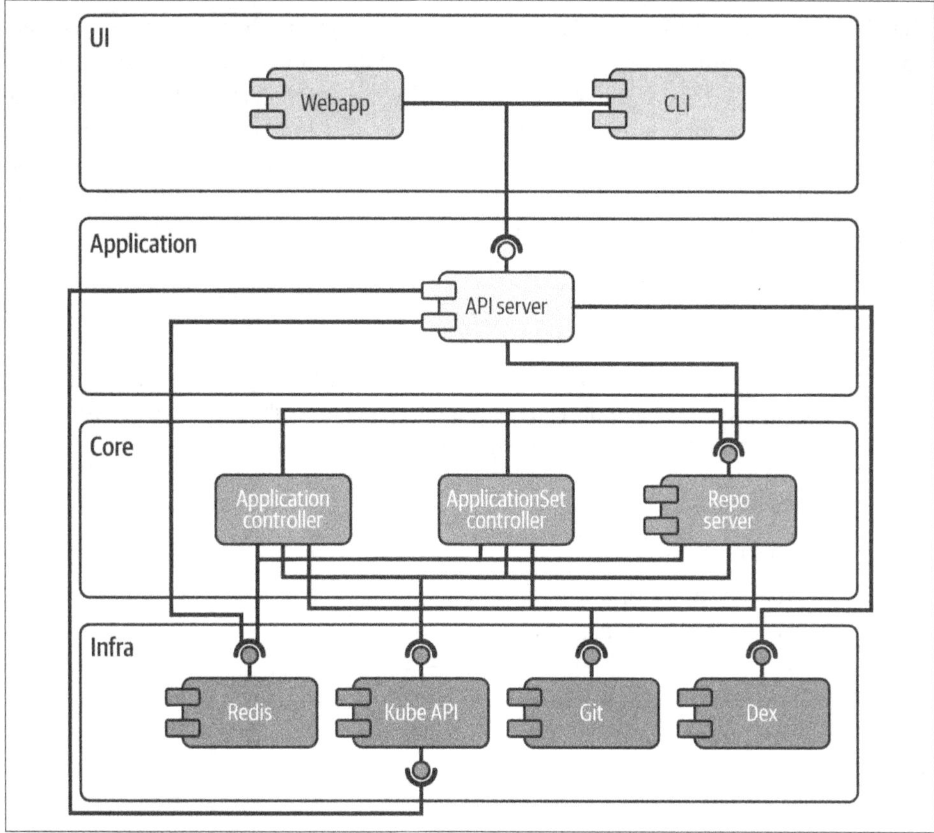


*Figure 2-1. Overall Argo CD architecture*

### Custom resources

Argo CD makes use of several custom resources to declaratively define business logic and APIs to implement GitOps management capabilities. Three custom resources are provided with each installation of Argo CD:

- Applications
- AppProjects
- ApplicationSets

The purpose of each custom resource will be described in more detail throughout the course of this book. However, it is important to note that Argo CD interacts with the Kubernetes cluster using these CRDs. This, effectively, makes these CRDs your interface for managing your Kubernetes cluster/clusters.

The Application controller and ApplicationSet controller are both Kubernetes Operators (and by definition, also controllers) that continuously monitor the state of `Application` and `ApplicationSet` resources, which represent an application instance deployed to environments where the live state in the Kubernetes clusters is compared against the desired state from source repositories. In addition, they are also responsible for performing lifecycle events associated with the content that they are reconciling, such as the ordering of resources as they are being applied. More details related to this feature are found in Chapter 5.

### Repository Server

The Repository Server maintains a local cache of the remote content source (either a Git or Helm repository) that will be translated into Kubernetes manifests. It is responsible for generating resources based on parameters, including:

- Repository type
- Repository source location
- Path within the repository
- Template tool-specific parameters

In addition, custom plugins (described in detail in Chapter 11) are also executed within this component, as they can influence the generation of the Kubernetes resources.

### API server

The API server is a gRPC/REST-based server (the API server accepts both) that exposes services for managing key configurations that are integral to the platform, including:

- Application management and status reporting
- Invocation of application operations including syncing, rollback, and additional user-defined actions
- Cluster and repository management
- RBAC enforcement

Several other components within the Argo CD ecosystem heavily rely on this asset for their normal operation including the UI, CLI, and external CI/CD systems.

In addition to acting as an API server, a web UI is also exposed, which provides a method for visualizing Application activity as well as supporting the management and configuration of Argo CD.

#### Redis

Redis is an in-memory database and provides local caching capabilities to reduce the dependency on external systems. While its primary purpose is to cache the contents of remote repositories, it also supports storing the state of the associated Kubernetes resources that users are managing from within repositories as well as the connection status of remote repositories and clusters. The content of the cache is not persisted and is always rebuilt at startup.

#### Command-line interface (CLI)

There is a command line–based utility for interacting with Argo CD. Support is available to manage the configuration of the platform itself as well as the lifecycle of applications. Communicates via the Argo CD API and includes a superset of the capabilities that are provided by the Argo CD user interface (UI).

#### Single Sign On (SSO)

Argo CD provides user management capabilities for interacting with the platform. These users can be defined locally within Argo CD or can be sourced from an external source. When integrating with an external source, OpenID Connect (OIDC) authentication is supported. For external identity providers that do not provide a direct OIDC integration, an instance of the Dex identity server is provided to act as a bridge between Argo CD and the remote identity provider.

#### Notifications

Notifications are included as part of the standard installation of Argo CD starting in version 2.3. This feature provides a mechanism for monitoring and triggering notifications to external systems based on the lifecycle of applications through the use of templating capabilities and a catalog of included triggers. Argo CD Notifications can be configured to send information to (but are not limited to) Slack and email, and can also invoke other webhooks. Understanding the current state of systems and environments is key when running production systems, and Argo CD notifications will be covered in greater detail in Chapter 13.

## Argo CD Key Patterns

As may be evident by this point, now that the foundational architecture has been introduced, Argo CD makes use of several key patterns; their significance will become even more apparent as each topic is described.

First, there is an emphasis on defining resources in a declarative fashion, whether they be one of the provided custom resources or a core configuration of the Argo CD server itself that is stored in a ConfigMap or Secret. Not only does this *trait* implement one of the most important concepts in GitOps, but it also enables the configuration of Argo CD itself to be managed via GitOps and Argo CD.

Building upon the first theme, where each resource is managed in a declarative fashion, Argo CD also makes use of a stateless architecture, meaning that configurations are the state of the system that can be rebuilt at any time. This approach makes Argo CD a stateless system from an architectural point of view. If there is either a desire or need for state to be tracked against a particular resource, the `status` field, a standard property and method found on many Kubernetes resources, can be used to provide historical context. In addition, while Redis is included as a caching mechanism within the Argo CD architecture, it is used as a volatile cache without any long-term persistence.

Finally, Argo CD enables extensibility. Not only are there multiple repository types from which GitOps-related content can be sourced, but there is also built-in support for templating resources using a number of popular tools, including Kustomize, Helm, and Jsonnet. Additional user-defined tools can also be added to not only integrate with additional external resources but also enhance how assets are rendered.

Now that we've covered the basics of the Argo CD architecture, including the primary components, let's shift gears to the methods that are supported for installing Argo CD.

# Installing Argo CD

Just as Argo CD supports the use of multiple methods and tools, such as Kustomize and Helm, to generate resources that can be applied to a Kubernetes cluster, many of these same tools and approaches can be used to install Argo CD itself. The determination of the particular approach depends largely on user preference as well as if there are any specific requirements or constraints, such as team or organizational guidance or restrictions. In addition to the tool that is used to facilitate the execution of the installation, Argo CD also supports several installation types, which influence the resources that are included in the deployment as well as the configuration of the deployed resources. Some of these topics will be expanded upon in subsequent chapters.

## Installation Types

Argo CD as a GitOps tool, similar to many other tools in this space, is utilized by a variety of personas who each have their own set of business domains and goals. Since there are a multitude of use cases and requirements that may be desired, Argo CD supports multiple installation configurations, and the determination of a particular configuration depends on the answer to these key decision points:

- Who are the users and consumers of the platform?
- What is the scope Argo CD should manage?
- Is high availability a concern?
- What are the security requirements?
- What are the bootstrapping and automation needs?

These options are illustrated in Figure 2-2.

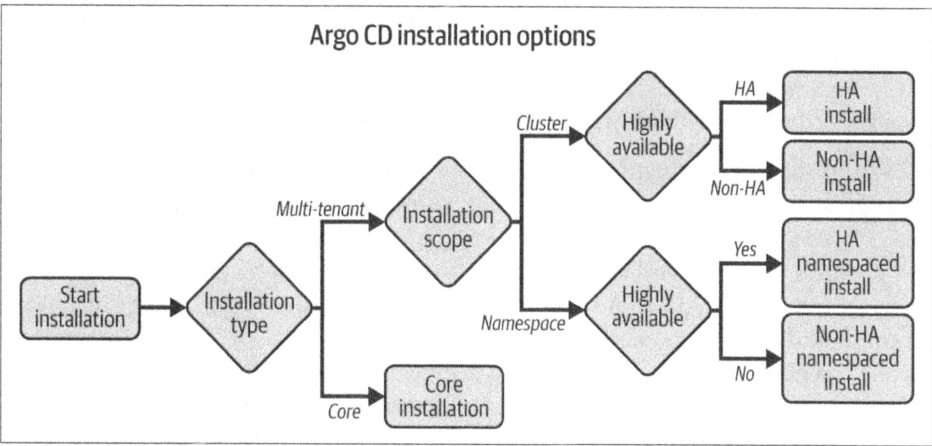


*Figure 2-2. The options and considerations when installing Argo CD*

The first decision point is the type of installation that Argo CD should serve. In most cases, Argo CD will be consumed by multiple individuals that may span across multiple teams within an organization. Additionally, most organizations desire to make use of the full set of features that are provided as part of a standard deployment of Argo CD (we covered these in the previous section). This is known as a *multi-tenant* type of installation, and it is most commonly utilized as it provides the full set of capabilities provided by Argo CD.

Alternatively, an option is available to perform an installation that includes only the minimal set of components to support normal operation—known as a *core install*. This approach does not include the API server or UI, SSO, or notification features. In addition, each component is also optimized to consume a minimum amount of resources in a non-highly available configuration (more on the topic of high availability later in this chapter). While a core deployment is not intended to appease the masses, this approach is beneficial for individual users who manage Argo CD from both an administrative and end-user perspective where there is not a desire to leverage the full multi-tenant feature set of Argo CD, but there is still a desire to take advantage of the primary GitOps capabilities.

The next decision point that must be addressed is the scope that Argo CD should manage. By default, Argo CD has the authority to control resources across an entire Kubernetes cluster they are deployed within as well as any external clusters under its management. This broad range of access is the preferred option, especially when Argo CD is being used by Kubernetes cluster administrators, as it does not introduce any limitations on the resources that can be managed. However, another approach, known as *namespaced* mode, that is available is to deploy Argo CD within a specific namespace and to allow Argo CD to only manage resources within specific namespaces. This option is used in multi-tenant environments where individual application teams are given the autonomy to operate their own instance of Argo CD but are not granted access to manage cluster-scoped resources. An in-depth look into the use of a namespaced deployment of Argo CD and its use case will be discussed in Chapter 8.

Finally, to support production environments, each of Argo CD's components can be configured in an optimized manner to ensure greater resiliency and performance needs. This approach is accomplished through a combination of increasing the replica count as well as enabling tunable parameters within each component. However, there are certain considerations that must be followed so that Argo CD can operate in an optimized fashion, as merely increasing the replica count of all components uniformly can actually cause a performance degradation. Fortunately, Argo CD provides manifests supporting both clustered and namespace-scoped deployments that illustrate the types of configurations necessary to enable a highly available deployment.

Now that both an overview of the Argo CD architecture and an understanding of the deployment approaches have been addressed, it's time to see Argo CD in action by working through the first hands-on activity.

## Deploying Argo CD

In due course throughout the remainder of this book, most of the installation types and approaches will be realized. However, let's start off by performing a basic installation of Argo CD to our `kind` environment.

### Deploying Argo CD using YAML manifests

The simplest and most straightforward option is to use one of the raw YAML-formatted manifests that include all of the resources and configurations within a single document, and in particular, a non-highly available, multi-tenant-based deployment of Argo CD.

High availability is covered in Chapter 13.

First, ensure that a fresh `kind` cluster is running:

```
kind create cluster
```

By default, the name of the cluster that the kind tool creates is called `kind`. You are free to change the default behavior by specifying an alternate name using the `--name` parameter of the `kind create cluster` command or by setting the environment variable `KIND_CLUSTER_NAME` with the desired name.

Once the cluster has started, your `kubectl` context will be automatically updated and ready to utilize the newly created cluster. Execute the following commands using `kubectl` to create a new namespace called `argocd` and to deploy Argo CD in the previously described configuration:

```
kubectl create namespace argocd
kubectl apply -n argocd \
-f https://raw.githubusercontent.com/argoproj/argo-cd/stable/manifests/install.yaml
```

After a few moments (to allow for the associated images to be downloaded to the `kind` cluster), the pods in the `argocd` namespace can be queried with a result similar to the following:

```
kubectl get pods -n argocd


NAME                                                READY   STATUS    RESTARTS   AGE
argocd-application-controller-0                     1/1     Running   0          46s
argocd-applicationset-controller-74575b6959-8dc7l   1/1     Running   0          46s
argocd-dex-server-64897989f8-qg8pm                  1/1     Running   0          46s
```

```
argocd-notifications-controller-566bc99494-7vj82   1/1     Running   0          46s
argocd-redis-79c755c747-867nk                      1/1     Running   0          46s
argocd-repo-server-bc9c646dc-6sd86                 1/1     Running   0          46s
argocd-server-757fddb4d7-xgdxh                     1/1     Running   0          46s
```

The standard deployment of Argo CD depicted here contains each of the primary components that are included with Argo CD, so it is an ideal baseline to work from.

The UI is one of the key features that sets Argo CD apart from other GitOps solutions. By default, the set of resources that were applied to the Kubernetes cluster did not include any configurations or resources to expose access to Argo CD outside the cluster. While there are several approaches that can be used to access Argo CD externally, such as creating a `LoadBalancer` service type or using an Ingress, to demonstrate baseline functionality, the port forwarding capability of the `kubectl` CLI can be used to connect to Argo CD without any additional actions.

Before moving on, confirm the successful installation of Argo CD by accessing the UI. To do this, execute the following command to initiate the forwarding of port 8080 from the local machine to the Argo CD server service, which will expose access to the UI:

```
kubectl port-forward svc/argocd-server -n argocd 8080:443
```

The command will establish a tunnel to facilitate the connection and block additional commands from being entered while the tunnel is established. If additional commands need to be executed while ports are forwarded, launch another terminal.

With access to the Argo CD UI available due to the `port-forward` tunnel, navigate to *https://localhost:8080*.

By default, Argo CD generates a self-signed TLS certificate to enable secure transmission between itself and the browser. Since this certificate is not trusted by the browser, a warning is displayed. Depending on the browser being used, there will be an option to proceed even though the certificate is not trusted, and then the Argo CD login page will be displayed.

To log in, `admin` is the username of the Argo CD administrator, and the password is a secret with the name `argocd-initial-admin-secret`. Obtain the password by executing the following command:

```
kubectl -n argocd get secret argocd-initial-admin-secret -o \
jsonpath="{.data.password}" | base64 -d; echo
```

Log in using `admin` as the username and the password that was obtained from the prior command. Upon successful login, the Argo CD dashboard is displayed, as shown in Figure 2-3.

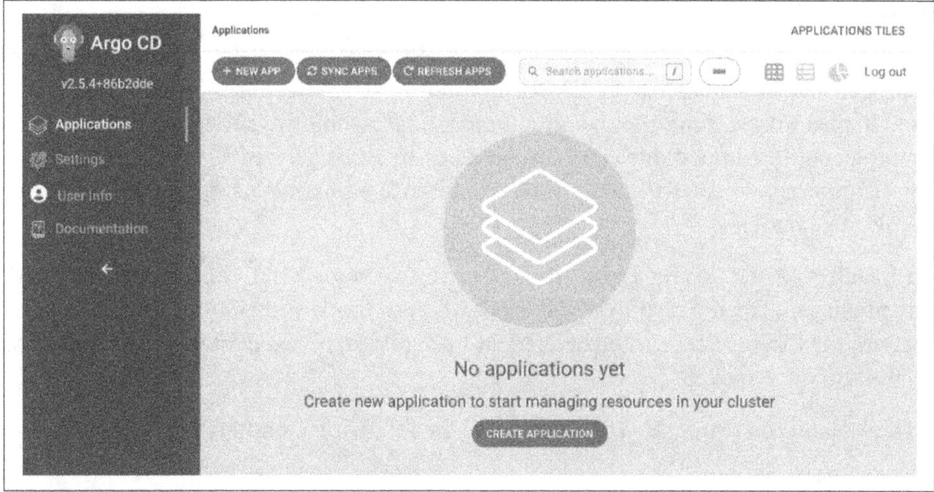


*Figure 2-3. The Argo CD Applications page*

The dashboard contains a list of the current *applications* that have been registered to Argo CD and their current status. Since this instance does not have any applications registered, the dashboard is empty. Feel free to navigate around the UI as you see fit. However, a more in-depth overview of the user interface will be covered in Chapter 3.

### High availability

The standard deployment of Argo CD is ideal for getting started but is not suitable for production environments due to the fact that there is only a single replica for each component. In case one of the components fails (due to an error or issue with the underlying infrastructure), it will cause a degradation of functionality as one or more of the resources will become unavailable. To mitigate these concerns, an alternate set of YAML definitions is available for both cluster and namespaced modes of operation. The key difference between these sets of resources and those that were deployed previously is that not only have additional tuning options been implemented, but multiple replicas of each service have also been defined. This means that if a failure does occur to one of the services, the remaining replica will be able to take on requests and continue normal operation in a degraded state until the original replica returns to normal operation.

Given that the topic of high availability is just one of the many traits of a production system, this will be expounded upon in Chapter 13 as part of the discussion on the considerations for operating Argo CD at scale.

### Deploying Argo CD using Helm

Argo CD can also be installed using a Helm chart. A Helm-based installation approach has advantages over YAML manifests, as the resources that are installed can be customized using the dynamic templating capabilities provided by Helm. For example, entire components can be enabled or disabled, as well as specific properties can be tailored, whereas these options would not be possible using the YAML-based manifest approach.

To install Argo CD using Helm, first be sure that your `kind` cluster does not have any previously created resources deployed. If Argo CD is still running from the prior section, the `kind` cluster can be deleted and re-created, or the contents from the prior section can be removed.

To delete and re-create the `kind` cluster, use the following commands:

```
kind delete cluster
kind create cluster
```

Alternatively, instead of needing to re-create the entire `kind` cluster, the YAML-based manifest installation of Argo CD can be uninstalled by removing the resources from the same manifest and then deleting the `argocd` namespace:

```
kubectl delete -n argocd \
-f https://raw.githubusercontent.com/argoproj/argo-cd/stable/manifests/install.yaml
kubectl delete namespace argocd
```

With a fresh `kind` cluster available, proceed to deploy Argo CD using Helm.

First, add the Argo CD Helm repository:

```
helm repo add argo https://argoproj.github.io/argo-helm
```

Install the Helm chart using the default configuration and create a new namespace called `argocd` using the following command:

```
helm upgrade -i argo-cd argo/argo-cd -n argocd --create-namespace
```

Either the `helm install` or `helm upgrade` command can be used to install the Argo CD chart. When the `helm upgrade` command is used with the `-i` parameter, Helm will check if there is an existing release found. If a release is not found, the chart will be installed instead of upgraded. The benefit of using `helm upgrade` in this situation is that the same command can be issued regardless of installing a chart for the first time or upgrading an existing release. The `helm install` command can only be used when installing a chart for the first time.

Another benefit of Helm is that chart creators can include additional information that is displayed whenever a chart is installed or upgraded, known as NOTES. After executing the `helm upgrade` command previously, the contents of the NOTES document in the chart was displayed, which provided a set of next steps, including how to access the Argo CD UI and how to obtain the password for the Argo CD admin user.

Query the running pods from the `argocd` namespace and take note that the set of resources are available, as they were using the YAML manifest approach (albeit with slightly different names, as the Helm chart prefixes each resource with the name of the Helm release):

```
kubectl get pods -n argocd
```

If desired, the Argo CD UI can be accessed in a similar manner, as described in the previous section, and the exact steps in this instance can be found within the provided Helm NOTES output.

While only a basic deployment of Argo CD was described in this section, the full set of tunable parameters provided by the Argo CD Helm chart can be viewed by listing the available chart *values*:

```
helm show values argo/argo-cd
```

The use of Helm values within the Argo CD Helm chart enables a greater level of customization and simplifies the initial configuration when deploying Argo CD. These values will be explored in subsequent chapters, especially in Chapter 13.

### Argo CD Operator

Another method to install Argo CD is the Argo CD Operator, which can be found on the OperatorHub (*https://oreil.ly/XAF4v*).

Beyond installation, the Operator helps to automate the process of upgrading, backing up, and restoring as needed, removing the human as much as possible. In addition, the Operator aims to provide deep insights into the Argo CD environment by configuring Prometheus and Grafana to aggregate, visualize, and expose the metrics already exported by Argo CD.

The Operator aims to provide the following, and is a work in progress:

- Easy configuration and installation of the Argo CD components with sane defaults to get up and running quickly
- Seamless upgrades provided for the Argo CD components
- The ability to back up and restore an Argo CD cluster from a point in time or on a recurring schedule

- Aggregated and exposed metrics for Argo CD and the Operator itself using Prometheus and Grafana
- Argo CD components that can autoscale as necessary to handle variability in demand

In this book, we will focus on using Helm as the way to install and manage Argo CD; however, it's good to get familiar with other installation methods.

## Summary

This chapter provided an overview of the architecture and components that are included as part of a deployment of Argo CD. In addition, two of the most common approaches for installing Argo CD, YAML manifests and Helm charts, were introduced and used to deploy Argo CD to a `kind` cluster. Finally, the Argo CD was accessed using the UI to confirm a successful installation. The next chapter expands upon the use of the UI and describes the various different methods available that can be used to manage and interact with Argo CD.

CHAPTER 3

# Interacting with Argo CD

Argo CD includes a fully declarative configuration model which supports a hands-off approach to GitOps and the management of a GitOps server. However, in some cases, more direct methods will be needed for interacting with the Argo CD server. In the previous chapter, we covered the Argo CD UI, which is one method for interacting with the platform as it provides a visual approach to the current state of GitOps. While the UI may be one of the most common methods for utilizing Argo CD, there are additional mechanisms to choose from, including a fully functional CLI and RESTful API. This chapter builds on the foundational concepts established in Chapter 2 for accessing and configuring Argo CD along with introducing several additional approaches that can be employed depending on the use case or preference.

## The User Interface in Depth

In Chapter 2, the UI was used as a way to access Argo CD. However, when deployed to the `kind` cluster, it required establishing a connection to the server component using the `kubectl port-forward` command. While this was acceptable for initial testing and validation, it is by no means how one should utilize a service long term. A more robust approach should be undertaken to provide a more reliable exposure of services.

One of the most common methods for exposing services and gaining access to resources within a Kubernetes cluster is to leverage an Ingress resource. An Ingress provides a means for exposing services outside of a cluster, and they are enabled by the use of an Ingress controller, which will map the incoming request to the backend service. There are many options as it relates to the available ingress controllers, where some have additional features and integrations with the operating environment, such as a cloud provider.

NGINX is one such popular ingress controller and there is support for deploying it to a `kind` cluster. `kind` clusters can be customized to include advanced configurations, such as setting options for kubeadm, the tool for deploying Kubernetes clusters, and to deploy multiple "nodes" to support simulating high-availability scenarios.

Another available option is to forward local ports to the `kind` node—a capability to enable Ingress into the Kubernetes cluster and, in this case, the NGINX ingress controller.

Create a new `kind` cluster and pass an inline definition of a `kind` configuration:

```
cat <<EOF | kind create cluster --config=-
kind: Cluster
apiVersion: kind.x-k8s.io/v1alpha4
nodes:
- role: control-plane
  kubeadmConfigPatches:
  - |
    kind: InitConfiguration
    nodeRegistration:
      kubeletExtraArgs:
        node-labels: "ingress-ready=true"
  extraPortMappings:
  - containerPort: 80
    hostPort: 80
    protocol: TCP
  - containerPort: 443
    hostPort: 443
    protocol: TCP
EOF
```

Alternatively, the configuration definition can be placed into a file and referenced using the same `--config` parameter when creating the cluster.

Once the cluster has started, deploy the NGINX ingress controller using Helm.

First, add the NGINX ingress controller Helm repository and install the NGINX ingress controller chart:

```
helm repo add ingress-nginx https://kubernetes.github.io/ingress-nginx
helm repo update
```

Once the repository has been added, create a new file called *values-ingress-nginx.yaml* to contain customized Helm values for the NGINX ingress controller with the following content:

```
controller:
  service:
    type: NodePort
  hostPort:
    enabled: true
  updateStrategy:
    type: Recreate
```

Install the Helm chart for the NGINX ingress controller using the customized values created previously using the following command:

```
helm -n ingress-nginx install ingress-nginx ingress-nginx/ingress-nginx --create-namespace \
-f values-ingress-nginx.yaml
```

Wait until the ingress controller is ready:

```
kubectl wait --namespace ingress-nginx \
  --for=condition=ready pod \
  --selector=app.kubernetes.io/component=controller \
  --timeout=90s
```

Query the pods and services in the `ingress-nginx` namespace to view the resources that were just deployed:

```
kubectl get pods -n ingress-nginx

NAME                                       READY   STATUS    RESTARTS   AGE
ingress-nginx-controller-56f6595fc8-74t7s  1/1     Running   0          3m33s

kubectl get svc -n ingress-nginx

NAME                                TYPE        CLUSTER-IP     EXTERNAL-IP   PORT(S)
ingress-nginx-controller            NodePort    10.96.33.103   <none>        80:30579 ...
ingress-nginx-controller-admission  ClusterIP   10.96.168.33   <none>        443/TCP  ...
```

Since the `kind` cluster was created binding port 80 and 443 of the local machine to the `kind` node, invoking the `curl` command against port 80 should verify communication to the ingress controller:

```
curl http://127.0.0.1

<html>
<head><title>404 Not Found</title></head>
<body>
<center><h1>404 Not Found</h1></center>
<hr><center>nginx</center>
</body>
</html>
```

While the 404 error may appear to be a failure, given that an Ingress resource has yet to be created, the fact that a response was provided and that it included `nginx` in the response body confirms the ingress controller has been deployed and is operating correctly.

Now that access to the ingress controller has been confirmed, an Ingress resource must be created so that access can be achieved through the ingress controller. Fortunately, the Argo CD Helm chart includes functionality for configuring this task. When utilizing an Ingress resource, one of the first steps that must be completed is to determine the hostname that is associated with the service.

Since NGINX is an Open Systems Interconnection (OSI) Layer 7 load balancer, routing is performed using the host header in the request. As requests are received, NGINX will inspect this header, determine if any of the defined Ingress resource matches the request, and if so, route the request to the associated backend service.

The hostname that will need to be specific for the Argo CD instance will most likely not have an associated value in a publicly accessible Domain Name System (DNS) server. To solve this challenge, two options are available:

- Modify the contents of the `/etc/hosts` file on the local machine.
- Use a hosted wildcard DNS service, such as nip.io.

While using the hosted service eliminates the need to make modifications on the local machine, it potentially introduces an unnecessary dependency on an external. As such, the manual modification approach will be demonstrated here.

`argocd.upandrunning.local` is the hostname that will be used to refer to the Argo CD instance deployed within the `kind` cluster. Modify the `/etc/hosts` file to add the loopback address of the local host and hostname so that queries are resolved and routed appropriately.

Append the following to the end of the `/etc/hosts` file:

```
127.0.0.1 argocd.upandrunning.local
```

With the ingress controller and hostname prerequisites complete, the Argo CD Helm chart has the capabilities available to support generating the necessary manifests to enable Argo CD to be accessed via an Ingress resource.

Create a file called *values-argocd-ingress.yaml* with the following content:

```
---

server:
  ingress:
    enabled: true
    hostname: argocd.upandrunning.local
    ingressClassName: nginx
  extraArgs:
  - --insecure
```

Deploy the Helm chart using the values file created previously:

```
helm upgrade -i argo-cd argo/argo-cd --namespace argocd --create-namespace \
-f values-argocd-ingress.yaml
```

This Helm release will appear similar to the release that was completed in Chapter 2. However, by specifying the appropriate values, a new Ingress resource was created, which can be verified by executing the following command:

```
kubectl get ingress -n argocd

NAME                    CLASS   HOSTS                       ADDRESS     PORTS   AGE
argo-cd-argocd-server   nginx   argocd.upandrunning.local   localhost   80      53s
```

Given that all of the pieces are in place in order to access Argo CD using an Ingress resource, open a web browser and navigate to *http://argocd.upandrunning.local*, which should display the Argo CD UI login page.

Argo CD can also be accessed securely through the ingress controller by using the analogous *https://* address. Similar to when the UI was accessed in Chapter 2, a warning will be displayed signifying that a connection is attempting to be established to an endpoint whose certificates are not trusted by the browser. One key difference is that the untrusted certificates are related to the ingress controller and not Argo CD. The default ingress configuration the Helm chart establishes terminates TLS traffic at the ingress controller instead of at Argo CD itself. The TLS options that can be configured in Argo CD will be discussed in more depth in Chapter 9.

Once again, obtain the password for the Argo CD admin user from the `argocd-initial-admin-secret` secret and log in. Refer back to Chapter 2 (see "Deploying Argo CD using YAML manifests" on page 17) for the command to retrieve the initial admin password.

Let's take an opportunity to explore the various configuration options that are available within the UI. The default landing page upon login contains the list of applications that have been registered to Argo CD. An Application is a source of GitOps content that targets a particular destination environment and is the primary focus for end users when using Argo CD. The UI enables the creation, management, and synchronization of application resources in a visual, user-friendly manner.

Deploying an application will be reviewed in depth in Chapter 4.

Aside from managing applications, the other primary purpose of the UI is to facilitate the management of the Argo CD server itself—from within the Settings page (see Figure 3-1).

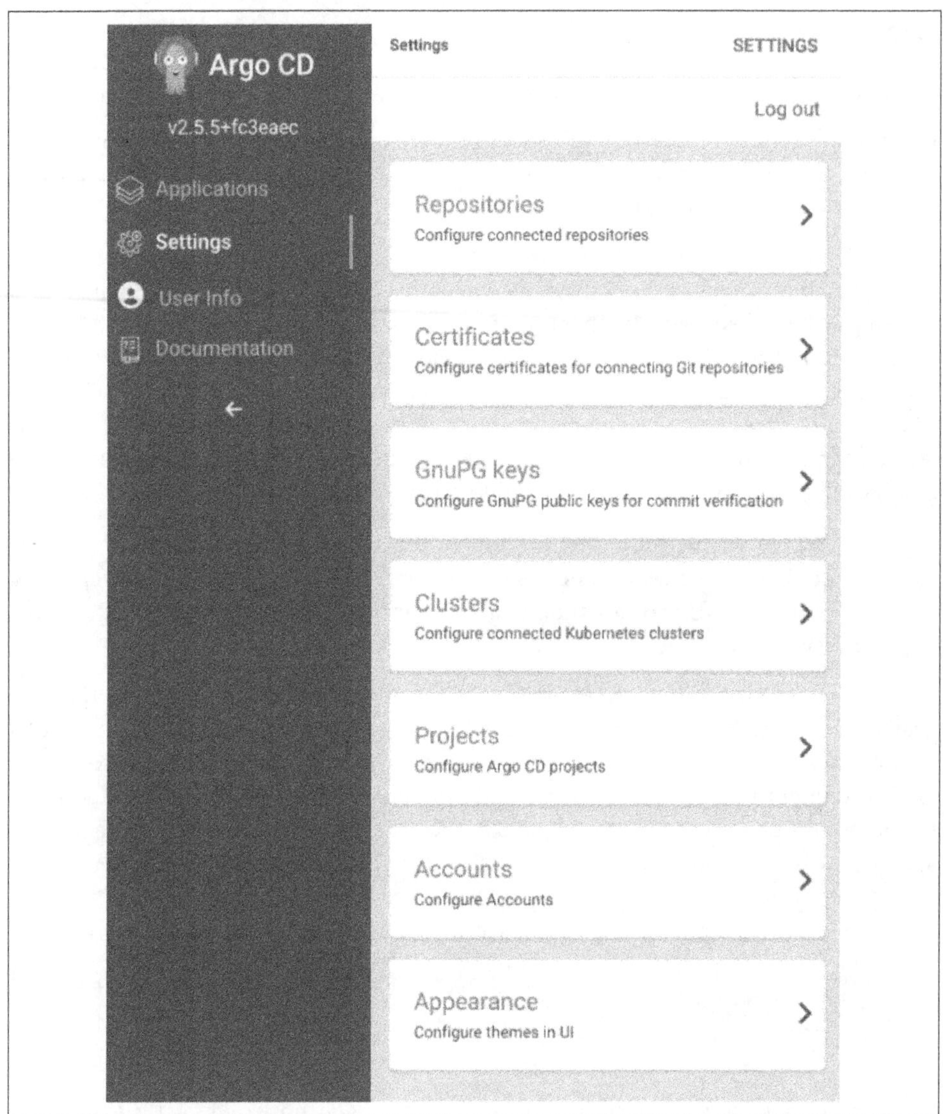


*Figure 3-1. Argo CD Settings page*

Table 3-1 details the configurable options that are made available from the Settings page of the UI.

*Table 3-1. Options available within the Argo CD Settings page*

| Setting | Description |
|---|---|
| Repositories | Configuration of remote locations containing resources that will be translated into Kubernetes manifests |
| Certificates | Management of transport mechanisms to facilitate secure connectivity to remote repositories |
| GnuPG keys | Key management to enable the verification of source control content |
| Clusters | Kubernetes environments that have content from source repositories applied |
| Projects | Logical groupings of applications with common configurations and permissions |
| Accounts | Management of local accounts stored within the Argo CD server |
| Appearance | Configuration of the look and feel of the UI |

In addition to being able to manage application and server settings, information related to the current authenticated user is available from the User Info page, which is helpful for associating identity details to enable role-based access control (RBAC) permissions that are used to manage access to Argo CD resources.

Even with all the parameters and settings that can be configured within the Argo CD UI, there are still a large number of properties that either cannot be managed using the UI or their values are read-only. When those situations do arise, the solution can be typically facilitated by using the Argo CD CLI. The next section introduces the capabilities included with the Argo CD CLI along with applying the appropriate settings to enable the management of the `kind` Argo CD environment.

# The Argo CD Command-Line Interface (CLI)

The Argo CD CLI (`argocd`) is a utility to control and manage the Argo CD server. Similar to the UI, the CLI leverages the API to facilitate the interaction with Argo CD. When certain options are not available from within the UI, such as adding remote clusters, the default option is to use the CLI, as it includes a more in-depth set of options and capabilities as compared to the UI.

Installing the Argo CD CLI can be performed on most major operating systems, as there are prebuilt binaries readily available. Other installation options are also available depending on the target operating system, and the CLI is also available in a number of formats, including a container image with the CLI included. Consult the Argo CD CLI installation documentation (*https://oreil.ly/y5ro5*) for the list of supported platforms and necessary steps to complete the installation.

Once the CLI has been successfully installed, execute the `argocd` command to see a list of functions that can be managed using the tool. Since the majority of the options enabled from within the CLI cannot be used unless a connection to an Argo CD environment is established, you will need to connect the CLI to the `kind` Argo CD instance using the `argocd login` command as shown next:

```
argocd login --insecure --grpc-web argocd.upandrunning.local
```

The `--grpc-web` parameter enables the use of the gRPC-Web protocol, which enables communication through the ingress controller. Additional configuration steps are needed to enable native gRPC connectivity, which will not be covered in this book.

When prompted, enter the Argo CD admin username and password to authenticate the CLI to the `kind` Argo CD instance.

As soon as successful authentication is achieved, a configuration file containing details related to the user, the Kubernetes context, and other connectivity data is created in a file located at `$HOMEDIR/.config/argocd/config`. `$HOMEDIR` uses an environment variable named `ARGOCD_CONFIG_DIR`, `HOME`, or `XDG_CONFIG_HOME` (XDG Base Directory Specification), depending on which value is resolved first.

One of the first steps that is typically taken after logging in via the CLI is to change the default admin password. Changing the admin password is an important step, as it increases the security posture of the Argo CD server. Kubernetes Secrets are not encrypted but are base64 encoded, which enables entities with access to query Secrets access to the default password.

Change the default admin password by executing the following command:

```
argocd account update-password
```

Enter the current admin password and the value of the desired password to reset the admin password.

Confirm the new password was applied properly by logging out of the current session and logging in once again with the updated password:

```
argocd logout <context>
```

The value of the `<context>` property refers to the argocd context to target. The list of argocd contexts can be queried by executing the `argocd context` command. After logging out, log in again using the `argocd login` command to confirm the password reset was successful.

Changing passwords for Argo CD users is just one action that cannot be accomplished using the UI and is one of the benefits provided by the CLI. The use of the CLI will become even more prevalent in upcoming chapters as it provides capabilities for not only administrators and users, but also its inclusion and integration into other systems and workflows.

However, what if there was no reason at all to use either the UI or the CLI but still get the benefits of being able to manage Argo CD? The final section of this chapter explores two additional methods for interacting with Argo CD.

## Additional Methods for Managing Argo CD

The Argo CD UI and CLI simplify how users interact with Argo CD—either through visualization and accessibility features from the perspective of the UI or by enabling a command-line-level approach with the CLI. One of the commonalities between these two components is that they both make use of the REST-based API that Argo CD exposes. End users can invoke the same APIs that Argo CD exposes without being limited based on the features that are included in either the UI or CLI.

The first question that may come to mind is: What type of information does Argo CD make available via the API? One approach could be to use the developer console included by the web browser to inspect the requests that are being invoked from the web console. But that would be somewhat tedious for being able to determine the exact endpoint and parameters that need to be included.

Fortunately, Argo CD provides an OpenAPI specification (sometimes called Swagger), which describes all of the APIs, including the acceptable inputs and provided outputs that are exposed, reducing the burden on the end user.

The OpenAPI specification provided by Argo CD is located at the endpoint `/swagger.json`.

OpenAPI is an open standard that is both machine and human readable for describing and visualizing web services. Additional information can be found at OpenAPI's website (*https://www.openapis.org*).

Open a web browser and navigate to *https://argocd.upandrunning.local/swagger.json* to view the contents.

Upon loading the OpenAPI specification document, one quickly realizes how verbose a specification can be. With a mature API, such as Argo CD, the document is quite large.

One of the tools provided by the Swagger project is a visualization component for OpenAPI specifications that avoids needing to become familiar with the intricate details of the OpenAPI specification. This utility is included with Argo CD and can be accessed by navigating to *https://argocd.upandrunning.local/swagger-ui*.

Now that there is an understanding of the API services to query, what are the steps necessary to invoke them? First, a session token must be generated by invoking the `/api/v1/session` endpoint with a valid username and password.

Execute the following command to obtain a session token, substituting the username and password in the appropriate fields:

```
curl -H "Content-Type: application/json" \
  -XPOST -k https://argocd.upandrunning.local/api/v1/session \
  -d '{"username":"<USERNAME>","password":"<TOKEN>"}' | jq -r
```

The `-k` argument disables TLS validation, which would have thrown an error similar to what was seen previously when navigating to the Argo CD UI from the web browser.

A successful authentication attempt will result in a similar response to the following:

```
{"token":"<TOKEN>"}
```

With a valid session token, the available API endpoints can be invoked.

One of the most important endpoints that is frequently queried, especially during the initial configuration of Argo CD, is the settings endpoint. This endpoint is exposed at `/api/v1/settings` and can also be verified within the Swagger UI interface by selecting SettingsService and viewing the GET request listed in Figure 3-2.

By expanding the responses, it is a wealth of information, much more than is provided by the CLI or the UI (see Figure 3-2).

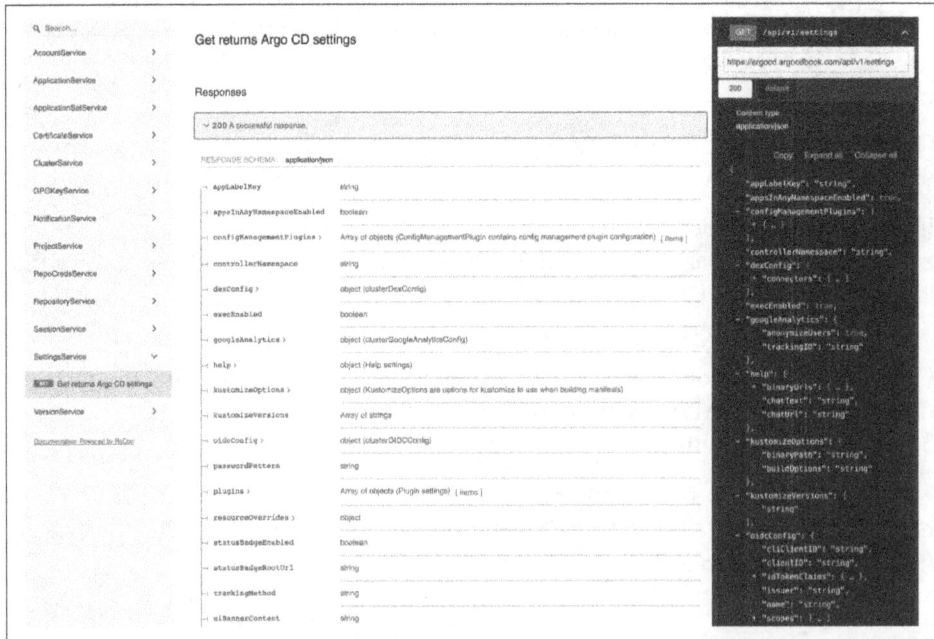


*Figure 3-2. The properties of the SettingsService as shown in the Swagger UI interface*

To invoke this endpoint, execute the following command, substituting the value of the bearer (session) token obtained previously:

```
curl -k -H "Authorization: Bearer <TOKEN>" \
    https://argocd.upandrunning.local/api/v1/settings | jq -r
```

A response similar to the following should be displayed:


```
{
  "appLabelKey": "argocd.argoproj.io/instance",
  "resourceOverrides": {
    "apiextensions.k8s.io/CustomResourceDefinition": {
      "ignoreDifferences": "jqPathExpressions: null\njsonPointers:\n- /status\n- ...
    }
  },
  "googleAnalytics": {
    "anonymizeUsers": true
  },
  "kustomizeOptions": {
    "BuildOptions": "",
    "BinaryPath": ""
  },
  "help": {
    "chatText": "Chat now!"
  },
  "passwordPattern": "^.{8,32}$",
  "controllerNamespace": "argocd"
}
```


Viewing server settings is just one of the many API endpoints that can be not only queried but also updated and adds an additional weapon to the already robust arsenal of tools that are used to manage Argo CD.

However, what if there was a desire to not leverage any of these tools or any services provided by Argo CD whatsoever but still retain the benefits and assurances of a well-maintained environment?

Recall back in Chapter 2 that Argo CD supports a declarative model for managing GitOps and that Argo CD implements the controller pattern to track the state of resources based on defined manifests. While Argo CD responds to changes to custom resources, such as applications and AppProjects, it also tracks additional resources, such as ConfigMaps and Secrets which are used to influence the configuration of the entire platform. So instead of using the UI, CLI, or invoking the API, the configurations can be applied directly to the Kubernetes cluster.

Each deployable in the Argo CD architecture makes use of configuration properties stored within ConfigMaps and Secrets in the same namespace that Argo CD is deployed within. Some of these resources use a well-known and established name, like a ConfigMap with the name `argocd-cm`, which contains the primary configuration properties for Argo CD, while others use metadata within each resource to signify their importance and intended capabilities. Indeed, the server settings API endpoint that was invoked previously queried the contents of this ConfigMap.

There are a number of Argo CD configurations that can be defined within ConfigMaps, and they are detailed in Table 3-2.

*Table 3-2. Common Argo CD configurations*

| Resource name(s) | Kind | Description |
|---|---|---|
| `argocd-cm` | ConfigMap | General Argo CD configuration |
| `argocd-cmd-params` | ConfigMap | Argo CD environment variable configurations |
| `argocd-rbac-cm` | ConfigMap | RBAC configuration |
| `argocd-ssh-known-hosts-cm` | ConfigMap | SSH known-host configuration data |

Additional resources that influence the configuration of Argo CD are stored within Secrets and do not make use of a standardized naming convention for the resource. Instead, a label with the key `argocd.argoproj.io/secret-type` is placed on the Secret to denote their significance.

For example, a secret with the label `argocd.argoproj.io/secret-type: repository` contains connection details to a remote content source repository. As Argo CD can manage content from multiple remote repositories at a time by using the label approach, similar content with distinct values for each repository can be applied within separate Secret resources and then correlated appropriately based on the content.

Table 3-3 provides an overview of the different Secret types and their significance.

*Table 3-3. Argo Secret types*

| Label | Description |
|---|---|
| `argocd.argoproj.io/secret-type: cluster` | The definition, configuration, and credentials associated with a remote cluster |
| `argocd.argoproj.io/secret-type: repository` | Consolidated configurations and credentials associated with a remote repository |
| `argocd.argoproj.io/secret-type: repo-config` | Configurations associated to a remote repository (not widely used) |
| `argocd.argoproj.io/secret-type: repo-creds` | Credentials for communicating with a remote repository |

As topics are introduced throughout the course of this book, the way in which these resources can be used will come into focus to enable an entirely hands-off approach for managing Argo CD server configuration.

## Summary

This chapter introduced several methods to aid in the management of Argo CD: a visual UI, an interactive command-line utility, a comprehensive API, and an entirely declarative model. These options empower a freedom of choice for Argo CD administrators and end users toward using a tool or approach they feel the most comfortable using. Chapter 4 focuses on one of, if not the most, foundational topics in the realm of Argo CD and how it is the center point for facilitating GitOps practices.

# CHAPTER 4
# Managing Applications

Argo CD manages the lifecycle of Kubernetes resources using a construct called Applications. An Argo CD Application is a custom resource that contains a logical collection of related Kubernetes resources (i.e., a collection of YAML or JSON files). An Argo CD Application is the smallest unit of work in Argo CD and is where Argo CD interfaces with Kubernetes in order to deploy Kubernetes objects.

Application templating is possible with ApplicationSets, which will be discussed in Chapter 10.

In this chapter, we will cover the basics of an Argo CD Application, the different components (including an overview of the types of sources Applications can connect to), and how to use different Kubernetes templating tools that Argo CD natively supports. To wrap up this chapter, we'll cover the lifecycle of an Argo CD Application.

## Application Overview

As previously mentioned, an Argo CD Application is the atomic working unit in Argo CD. It defines the end state of the desired set of resources within a Kubernetes cluster, more specifically, it defines which objects need to be applied to the running Kubernetes cluster. Let's take a look at an example of an Argo CD Application:

```
apiVersion: argoproj.io/v1alpha1
kind: Application
metadata:
  name: guestbook
  namespace: argocd
spec:
```

```
  project: default
  source:
    repoURL: https://github.com/argoproj-labs/argocd-example-apps/
    targetRevision: main
    path: guestbook/
  destination:
    server: https://kubernetes.default.svc
    namespace: example
```

This is a minimal example of what is needed for an Argo CD Application to be functional within a cluster. Things like adding Kustomize post-rendering and sync options are also possible using the Application CRD. For the time being, the two main pieces of information that you should focus on are the `.spec.source` and `.spec.destination` sections:

`.spec.source`
: This defines the location containing resources that Argo CD should interface with. This property includes key options, such as `repoURL`, which defines where the Git repository or a Helm chart repository that holds the manifests are located. The `targetRevision` is where you can define what branch or tag should be targeted, or in the case of a Helm chart, the version of the Helm chart you want deployed. And finally, the `path` is where you can find the Kubernetes manifests relative to the `repoURL`.

`.spec.destination`
: This specifies the target Kubernetes cluster to apply the manifests defined under the `.spec.source` section. Here you'll specify the Kubernetes API endpoint in the `server` section (here, `https://kubernetes.default.svc` is used as a way to indicate to Argo CD to deploy to the cluster Argo CD is running on), and the `namespace` section indicates which namespace to target on that cluster. Omitting the `namespace` section will cause Argo CD to default to the `default` namespace during deployment.

The `namespace` in the `Application` YAML should match the `namespace` of where your Argo CD instance is installed—this is typically the default `argocd` namespace, and we show this in our example. Starting in Argo CD version 2.5, support was added to enable sourcing Applications from namespaces other than where Argo CD is deployed. Although this is a very useful feature, it will not be used in the examples found within this publication.

The Argo CD Project Git repository (*https://oreil.ly/lfoSM*) provides a comprehensive view of all of the options available to you.

Other sections of note that we will cover in detail in subsequent chapters are the options for when Applications are synchronized against cluster(s) within the `syncPolicy` property as well as how differences between the expected rendered state of resources and the actual state within a cluster are handled. Understanding and managing resources beyond their initial creation is related to a concept called *drift management* and is one of the key benefits provided by Argo CD.

## Application Sources

Argo CD takes the desired state defined in the Application Custom Resource Definition (CRD) and attempts to modify the current running state on the Kubernetes cluster based on the defined content. Argo CD was built from the ground up with GitOps in mind, and it therefore supports two sources as the source of truth: Git and Helm.

Drift detection happens out of the box with Argo CD, but self-heal needs to be enabled. The examples in this book enable self-healing, but it's important to note that it's not the default.

The `source` field in an Argo CD Application has a 1:1 relationship with the application specification. In other words, only one source can be configured per application.

Starting with Argo CD v2.6, you can have a `sources` field now and specify more than one source. An example of a multisource application is as follows:

```
spec:
  sources:
    - repoURL: https://github.com/christianh814/gitops-examples
      path: applicationsets/rollingsync/apps/pricelist-config
      targetRevision: main
    - chart: mysql
      repoURL: https://charts.bitnami.com/bitnami
      targetRevision: 9.2.0
      helm:
        releaseName: pricelist-db
        parameters:
          - name: serviceAccount.name
            value: "pricelist-db"
          - name: auth.database
            value: "pricelist"
          - name: auth.username
            value: "pricelist"
          - name: auth.password
            value: "pricelist"
          - name: secondary.replicaCount
    - repoURL: https://github.com/christianh814/gitops-examples
      path: applicationsets/rollingsync/apps/pricelist-frontend
      targetRevision: main
```

Using the `sources` field will cause Argo CD to ignore the `source` field.

A multisource Application takes, as the name suggests, multiple sources of truth for an Application. Typically this is used when you are deploying a Helm chart, but store the values file in a separate Git repository. Although a great feature, we will not be deploying any examples using this method.

### Git

Using Git as a source is a natural starting point for Argo CD users, as it's the focal point of where *GitOps* gets its name. Git is not only the de facto source code management (SCM) system for developers, but is also the place where site reliability engineers (SREs) and platform engineers store their infrastructure as code (IaC) configurations. Many users making the switch to Argo CD and/or GitOps find that they are storing a lot of things on Git already.

Storing resources in Git, as an Argo CD Application source, can be as simple as having raw YAML stored containing Kubernetes resources within a directory. However, it doesn't have to be raw YAML. The declarations can also be stored and managed via templating tools, such as Kustomize (covered later in this chapter) or Helm (covered next).

### Helm

Helm has become the de facto package manager for Kubernetes applications and deployments. At its core, Helm includes a templating engine for use with Kubernetes manifests so that they are reusable, reproducible, and stable. Many organizations have adopted Helm, and it's a natural choice for developers and system administrators alike because of its ease of use and flexibility.

Since many organizations have widely adopted Helm, it was a natural fit for Argo CD. Argo CD can use Helm by directly consuming the Helm chart stored in a standard Helm repository, OCI registry, or embedded within a Git repository.

## Destinations

In Argo CD, the *destination* refers to a Kubernetes cluster. This destination cluster can either be the cluster that is running Argo CD or another remote cluster (which can be thought of as "hub and spoke," where there is a central control plane managing remote systems).

The destination cluster is noted under `.spec.destination` in the Argo CD Application manifest. Here is a snippet of the configuration:

```
spec:
  destination:
    server: https://kubernetes.default.svc
    namespace: bgd
```

In this example, the `server` field is set to `https://kubernetes.default.svc`, which refers to the cluster that Argo CD is running on. You can also specify `name` instead of `server`, which is a reference to the `name` field in the cluster secret. This will be discussed in depth in Chapter 7. The `namespace` field indicates which namespace to target.

The `namespace` field *does not* overwrite the `.metadata.namespace` field if they are declared within your manifests.

Clusters can be added either declaratively or via the `argocd` CLI, resulting in a new Secret to be added to the namespace Argo CD is deployed within.

For example, you can see any clusters that Argo CD is managing by listing Secrets using the `kubectl` command:

```
$ kubectl get secrets -n argocd -l argocd.argoproj.io/secret-type=cluster
NAME                                 TYPE  DATA   AGE
cluster-192.168.1.254-1289728133   Opaque   3    31s
```

More information about adding and managing clusters within Argo CD will be covered in depth in Chapter 7.

# Tools

One of the main tenets of GitOps is that declarations/configurations must exist in an immutate format (the second OpenGitOps principle). In a Kubernetes environment, this means that YAML is stored inside a Git repository. After a while, those who are just starting out in their GitOps journey ask themselves: How do I declaratively describe my resources in Git without copying and pasting *the same* YAML all over the place?

It might seem like you'll have to duplicate a lot of the same YAML after you take things like environments, clusters, regulatory restrictions, and anything else in your organization that might force you to create a lot of YAML with only slight variations between files into consideration. After a while this simple YAML that should be applicable "anywhere"...all of a sudden doesn't fit anywhere. Luckily, there are tools that can help you mitigate the issue of having to copy and paste the same YAML all over the place while making only small modifications.

## Helm

As mentioned previously, Helm has become the de facto package manager and delivery mechanism for applications and controllers alike in a Kubernetes-based environment. If you've ever worked on a Kubernetes cluster, you have most likely used Helm at some point to deploy software from an independent software vendor (ISV), stacks, or even deliver your own application by leveraging its automation benefits. Helm provides not only a method of packaging an application and parameterizing YAML manifests, but also a templating engine that can be used to deploy your application to different environments.

Helm consists of different parts, as shown in Figure 4-1. Charts are templatized versions of your application's YAML manifests that are parameterized so that you can inject values into the defined templates. Helm combines the templatized manifests with parameters, called *values*, to produce the resources to apply to the Kubernetes cluster. The specific installation of a chart within a cluster is known as a *release*. The end state representation of the produced release manifests is stored as a Secret within the installed namespace on the Kubernetes cluster.

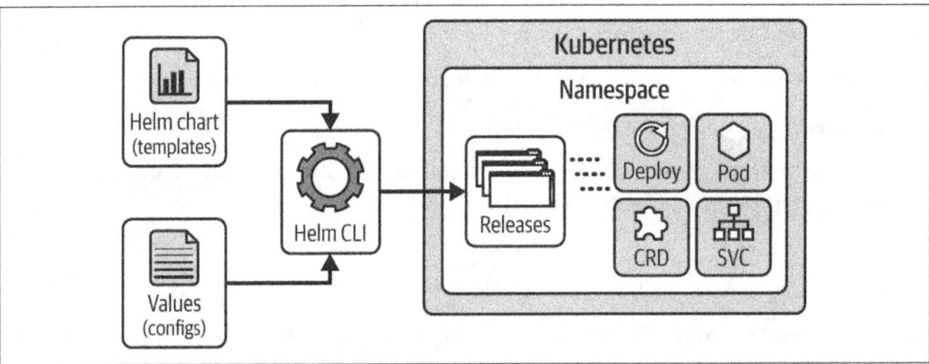


*Figure 4-1. Helm architecture*

Secrets are the default backend storage (i.e., stores installation information) for Helm 3. Consult the Helm documentation for more information.

Helm has a large ecosystem and many repositories that end users can draw on to deploy prebuilt applications. If your organization uses Helm heavily, you're in luck! Most GitOps tools support deploying Helm charts.

## Kustomize

Kustomize is a framework built within the Kubernetes community that lets you patch Kubernetes manifests without needing to modify the original Kubernetes manifests. While patching can be done via JSON patches, the manifest that it modifies needs to be in YAML.

Kustomize is hierarchically organized using a directory structure based on a concept of *bases* and *overlays*. While each of these directories have their own purpose within Kustomize, they must contain a `kustomization` file (`kustomization.yaml`), which defines how to process the contents within the current directory along with importing content from other relative or remote sources.

The following is a simple example of a `kustomization.yaml`:

```
apiVersion: kustomize.config.k8s.io/v1beta1
kind: Kustomization

namePrefix: kustomize-

resources:
- guestbook-ui-deployment.yaml
- guestbook-ui-svc.yaml
```

When using Kustomize against the prior example, two Kubernetes resources will be produced with their names prefixed with `kustomize-`, as defined in the `namePrefix` property.

Kustomize is a powerful tool, and since it is built within the Kubernetes community, support is available within the `kubectl` CLI. Adding the `-k` flag when using `kubectl create` and `kubectl apply` commands will activate Kustomize processing. However, by using the `kubectl kustomize` subcommand instead, the full feature set of the `kustomize` CLI can be achieved.

Kustomize truly is a powerful tool because it eliminates the duplication of YAML and enables the ability to reuse by providing a method of patching the YAML to fit the need of the deployment. This means that you can store differences (for example, between environments) as deltas instead of copying the YAML for each use. The Kustomize structure provides flexibility by creating overlays that can leverage other bases and other overlays, creating a cascading sequence of files. Those overlays can refer to remote repositories as well. Kustomize can even process Helm charts, which can be achieved within Argo CD.

## Beyond Helm and Kustomize

While Helm and Kustomize are the two primary tools that are used in Argo CD to render resources within a Kubernetes cluster (aside from raw YAML), other tools are also supported. Argo CD natively supports the JSON templating language Jsonnet and will process any file containing the **.jsonnet* extension. Nonnative tooling can also be included through the use of a config management plugin (like Cue, for example), eliminating restrictions to customizing how Kubernetes resources are produced. More information on config management plugins and their use can be found in Chapter 11.

# Deploying Your First Application

Now that you're familiar with what an Argo CD Application is and its basic functionality, it's time to deploy your first Argo CD Application! Yes, we did walk through deploying an Application back in Chapter 2 when Argo CD was first installed, but by now, you have a better understanding of the purpose of an Application and how they can be used. Throughout the rest of this book, you'll be exploring many ways of deploying an Application, but for this example, we'll be going with deploying from a Helm chart.

For this example, create the following Argo CD Application YAML in a file called `quarkus-app.yaml`.

Here, we are going to define the name of the `Application` to be `quarkus-app` and we will be deploying the `Application` to the same cluster as Argo CD is running (denoted by `in-cluster` in the `.spec.destination.name` field). We are targeting the `demo` namespace on the destination cluster (i.e., which namespace to deploy the manifests to):

```
apiVersion: argoproj.io/v1alpha1
kind: Application
metadata:
  name: quarkus-app
  namespace: argocd
spec:
  project: default
  destination:
    namespace: demo
    name: in-cluster
  source:
    helm:
      parameters:
        - name: build.enabled
          value: "false"
        - name: deploy.route.enabled
          value: "false"
        - name: image.name
          value: quay.io/ablock/gitops-helm-quarkus
    chart: quarkus
```

```
    repoURL: https://redhat-developer.github.io/redhat-helm-charts
    targetRevision: 0.0.3
  syncPolicy:
    automated:
      prune: true
      selfHeal: true
    syncOptions:
    - CreateNamespace=true
```

The keyword `in-cluster` is a special keyword that means "target the cluster that the instance of Argo CD is running in."

We are deploying the `quarkus` chart version `0.0.3` from the repo denoted in the `repoURL` field. We are also providing any parameters in the `.spec.source.helm.parameters` field, which represent Helm values being set against the chart. Also take note: we are adding the `CreateNamespace=true` option in the `syncOptions` field (in order to make sure the namespace exists before deploying the manifests). This example deployment of a Helm chart using an Argo CD `Application` is analogous to the following command:

```
$ helm install quarkus-app --namespace demo --create-namespace --version 0.0.3 \
--set build.enabled=false \
--set deploy.route.enabled=false \
--set image.name=quay.io/ablock/gitops-helm-quarkus \
redhat-helm-charts/quarkus
```

To make use of the sample `helm install` command, the Helm chart repository containing the `quarkus` chart must be added to the local machine using the `helm repo add <repo URL>` command. If the chart is installed using the Helm CLI, be sure that it is uninstalled prior to defining the chart using Argo CD. Otherwise, errors will be produced.

To create this Argo CD `Application` within the Kubernetes cluster, you can apply it using the following `kubectl` command:

```
kubectl apply -f quarkus-app.yaml
```

You should see the Application appear in the Argo CD UI, as shown in Figure 4-2.

*Figure 4-2. Sample Helm chart application*

See Chapters 2 and 3 for more information about connecting to the Argo CD UI.

You should also be able to see the manifests deployed on the cluster using the Kubernetes CLI client. For example:

```
$ kubectl get deploy,service,pods -n demo
NAME                         READY   UP-TO-DATE   AVAILABLE   AGE
deployment.apps/quarkus-app   1/1     1            1           9m24s

NAME                    TYPE        CLUSTER-IP       EXTERNAL-IP   PORT(S)
AGE
service/quarkus-app    ClusterIP    10.106.53.207    <none>
8080/TCP    9m24s

NAME                               READY   STATUS   RESTARTS     AGE
pod/quarkus-app-57cf4d4b5c-q5jb8    1/1     Running    0           9m24s
```

One very important thing to note is the behavior in comparison to using the Helm CLI directly. Running `helm ls -n demo` against the namespace that contains an Argo CD–managed Helm chart will not return any results:

```
$ helm ls -n demo
NAME    NAMESPACE       REVISION        UPDATED STATUS   CHART    APP VERSION
```

Why? Argo CD takes the philosophical approach of only working with "RAW Kubernetes manifests" directly. This means that Argo CD wants to "own" the manifests and not have to rely on trying to interface with another tool. Argo CD achieves this by doing the equivalent of running: `helm template <options> | kubectl apply -f -`.

You may see other Helm releases running, but you won't see anything deployed via Argo CD.

A release is only created whenever the `install` or `upgrade` subcommands of the Helm CLI is used, which explains why a release is not present for Helm charts maintained by Argo CD.

## Deleting Applications

Regardless of the tool being used to produce Kubernetes resources or the destination where these resources will be created, there may be a need to remove the Application so that the generated resources are no longer managed by Argo CD. Deleting an Application, similar to creating an Application, can be facilitated by using the `kubectl` command.

Execute the following command to delete the Application:

```
kubectl delete application quarkus-app -n argocd
```

Once the Application has been deleted, the tile representing the Application will no longer be present in the Argo CD interface. You should see something like in Figure 4-3.

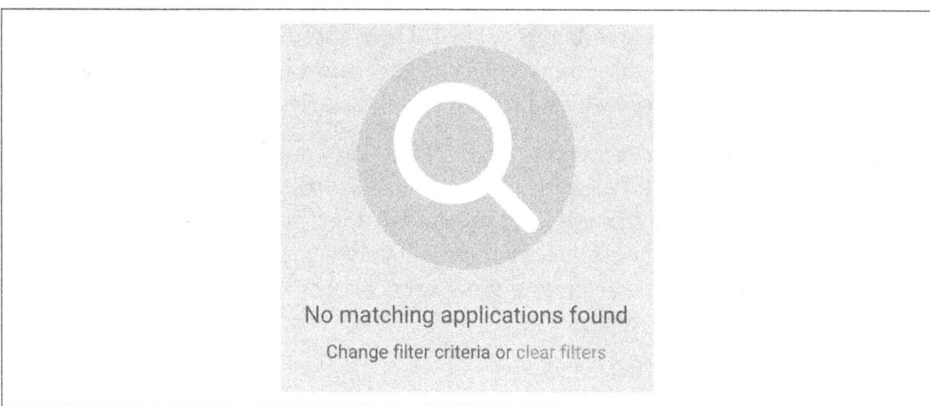
No matching applications found
Change filter criteria or clear filters

*Figure 4-3. Application deleted*

It is important to note, and you may have discovered this already, that even though the Application was deleted, the resources that were managed by the Application still remain within the `argocd` namespace.

"Why is that the case?" you may wonder.

Argo CD makes the assumption that even though there is no longer a desire to manage these sets of resources, there will still be a need for them to remain within the cluster after the Application is deleted. This is mainly due to the motivation of avoiding data loss of the resources and so that anything dependent on them remains available. This approach is similar to how `PersistentVolumes` are managed within `StatefulSets` upon the removal of the `StatefulSet` itself or one of the replicas.

To remove the resources that are managed by an Application, the `resources-finalizer.argocd.argoproj.io` finalizer can be set on the Application:

```
apiVersion: argoproj.io/v1alpha1
kind: Application
metadata:
  name: quarkus-app
  namespace: argocd
  finalizers:
    - resources-finalizer.argocd.argoproj.io
```

If an Application has this finalizer present (either by an administrator or ApplicationSet), upon deletion, the Argo CD controller will perform a cascading deletion of all of the resources that it is managing.

## Finalizers

Finalizers are a feature of Kubernetes associated with garbage collection that controls when a resource is deleted. When a resource is deleted, the `.metadata.deletionTimestamp` field is populated, which triggers controllers to clean up any resource that is owned by the resource being deleted. Once the cleanup process completes, the associated controller will remove the finalizer from the resource. Only when all finalizers have been removed will the resource itself be deleted.

When deleting dependent resources, Argo CD makes use of the *foreground* cascade deletion policy, which will delete the dependent resources first and then delete the Application afterward. If there is a desire to use the *background* cascade deletion policy, which will delete the Application immediately while the controller deletes the associated resources, the `resources-finalizer.argocd.argoproj.io/background` finalizer can be set on the Application:

```
apiVersion: argoproj.io/v1alpha1
kind: Application
metadata:
  name: quarkus-app
  namespace: argocd
  finalizers:
    - resources-finalizer.argocd.argoproj.io
    - resources-finalizer.argocd.argoproj.io/background
```

## Summary

This chapter focused on managing Kubernetes resources through Argo CD Applications, which are Custom Resource Definitions (CRDs) representing a logical collection of related resources. These Applications are the smallest unit of work in Argo CD, defining the desired state of resources within a Kubernetes cluster. This chapter covers the essential components of an Argo CD Application, including the source and destination specifications, and introduces the templating tools supported by Argo CD, such as Helm and Kustomize.

An Argo CD Application specifies the source of resource manifests, typically located in a Git repository or Helm chart repository. With the introduction of multisource applications in Argo CD version 2.6, users can now specify multiple sources for a single application. Templating tools like Helm and Kustomize help manage and deploy Kubernetes manifests efficiently, avoiding redundancy and facilitating modifications.

This chapter also provided a guide for deploying applications using Argo CD, focusing on Helm chart deployments. It explains the synchronization policies and the importance of finalizers in managing application deletions. Finalizers ensure that dependent resources are cleaned up properly, preventing data loss and maintaining resource availability. This chapter emphasizes Argo CD's approach to managing raw Kubernetes manifests, ensuring consistency and control over the deployment process.

CHAPTER 5

# Synchronizing Applications

Argo CD's synchronization process makes it easy to be able to take Kubernetes resources stored within Git or Helm repositories and apply them to a target cluster. Given that this capability is one of the core features of Argo CD, there are a variety of options available for determining when the synchronization process will be triggered and how the Kubernetes resources will be applied. This level of control is important, as there may be a need to guard exactly how and when content is applied (for example, if certain resources need to be applied in a specific order). In this chapter, we will explore the options available when synchronizing Argo CD Applications, their impact against the lifecycle of the application itself, the Argo CD server, and ultimately the target Kubernetes cluster.

## Managing How Applications Are Synchronized

Given that the synchronization of content from source to target Kubernetes cluster is a fundamental concept in Argo CD, it is important to first understand the defaults that Argo CD applies and the various levels of customizations that are available. If you recall in Chapter 4, we briefly introduced synchronization and covered how the configurations can be defined within the `.spec.syncPolicy` property of an Application.

By default, when Applications are created, none of the rendered resources are applied to the Kubernetes cluster. This may surprise many new Argo CD users given that Argo CD is a tool that manages assets that are destined for Kubernetes. However, there are a number of reasons why this is Argo CD's default behavior:

- As the configurations for an Application are refined, there may be a need or desire to "preview" the changes that would be applied without performing any change.
- It may be important to control when and how resources are applied.
- Organizational policies may prohibit automating changes to infrastructure.

The Argo CD UI and application resource provide a glimpse of the resources that would be affected, but any synchronization against the cluster needs to be performed in a manual fashion. Synchronization of manifests can be achieved through the UI by selecting the Sync button on the application or from the Argo CD CLI using the `argocd app sync` command.

Syncs can also be initiated by running the `kubectl` patch command. More information can be found in the Argo CD documentation (*https://oreil.ly/qXR9u*).

Since most users would want to take advantage of an automated synchronization of an application, let's illustrate the ways that this can be achieved:

- Specify the sync policy for the application using the `argocd` CLI:

```
$ argocd app set <APPNAME> --sync-policy automated
```

- Select the Enable Auto-Sync button within the Argo CD UI.
- Define the configuration explicitly within the Application resource:

```
spec:
  syncPolicy:
    automated: {}
```

Regardless of the option chosen (either manual or automated), as soon as the source content differs from the live state of the cluster, the application will be synchronized.

## Sync Options

Aside from the fundamental determination of whether an application should be synchronized automatically or manually, Argo CD can be configured to perform a customized operation of how it synchronizes the desired state to the target cluster through the `.spec.syncPolicy.syncOptions` property. These customizations can, for the most part, be configured on the application resource itself. However, others can be defined as annotations within each individual resource that is associated with an application. This is especially useful when you want a specific action to occur against a set of resources, but not in all of the manifests associated within an Argo CD Application.

Let's first take a look at how Sync Options can be used within an Argo CD Application.

## Application-Level Options

As mentioned previously, synchronization options are specified under the `.spec .syncPolicy.syncOptions` in the application manifest. These options will affect all resources that are associated with the Argo CD Application. The following example `Application` manifest goes through the sync options available:

```
apiVersion: argoproj.io/v1alpha1
kind: Application
metadata:
    name: sample-app
    namespace: argocd
spec:
  syncPolicy:
    syncOptions:
      - Validate=true
      - ApplyOutOfSyncOnly=true
      - CreateNamespace=true
      - PrunePropagationPolicy=foreground
      - PruneLast=true
      - Replace=false
      - ServerSideApply=true
      - FailOnSharedResource=true
      - RespectIgnoreDifferences=true
```

Let's dive a little deeper into the `syncOptions` configurations:

`Validate=false`
: By default, Argo CD uses Kubernetes API validation and will fail the sync operation if the manifest is not valid (equivalent to running: `kubectl apply --validate=false`). The default value is: `true`.

`ApplyOutOfSyncOnly=true`
: By default, Argo CD applies every object in an Argo CD Application. This could pose a problem if you have thousands and thousands of objects. This option only synchronizes/applies to objects that are out of sync.

`CreateNamespace=true`
: This option creates the namespace (in the `spec.destination.namespace` section of the Argo CD Application), if it does not already exist, before Argo CD attempts to apply the objects in an application.

`PrunePropagationPolicy=foreground`
: This option shapes how the application handles pruning/deleting of resources (known as *garbage collection*). The default is `foreground`, and other options available are `background` and `orphan`.

`PruneLast=true`
: This option allows the ability for resource pruning to happen as a final part of a sync operation, after the other resources have been deployed and become healthy, and after all other waves are completed successfully.

`Replace=false`
: By default, Argo CD does the equivalent of `kubectl apply`. This sometimes poses an issue when the object is too big to fit into `kubectl.kubernetes.io/last-applied-configuration` annotation. Note, this option could be dangerous if set to `true`, as a Replace operation effectively does a Delete and the Recreate operation. Deleting things like storage claims or CRDs can cause production outages.

`ServerSideApply=true`
: This option enables Argo CD to use server-side apply when running a sync operation. This is equivalent to running `kubectl apply --server-side`. Most of the time, since this option is used to apply deltas of changes, the `Validate=false` option is frequently used in conjunction with this option.

`FailOnSharedResource=true`
: With this option, Argo CD will mark the application as failed whenever it finds a resource associated with the application that has already been applied in the cluster via another application.

`RespectIgnoreDifferences=true`
: By default, Argo CD uses the `ignoreDifferences` config, found in `.spec.ignoreDifferences`, only for calculating the difference between the live and desired state (but still applies the object as it is defined in Git). This option also takes it into consideration during the sync operation.

## Resource-Level Options

Along with the sync options on the Argo CD Application level, users can also apply these configurations/options at the object/individual resource level. This means that you don't have to apply any of the sync options against all resources contained within the entire Argo CD Application, but to only specific objects. A subset of the application sync options are available to individual objects, as well as several other additional options.

These resource-level options can be set by annotating the resource you want the option to apply to. You can do this by defining the `argocd.argoproj.io/sync-options` annotation under `metadata.annotations` on the resource you would like to apply the option to. For example, to skip Kubernetes validation on a specific object:

```
metadata:
  annotations:
    argocd.argoproj.io/sync-options: Validate=false
```

By implementing this approach, only the object with this annotation will skip Kubernetes validation while the rest of the objects within the Argo CD Application will be validated. The options available via the `argocd.argoproj.io/sync-options` annotation are:

- `Validate`
- `PruneLast`
- `Replace`
- `ServerSideApply`

In addition, the following options are available for individual resources using the `argocd.argoproj.io/sync-options` annotation:

`Prune=false`
: This prevents the annotated object from being pruned.

`SkipDryRunOnMissingResource=true`
: Argo CD, by default, performs a "dry run" of applying the manifests (equivalent to using the `--dry-run` option with `kubectl`); this option skips the dry run step. This is especially useful if you are deploying CRDs or Operators, as the associated resource may not be available as a registered resource at the specific validation time. This option is commonly paired with the retry strategy, which will perform subsequent attempts to synchronize the Application where a failure no longer occurs, as the desired resource has become available.

Users can specify multiple options in the annotation by separating the options with a comma (,) between each of the desired options. For example, to disable validation and use server-side apply within a resource, you can set the following in your object:

```
metadata:
  annotations:
    argocd.argoproj.io/sync-options: Validate=false,ServerSideApply=true
```

Using this configuration, the object with this annotation will disable validation *and* use server-side apply.

## Sync Order and Hooks

Argo CD has the ability to customize the order in which the manifests are applied. Furthermore, Argo CD incorporates different sync phases so that users can further fine-tune how objects are applied to the target cluster.

### Hooks

Argo CD has the ability to set up different sync phases by allowing the user to utilize hooks. These injection points within the application lifecycle enable additional automation, such as running scripts before, during, and/or after a sync has completed to supplement applying the standard set of resources. You can also use hooks in the event a sync has failed for whatever reason. While hooks can be implemented as any Kubernetes object, they are usually as Pods or Jobs.

There are four hooks that can be used in your Argo CD sync process:

`PreSync`
: This phase occurs prior to the `Sync` phase. This is typically used for actions that need to occur before the Application is synced. A common use case is running a script that performs a schema update against a database.

`Sync`
: This is the standard (default) phase for Argo CD and is executed once the `PreSync` phase has finished. This is typically used to aid the Argo CD Application deployment process in the event more complex activities within the Application need to occur.

`PostSync`
: This phase occurs after the `Sync` phase has been completed. This can be used to send a notification that the phase has been completed or to trigger a CI progress or continue a CI/CD workflow.

`SyncFail`
: This is a special hook that is run only if a sync operation has failed. This is normally used for alerting or performing cleanup activities.

`PostDelete`
: This is typically used for any cleanup tasks after all other resources have been deleted.

When setting up an Argo CD Application, the resources that are in your source of truth are applied to the destination cluster during the `Sync` phase. The other phases are used to perform pre- or posttasks before and/or after the objects are applied in the `Sync` phase.

It is important to note that each phase is dependent on the success of the previous phase (with the exception of the `SyncFail` phase). For example, if an error occurs in the `PreSync` phase, the `Sync` phase will not run.

In order to indicate which resource in your Git repository belongs to which phase, you will have to annotate the desired resource with `argocd.argoproj.io/hook` with the value of the phase that it should execute within (the absence of the hook annotation results in the resource being applied during the `Sync` phase). For example, for a Job to be executed in the `PostSync` phase, the following annotation is applied:

```
metadata:
  annotations:
    argocd.argoproj.io/hook: PostSync
```

Resources that make use of hooks can be deleted when a sync operation is performed by using the `argocd.argoproj.io/hook-delete-policy` annotation. The following hook deletion policies are available:

`HookSucceeded`
: The hook resource/object is deleted once it has successfully completed.

`HookFailed`
: The hook resource/object is deleted if the hook has failed.

`BeforeHookCreation`
: Any hook resource/object will be deleted before the new one is created. This is the default if no hook deletion policy is specified.

Here is an example of a `PostSync` hook with a deletion policy of `HookSucceeded`:

```
metadata:
  annotations:
    argocd.argoproj.io/hook: PostSync
    argocd.argoproj.io/hook-delete-policy: HookSucceeded
```

It is important to note that hooks that are named (i.e., ones with `.metadata.name` defined) will be created/run only once. If you want a hook to be re-created or re-run each time there is a sync operation, either use the `BeforeHookCreation` deletion policy or use `.metadata.generateName` in your resource/object.

Note: As of the time of this writing, certain tools, such as Kustomize, have limited support for the use of the `generateName` property.

## Sync Waves

Argo CD applies manifests in a specific order. You can see this order by inspecting the code (*https://oreil.ly/QbCwy*). In most cases, the default order that Argo CD applies resources should work. However, complex deployments may inevitably require changes to this default order. This is where sync waves come in.

Sync waves work best if proper Application health checks are in place. This will be reviewed in depth in Chapter 10.

The concept of sync waves is pretty straightforward. The desired resource is annotated with the order in which you wish Argo CD to apply your manifests using `argocd.argoproj.io/sync-wave` key with an integer value denoted as a string:

```
metadata:
  annotations:
    argocd.argoproj.io/sync-wave: "5"
```

By default, every resource gets assigned "wave 0," unless otherwise specified via the annotation. Numbers can be negative as well. So, for example, consider the following:

- Namespace as wave "–1"
- Service Account as wave "0"
- Deployment as wave "1"

The Namespace would be applied first, then the Service Account, and then finally the Deployment.

A good use case for sync waves is to apply CRDs first before the corresponding custom resource.

Sync waves can also be used within the confines of a hook. This means that you can have resources within a `PreSync` hook phase be applied in a specific order, within that phase, without affecting other hook phases. In the following example, the Job will be applied in wave "3" within the `PreSync` hook phase:

```
apiVersion: batch/v1
kind: Job
metadata:
  name: create-tables
  annotations:
    argocd.argoproj.io/sync-wave: "3"
    argocd.argoproj.io/hook: PreSync
```

Now, you can also have the following resource in a `PostSync` hook:

```
apiVersion: batch/v1
kind: Job
metadata:
  name: test-deployment
metadata:
  annotations:
    argocd.argoproj.io/sync-wave: "1"
    argocd.argoproj.io/hook: PostSync
```

In these two examples, the `create-tables` will be applied before the `test-deployment` even though `test-deployment` is a lower wave. This is due to the fact that the `create-tables` resource is in a different hook phase. The important thing to note when considering sync waves with hooks is that sync waves are scoped within each hook phase. This provides administrators with flexibility in how manifests get applied to the destination.

# Comparing Options

There might be cases where you will need to exclude resources from the overall status of your application—for example, if you have a resource created by another controller (this is common when working with Kubernetes Operators). This can be achieved with the following annotation:

```
metadata:
  annotations:
    argocd.argoproj.io/compare-options: IgnoreExtraneous
```

This only affects the sync status. If the resource's health is degraded, then the application will also be degraded.

For example, the following Secret instructs the OpenShift OAuth operator to create another Secret for the OpenShift OAuth controller to consume. By doing so, Argo CD will mark your Argo CD Application "out of sync." To work around this issue, use the aforementioned `argocd.argoproj.io/compare-options: IgnoreExtraneous` annotation:

```
apiVersion: v1
kind: Secret
type: Opaque
metadata:
  name: htpass-secret
  namespace: openshift-config
  annotations:
    argocd.argoproj.io/compare-options: IgnoreExtraneous
data:
  htpasswd: bm90VGhlRHJvaWRzWW91cmVMb29raW5nRm9y
```

This will mark your Application as "healthy" in Argo CD, but it's important to note that it'll mark the created resource as "out of sync." However, the overall Application health is not affected.

# Managing Resource Differences

Argo CD allows you to manage how you handle differences from your source of truth and current state within Kubernetes by the way of ignoring differences. There are several locations where ignoring differences can be configured. This configuration can be applied on a per–Argo CD Application basis or for the whole Argo CD system (where all the Applications in an Argo CD installation are affected).

## Application-Level Diffing

As the name suggests, *application-level diffing* allows you to ignore differences within individual applications at a specific JSON path, using RFC6902 JSON patches (*https://oreil.ly/ncPGa*) and jq path expressions (*https://oreil.ly/Y-31-*). Using the JSON path, you can specify paths referencing properties that Argo CD should ignore when it compares the running state with the desired state defined. Here is an example:

```
apiVersion: argoproj.io/v1alpha1
kind: Application
metadata:
  name: myapp
spec:
  ignoreDifferences:
  - group: apps
    kind: Deployment
    jsonPointers:
    - /spec/replicas
```

The `ignoreDifferences` setting allows you to specify the name of the resource and the namespace as well as the Group Version Kind (GVK). For more complex manifests, you can use the jq path expression to define specific items to ignore in a more granular fashion. For example:

```
apiVersion: argoproj.io/v1alpha1
kind: Application
metadata:
  name: myapp
spec:
  ignoreDifferences:
  - group: apps
    kind: Deployment
    jqPathExpressions:
    - .spec.template.spec.initContainers[] | select(.name == "injected-init-container")
```

Visit *https://jqlang.org* for more on the jq expression language and how to use the jq path expression option.

You can also ignore fields owned by specific managers by using `managedFieldsManagers` and listing the specific managers to ignore.

An additional item to note: most users will use the `RespectIgnoreDifferences` sync option in conjunction with this `ignoreDifferences` setting.

### System-Level Diffing

Argo CD can also be set up to ignore differences at a system level. This allows administrators to be able to set global ignore settings for the specific Argo CD installation. These configurations can be set up for a specified group and kind by using the `resource.customizations` key of `argocd-cm` ConfigMap using the following format:

```
data:
  resource.customizations.ignoreDifferences.apps_Deployment: |
   jsonPointers:
    - /spec/replicas
```

Take note that the `resource.customizations` key also includes the keyword `ignoreDifferences` with the GKV demarcated by an underscore (_), using a flattened approach. For more information about how to formulate these settings, please see the official Argo CD documentation site on system-level diffing (*https://oreil.ly/xp47q*). There you can see more specific examples of modifying how Argo CD handles diffs as a global setting.

## Use Case: Database Schema Setup

With an understanding of some of the ways to customize the synchronization and the associating current state for applications, let's see it in action with one of the most common use cases: a database schema setup.

We are going to be deploying an Application that is going to consist of a backend database. The database will be set up at deploy time, which means that the database schema will need to be loaded as a part of the deployment. Furthermore, the database schema setup needs to run after the database is up and running. For this specific use case, we are going to be making use of sync waves and Argo CD Application Sync Options.

## Argo CD Application Overview

All the artifacts we will be using are in the aforementioned companion repository (*https://github.com/sabre1041/argocd-up-and-running-book*)—make sure you've cloned this repository if you have not done so already, and ensure that you are in the root directory of this repository.

Inspect the Argo CD Application for this use case, which is located in the *ch05* directory.

Execute `cat ch05/pricelist-app.yaml` from the root directory of the repository and you will see the following manifest:

```
apiVersion: argoproj.io/v1alpha1
kind: Application
metadata:
  name: pricelist-app
  namespace: argocd
  finalizers:
    - resources-finalizer.argocd.argoproj.io
spec:
  project: default
  source:
    path: ch05/manifests/
    repoURL: https://github.com/sabre1041/argocd-up-and-running-book
    targetRevision: main
  destination:
    namespace: pricelist
    name: in-cluster
  syncPolicy:
    automated:
      prune: true
      selfHeal: true
    syncOptions:
      - CreateNamespace=true
    retry:
      limit: 5
      backoff:
        duration: 5s
        factor: 2
        maxDuration: 3m
```

This manifest should look familiar if you have already completed Chapter 4. There are several items of note to point out:

- The `.spec.syncPolicy` has the `automated` options of `prune: true` and `selfHeal: true`. This means that Argo CD will synchronize this application automatically whenever it's out of sync. In addition, it will also delete resources that it is not keeping track of.
- Under `.spec.syncPolicy`, the `CreateNamespace=true` option under `syncOptions` is also defined, which specifies that Argo CD will create the destination namespace if it doesn't already exist.

- Retries under that `.spec.syncPolicy.retry` property have also been defined. This option specifies how many times to retry the sync before Argo CD marks the sync process as "Failed."

One final item to note is that Argo CD will be deploying manifests under the *ch05/manifests/* directory from the repository as denoted in the `.spec.source.path` section. This last item is what we will cover in the next section.

## Manifest Sync Wave Overview

If you take a look under the *ch05/manifests/* directory, you will see a `kustomization.yaml` file, which for the purposes of this example, aggregates the manifests that need to be applied. It's a simple list; basically, it is the resources that we want applied to the cluster:

```
apiVersion: kustomize.config.k8s.io/v1beta1
kind: Kustomization
namespace: pricelist
resources:
- pricelist-db-pvc.yaml
- pricelist-db-svc.yaml
- pricelist-db.yaml
- pricelist-deploy.yaml
- pricelist-job.yaml
- pricelist-svc.yaml
```

For more information about Kustomize, please see Chapter 4.

Normally, Argo CD would apply these manifests in the same order as the output of `kustomize build` in this directory. However, we've added a sync wave annotation to customize the order Argo CD should apply these manifests.

Prior to any other resource in this Application being applied, we want the database and any backend storage to be up and running first. Therefore, we've annotated the `pricelist-db-pvc.yaml` (PersistentVolumeClaim for the database) and `pricelist-db.yaml` (database deployment) manifests with the `argocd.argoproj.io/sync-wave: "1"` annotation to denote that we want these two manifests to be applied first. They both should have the following annotation:

```
metadata:
  annotations:
    argocd.argoproj.io/sync-wave: "1"
```

This will not only make Argo CD apply these manifests first, but the annotation also causes Argo CD to wait until these manifests are in a "ready" state before attempting to go on the next manifest. Once all the manifests in wave 1 are applied and reporting a ready state, the next wave is applied.

In our use case, the next wave is the `pricelist-db-svc.yaml` file, which has the `argocd.argoproj.io/sync-wave: "2"` annotation:

```
apiVersion: v1
kind: Service
metadata:
  name: mysql
  annotations:
    argocd.argoproj.io/sync-wave: "2"
```

Since this is the only manifest with that sync wave annotation, this `pricelist-db-svc.yaml` file will be applied after wave 1.

You can inspect the other manifests in the *ch05/manifests/* directory to inspect the order that they will be applied in:

- `pricelist-db-pvc.yaml` and `pricelist-db.yaml` as sync wave 1
- `pricelist-db-svc.yaml` as sync wave 2
- `pricelist-deploy.yaml` as sync wave 3
- `pricelist-svc.yaml` as sync wave 4
- `pricelist-job.yaml` in a `PostSync` hook in sync wave 0

Before moving on, it's important to note that when you inspect the `pricelist-job.yaml` manifest, this Job is responsible for setting up the database schema. This Job also runs as a `PostSync` hook, which means that it will be applied after all the manifests in the sync phase have been applied. Also note that the Job has a sync wave of 0. Although a sync wave of 0 is the default, the annotation was added to illustrate that sync waves work within phases.

It's good practice to make your hooks be idempotent, given that the hooks, depending on the specific hook, will run multiple times.

Taking a look at the annotations in the `pricelist-job.yaml` manifest:

```
apiVersion: batch/v1
kind: Job
metadata:
  name: pricelist-postdeploy
  annotations:
    argocd.argoproj.io/sync-wave: "0"
    argocd.argoproj.io/hook: PostSync
    argocd.argoproj.io/hook-delete-policy: BeforeHookCreation
```

Another important item to note is the use of a hook deletion policy. This annotation ensures that this Job object should be deleted before the hook phase starts in subsequent sync runs if it is present. To learn more about hook deletion policies, please consult the official Argo CD documentation on resource hooks (*https://oreil.ly/YhDrF*).

## Importance of Probes

Argo CD uses several different sources to determine the overall health of the Application being deployed. One of the important metrics used is health status from the Kubernetes API. In order for this capability to be utilized, it's very important to have readiness/liveness probes set up correctly for each object that needs it. In Kubernetes, liveness probes determine when to restart a container. Readiness probes determine when a container is ready to start accepting traffic.

For more information about how Argo CD handles Application health, please consult the official documentation. We will also go over this in Chapter 10.

In our particular use case, the resources that require probes to be defined in order to achieve the desired goal are the database deployment and the web app deployment. Taking a look at the `pricelist-db.yaml` file, you'll see the following probes:

```
spec:
  template:
    spec:
      containers:
      - image: mysql:8.0.41
        name: mysql
        livenessProbe:
          tcpSocket:
            port: 3306
          initialDelaySeconds: 12
          periodSeconds: 10
        readinessProbe:
          tcpSocket:
            port: 3306
          initialDelaySeconds: 12
          periodSeconds: 10
```

In this instance, TCP port 3306 is waiting to become active before considering the database deployment alive and ready to receive requests. For the web app, which is the `pricelist-deploy.yaml` file, you will see the following probes configured:

```
spec:
  template:
    spec:
      containers:
      - image: quay.io/redhatworkshops/pricelist:latest
        readinessProbe:
          httpGet:
            path: /
            port: 8080
          initialDelaySeconds: 5
          periodSeconds: 2
        livenessProbe:
          tcpSocket:
            port: 8080
          initialDelaySeconds: 5
          periodSeconds: 2
```

In the web app Deployment, we are considering the web app alive when TCP port 8080 is active. The app will not be considered ready until an HTTP GET request returns a response code of 200 on port 8080.

In both cases (the database Deployment and web app Deployment), both probes need to be successful before Argo CD considers the Application "healthy" and "synced."

For more information on probes and how to set them up, please see the official Kubernetes documentation (*https://oreil.ly/patGK*) on probes.

## Seeing It in Action

Now that we've reviewed the use case in detail, let's see it in action by using these manifests in our `kind` instance. From the root directory of the companion Git repository, apply the Application manifest by running the following command:

```
kubectl apply -f ch05/pricelist-app.yaml
```

An Argo CD Application tile should appear in the Argo CD UI as a result. The tile will appear similar to what is depicted in Figure 5-1.

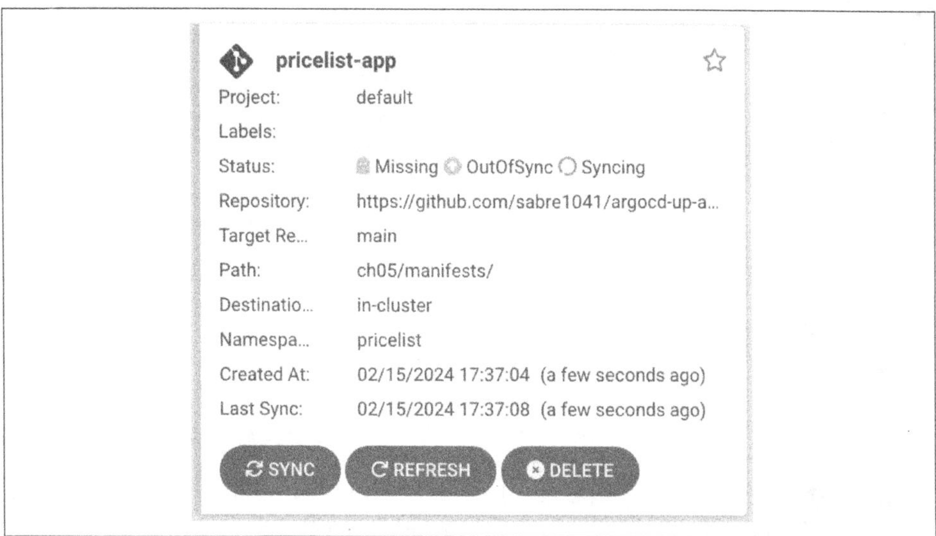


*Figure 5-1. Pricelist Application tile*

The first thing Argo CD does is apply the first sync wave, which is our storage and database Deployment. After clicking on the Application tile, you should be able to see these resources enter the syncing phase first while the other resources are in the "missing" state. Take a look at Figure 5-2 for an example of how this is displayed.

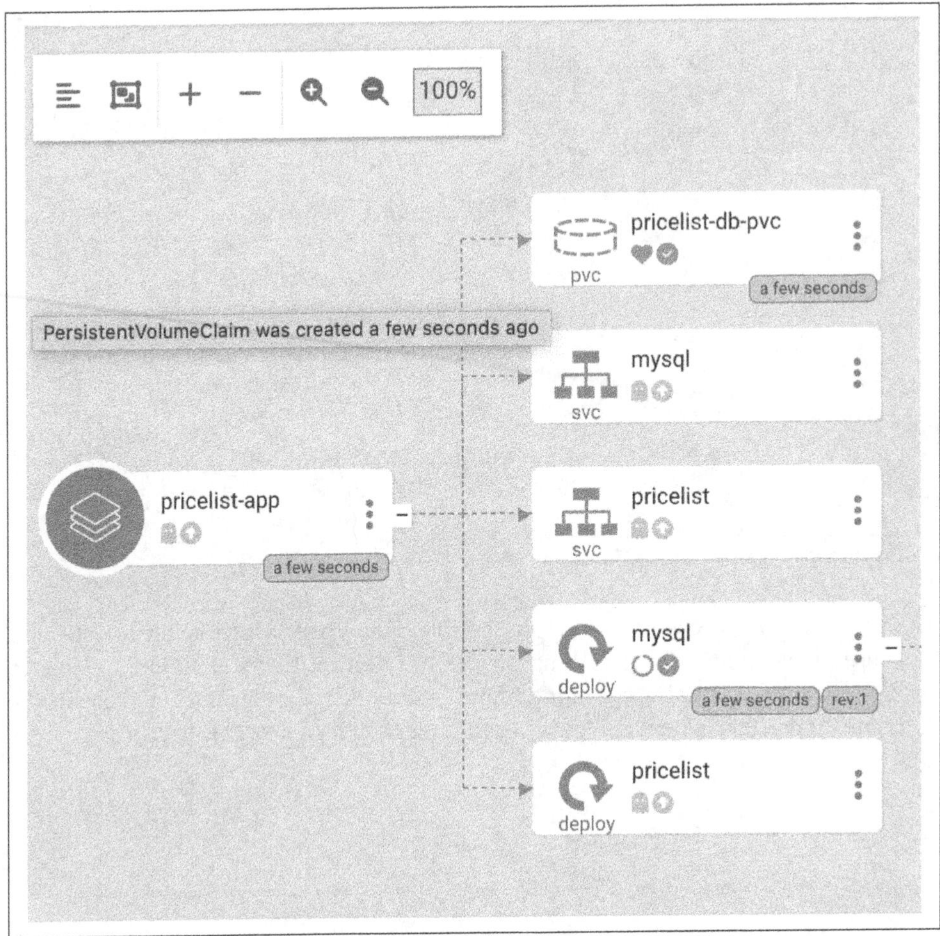


*Figure 5-2. Pricelist sync wave 1*

When the storage is provisioned and the MySQL database is deployed, the next object that Argo CD will apply in our use case is the MySQL service. The Application overview will appear similar to Figure 5-3.

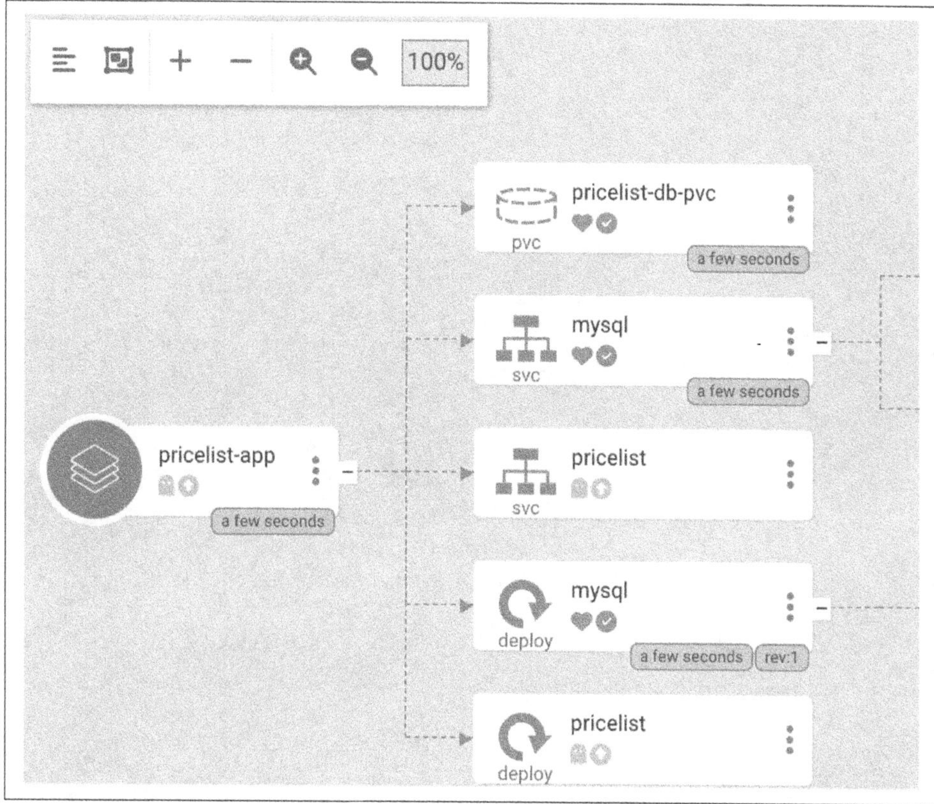


*Figure 5-3. Pricelist sync wave 2*

After the service is healthy, Argo CD will apply the web app Deployment, as seen in Figure 5-4.

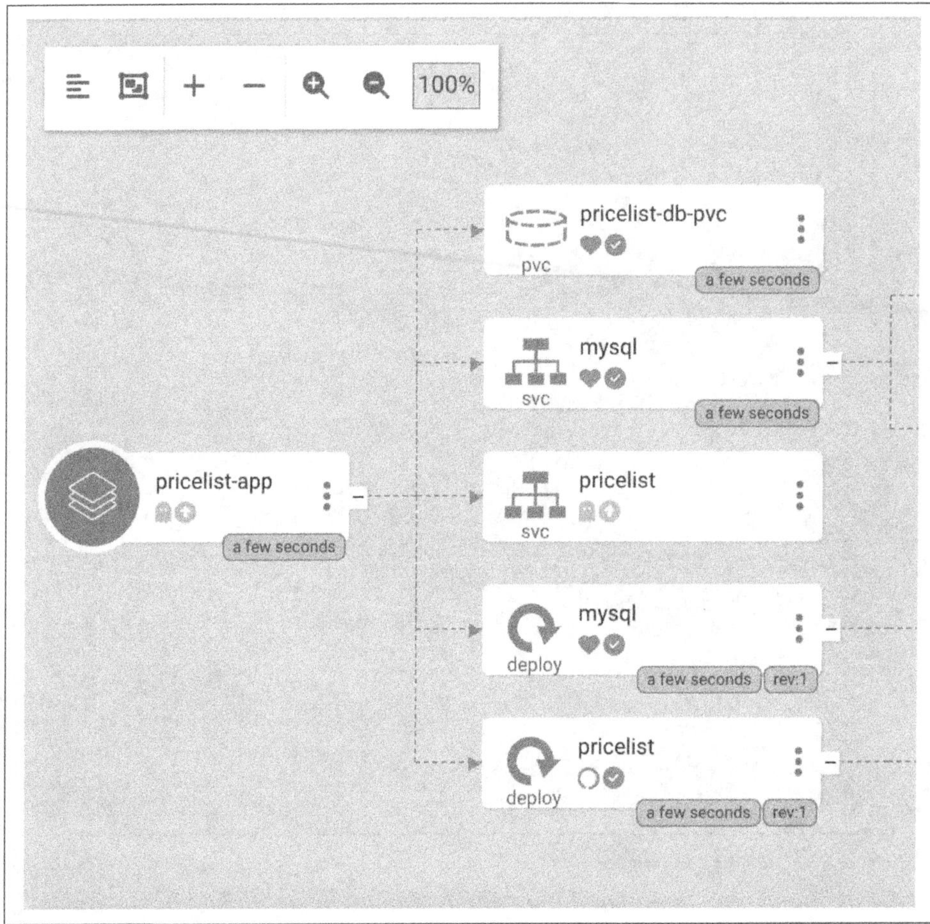


*Figure 5-4. Pricelist sync wave 3*

Once the web app is deployed, the service for the web app is applied, as denoted in Figure 5-5.

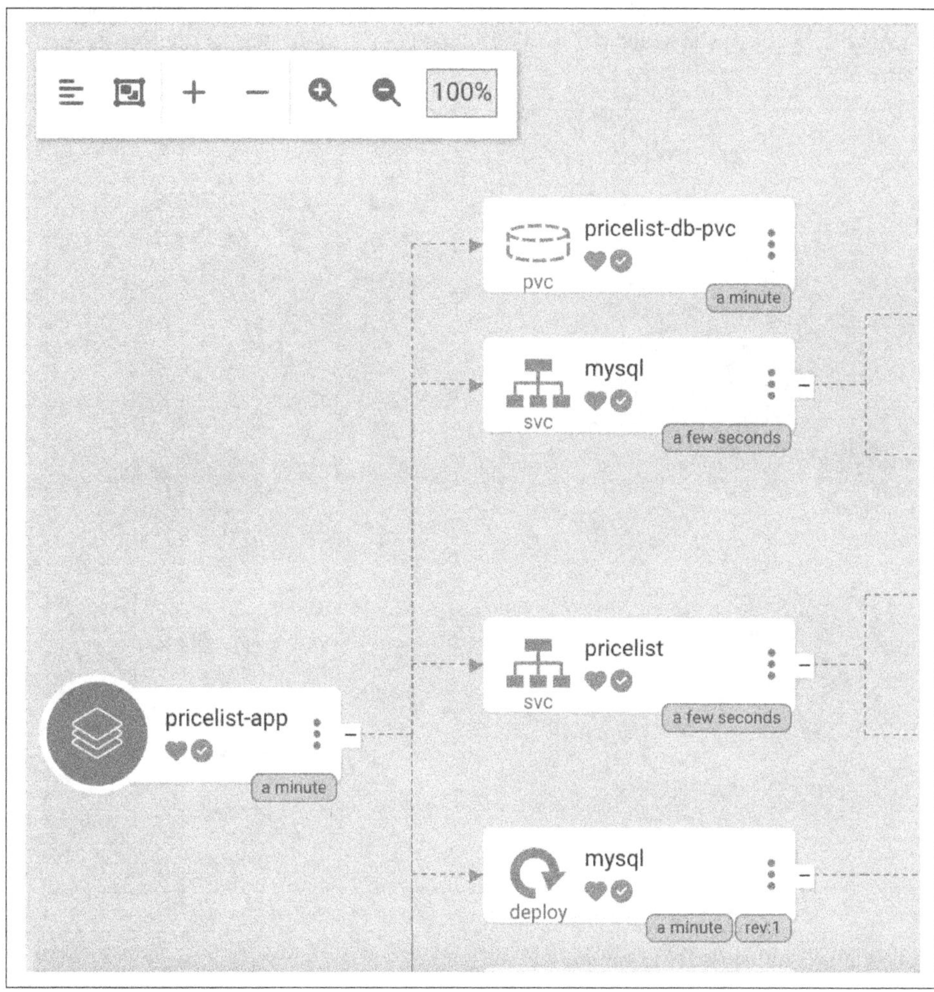


*Figure 5-5. Pricelist sync wave 4*

Once the web app service is deployed and in a healthy state; the `Sync` phase is considered complete, and Argo CD will enter the `PostSync` phase. The final step that Argo CD performs is applying the Job that facilitates the database schema setup. In the Argo CD UI, this is indicated by an anchor (⚓) symbol within the Job, as seen in Figure 5-6.

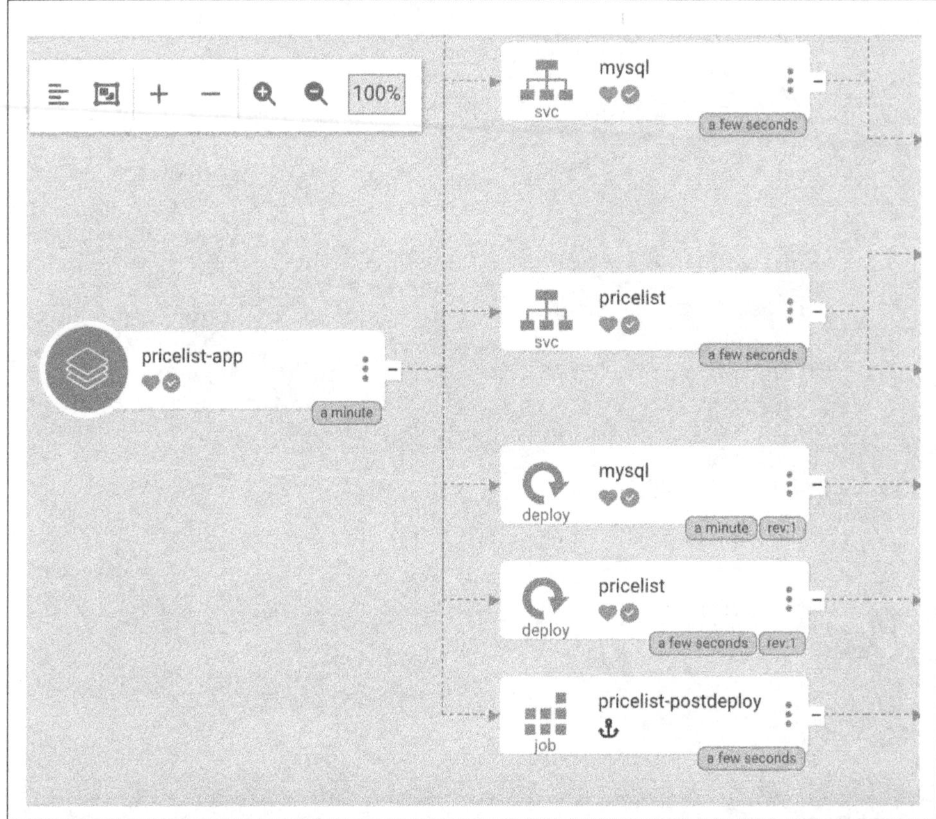


*Figure 5-6. Pricelist `PostSync` hook*

Once the `PostSync` phase finishes, you should now see the Argo CD Application tile for the Application show Healthy and Synced status in the Application overview page. See Figure 5-7 for how this appears.

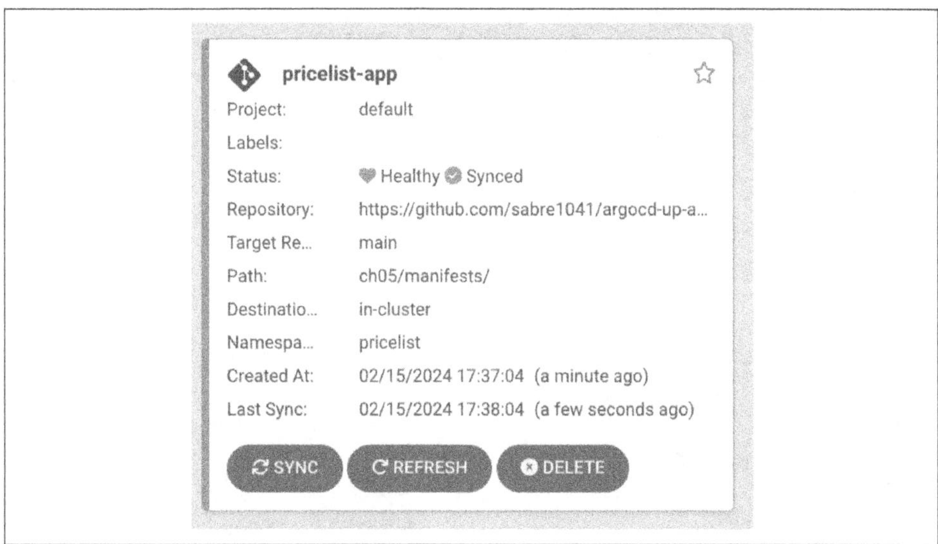


*Figure 5-7. Pricelist synced and healthy*

# Summary

In this chapter, we covered how Argo CD synchronizes applications and how you can customize the method in which Argo CD performs synchronizations on the individual application level and the system as a whole. We also reviewed how to further refine your synchronizations by implementing ordering with sync waves and sync hooks. Finally, we reviewed in detail a use case where sync waves and sync hooks were used to perform a database schema setup during an Argo CD deployment of an application.

# CHAPTER 6

# Authentication and Authorization

Included as part of the standard platform deployment, Argo CD contains a default management user providing unrestricted access to configure the platform using either the UI or via the API/CLI. By providing this functionality out of the box, it simplifies the getting started experience and enables end users to realize the capabilities provided by Argo CD and the concepts embraced by GitOps methodologies.

As adoption grows beyond a single individual managing and utilizing Argo CD, there becomes a need to support additional users aside from a single elevated management user along with integrating with a centralized user management system, such as LDAP or a compatible OIDC provider. While at the same time, when providing the capability to support additional users, there must also be a way to define and govern the level of access that each entity is entitled to.

In this chapter, we will explore how users are managed in Argo CD, including where and how they are defined, the ways that they can perform actions against the tool, and the capabilities to define role-based access control (RBAC) policies to govern their access.

## Managing Users

While Argo CD supports the ability to define and leverage multiple users, upon initial deployment, there is only a single user available for use—"admin." The admin user, as discussed previously, is provided both as a convenience for quickly getting up to speed with the capabilities provided by Argo CD and for allowing unrestricted access to the entire set of features included by the tool. It can be used as the sole entity when Argo CD is utilized by a single individual, complement the incorporation of additional users once they are introduced, or be disabled entirely. Let's look into this admin user and how it can be leveraged at various phases in Argo CD, at initial deployment time and the use afterward.

## The Admin User

When Argo CD is first deployed, a secret named `argocd-initial-admin-secret` is created within the namespace for which Argo CD has been deployed, containing the password for the admin user. Assuming Argo CD has been deployed to the `argocd` namespace, the password can be obtained by using the following command:

```
kubectl -n argocd get secret argocd-initial-admin-secret \
-o jsonpath="{.data.password}" | base64 -d
```

This method for obtaining the admin password was introduced in earlier chapters as we explored the various ways to interact with Argo CD. Let's now explore how we can manage the admin user in further detail.

Using the `argocd` CLI, log in to Argo CD deployed to the `kind` cluster deployed earlier using the previous command to obtain the admin password:

```
argocd login --insecure --grpc-web --username admin \
--password=$(kubectl -n argocd get secret \
argocd-initial-admin-secret \
-o jsonpath="{.data.password}" | base64 -d) argocd.upandrunning.local
```

It is important that the `kind` cluster that is used for this chapter has an ingress controller deployed. Steps to enable the required `kind` cluster environment can be found at the beginning of Chapter 3.

Details relating to the user can be found by using the `argocd account get-user-info`. Use this command to obtain information about the admin user:

```
argocd account get-user-info

Logged In: true
Username: admin
Issuer: argocd
Groups:
```

This output confirms that we successfully authenticated and have an active session as the admin user.

The initial password for the admin user should only be used for initial access and should be changed to prevent unwanted use, given that anyone with the ability to read secrets in the Argo CD namespace can gain access to the password for a privileged user.

The `argocd account update-password` command can be used to change the password for a user. Update the password for the admin user, replacing *<new_password_value>* with the desired password, by executing the following command:

```
argocd account update-password \
--account=admin \
--current-password \
$(kubectl -n argocd get secret argocd-initial-admin-secret \
-o jsonpath="{.data.password}" | base64 -d) --new-password=<new_password_value>
```

By default, the `argocd account update-password` command will update the account of the current user, and in this case, could have been omitted. However, the `--account` flag was included to explicitly select the user for which the password would be updated as well as to demonstrate how to target a different user, if desired.

With the account details updated, let's confirm the updated password works successfully by authenticating to the Argo CD web interface. Launch a browser and enter **`admin`** in the username field and the value of the updated password in the password field. If the credentials were accepted, you have successfully updated the admin password.

Now that the password for the admin user has been changed, the secret containing the initial password can be safely removed, if you choose to do so. Execute the following to delete the initial admin secret:

```
kubectl delete secret argocd-initial-admin-secret -n argocd
```

## Local Users

To give individuals the ability to access Argo CD without needing to use the admin user, Argo CD includes the functionality to manage users that are defined locally within the tool. Local users serve two primary purposes:

- They provide a facility to generate authentication tokens for use by tools integrating to perform management functions. Examples include CI/CD, configuration management tooling, and monitoring tools.
- The creation of additional users to support small teams or environments where integrating an external user management tool is not needed or desired.

Additional users are defined within the `argocd-cm` ConfigMap using the format `accounts.`*<username>* as the key along with one of the available capabilities that can be granted to a user.

The following is an example of how a new local user named `alice` can be defined within the `argocd-cm` ConfigMap:

```
apiVersion: v1
kind: ConfigMap
metadata:
  name: argocd-cm
  namespace: argocd
  labels:
    app.kubernetes.io/name: argocd-cm
    app.kubernetes.io/part-of: argocd
data:
  accounts.alice: apiKey, login
```

Adding the user `alice` to the `argocd-cm` can also be achieved using `kubectl` by patching the `argocd-cm` ConfigMap using the following command:

```
kubectl patch -n argocd cm argocd-cm --type='merge' \
-p='{"data": {"accounts.alice": "apiKey, login"}}'
```

Once the ConfigMap has been updated with the new user, their details can be displayed by using the `argocd account list` command:

```
NAME   ENABLED  CAPABILITIES
admin  true     login
alice  true     apiKey, login
```

At the present time, only two capabilities can be associated with a local user: `login` and `apiKey`:

`login`
: Provides the ability to access the web UI

`apiKey`
: Allows for authentication tokens to be generated to interact with the Argo CD API

For the majority use cases when creating local users, login is the only capability that will be needed, as it is typically associated with a human actor. However, for the purposes of this exercise, we provided both available capabilities to the user `alice`.

Similar to the admin user, the first step that should be taken when creating new local users is to reset their password since no password is initially defined and they would be unable to log in. Use the `argocd account update-password` to update the password of the user `alice`, as shown next. Replace *<new_password>* with the desired password that should be associated with the user `alice`:

```
argocd account update-password --account=alice --new-password=<new_password>
```

You will then be prompted to enter the password of the current user, and once entered, the password will be changed.

Confirm that the new user Alice can authenticate successfully by launching a web browser, navigating to the Argo CD web console, and logging in with the username `alice` and the password previously specified.

If the credentials are accepted, the new user has been created successfully and is ready for use.

Alternatively, instead of using the Argo CD CLI to update the password for a user, passwords can be defined in a declarative fashion by setting the `accounts.<username>.password` and `accounts.<username>.passwordMtime` properties within the `argocd-secret` Secret. `accounts.<username>.password` is a bcrypt hash containing the password, while `accounts.<username>.passwordMtime` contains the date that the password was last modified.

The Argo CD CLI includes the `argocd account bcrypt` helper function for generating a bcrypt hash that can be used to specify the desired password for a user.

Generate a password that will be used for the user `alice` to authenticate using the following command:

```
argocd account bcrypt --password <new_password>
```

Update the password by patching the `argocd-secret` with the value generated previously, using the following command:

```
kubectl -n argocd patch secret argocd-secret \
  -p '{"stringData": {
    "accounts.alice.password": "<BCRYPT_PASSWORD>",
    "accounts.alice.passwordMtime": "'$(date -u +"%Y-%m-%dT%H:%M:%SZ")'"
  }}'
```

Once again, authenticate as `alice` using the newly updated password in the Argo CD UI.

### Disabling users

Once users have been created in Argo CD, their access can be disabled. By setting the `accounts.<username>.enabled` property to `false` in the `argocd-cm` ConfigMap, their access to both the UI and CLI can be disabled.

For example, to disable access for the user Alice previously created, set `accounts.alice.enabled` to `"false"` in the `argocd-cm` ConfigMap as shown next:

```
apiVersion: v1
kind: ConfigMap
metadata:
  name: argocd-cm
  namespace: argocd
  labels:
    app.kubernetes.io/name: argocd-cm
    app.kubernetes.io/part-of: argocd
data:
  accounts.alice: apiKey, login
  # Disables Alice's Local User Account
  accounts.alice.enabled: "false"
```

The ConfigMap can also be updated directly using `kubectl` by performing the following command:

```
kubectl patch -n argocd cm argocd-cm --type='merge' \
-p='{"data": {"accounts.alice.enabled": "false"}}'
```

Confirm the user `alice` can no longer access Argo CD by launching a web browser and attempting to authenticate using the `alice` user. You will be greeted with a message indicating the user account is disabled.

To reinstate the account, either set the `accounts.alice.enabled` field to `true` or remove the field entirely. The following is how to reenable the `alice` user account by removing the property patching the `argocd-cm` ConfigMap using `kubectl`:

```
kubectl patch -n argocd cm argocd-cm --type=json \
-p='[{"op": "remove", "path": "/data/accounts.alice.enabled"}]'
```

Once the property has been removed from the `argocd-cm` ConfigMap, the user `alice` will be able to authenticate once again.

In addition to being able to disable local user accounts, the Argo CD admin account can also be disabled. Once local users have been established and at least one of these accounts has been granted access to perform elevated actions, it is recommended that the admin account be disabled to enhance the overall security posture of Argo CD. Comparable to disabling a local user, the admin user can be disabled by setting the `admin.enabled` field to `"false"` in the `argocd-cm` ConfigMap:

```
apiVersion: v1
kind: ConfigMap
metadata:
  name: argocd-cm
  namespace: argocd
  labels:
    app.kubernetes.io/name: argocd-cm
    app.kubernetes.io/part-of: argocd
data:
  # Disables the admin account
  admin.enabled: "false"
```

This action can also be performed using `kubectl` by executing the following command:

```
kubectl patch -n argocd cm argocd-cm --type='merge' \
-p='{"data": {"admin.enabled": "false"}}
```

### Auth tokens

Aside from being able to define additional users to access Argo CD, local users serve another function—the ability to define and generate authentication tokens, which can be leveraged by external systems to perform automation actions. Examples of when auth tokens can be used include CI/CD tools to control and monitor the synchronization of Applications as part of an application release pipeline or within an automation tool to perform actions against Argo CD.

You may have noticed that when users are defined, they have the ability to have two associated capabilities: `login` and `apiKey`. While we previously covered the use case for the `login` capability where a user is granted the ability to access the Argo CD web console, the `apiKey` capability allows for the generation of an auth token that is associated with their account.

Let's walk through how an auth token can be generated and used.

First, create a new local user called "automation," which will be used to demonstrate how auth tokens can be created, managed, and utilized, by patching the `argocd-cm` ConfigMap with the following command:

```
kubectl patch -n argocd cm argocd-cm --type='merge' \
-p='{"data": {"accounts.automation": "apiKey"}}'
```

Auth tokens can be generated using the `argocd account generate-token` command. Individual user accounts for which the token will be generated can be targeted using the `--account` flag. Otherwise, a token will be generated for the current logged-in user.

To generate an auth token for the newly created automation user, execute the following command:

```
argocd account generate-token --account automation
```

An auth token consisting of a JSON Web Token (JWT) will be displayed as the output of the command. This token can be used to interact with the Argo CD CLI or API. Within the CLI, the `--auth-token` parameter can be used when invoking any command. So, to confirm that the user backing the token is being honored by the CLI, execute the following command, which will display information about the user invoking the command:

```
argocd account get-user-info --auth-token=<token>
```

Replace the value of *`<token>`* with the token value generated previously. A response similar to the following should be displayed:

```
Logged In: true
Username: automation
Issuer: argocd
Groups:
```

Alternatively, the `ARGOCD_AUTH_TOKEN` environment variable allows for the auth token to be defined once and avoids needing to provide it as a parameter for each invocation of the CLI.

Specifying an auth token either through the flag or environment variable has a higher precedence than any other previously authenticated user.

Auth tokens, by default, have no expiration, which could be seen as a security risk. To increase the security posture surrounding auth tokens, it is recommended that they expire after a certain amount of time. The `--expires-in` flag can be used to specify a duration for which the token is valid (such as 1h, 90d, etc.).

Generate a timebound auth token of 90 days using the `--expires-in` parameter using the following command:

```
argocd account generate-token --account automation --expires-in 90d
```

Tokens associated with a user can be displayed using the `argocd account get` command. Display details about the automation user, including the two tokens previously generated using the following command:

```
argocd account get --account automation

Name:               automation
Enabled:            true
Capabilities:       apiKey

Tokens:
ID                                    ISSUED AT                  EXPIRING AT
89ec94b0-aff8-47c6-b59a-229c4b564688  2024-01-20T14:15:16-06:00  2024-04-19T15:15:16-05:00
70cf36ea-b365-4f04-9fc0-56229cd41620  2024-01-20T12:39:16-06:00  never
```

Notice how one token has an infinite lifespan, whereas the other token will expire at a time relative to the time it was generated.

Tokens can be explicitly revoked whenever there is a desire to do so. Examples of when one might want to revoke an auth token are when it has been accidentally exposed or is being used by a member of the team who no longer requires access. Tokens are tracked within the `argocd-secret` Secret in a key called `accounts.<account>.tokens` and while this property can be modified manually, it is much more straightforward to use the Argo CD CLI.

Delete one of the tokens previously generated by using `argocd account delete-token` command and specifying the name of the account the token is associated with and the ID of the token. The ID of all auth tokens is shown when invoking the `argocd account get` command and is a Universally Unique Identifier (UUID) that is generated at token creation time. To use a more friendly name, use the `--id` flag of the `argocd account generate-token` command.

Revoke an auth token by executing the following command:

```
argocd account delete-token --account <account> <ID>
```

## SSO

Local users are a great way to onboard a small team into Argo CD or leverage an auth token to perform automation actions. As Argo CD adoption grows, especially within a large organization, the management of users within Argo CD through the use of the local users feature can become untenable. Fortunately, Argo CD has the capability to integrate with external user management tools to offload the capability to an external system.

Two forms of SSO are available:

- Dex OIDC provider
- Direct OIDC integration

Either option uses the OpenID Connect (OIDC) authentication protocol to facilitate how users authenticate and how their details are consumed by Argo CD.

### Dex

Dex is an identity service that is bundled with Argo CD and runs as a separate pod, acting as a bridge between one or more identity providers through the use of connectors. These connectors provide advanced and provider-specific functionality that maps user details into a format that Argo CD can understand in a standardized manner. Supported connectors include Git-based services, like GitHub and GitLab; enterprise integrations from Google and Microsoft; and lightweight directory access protocol (LDAP) for integrating more traditional user-management platforms. Multiple connectors can be specified to account for one or more identity services that contain users who would like to access and leverage Argo CD.

### Direct OIDC

If the desired user management tool exposes an OIDC interface (for example, Microsoft, Google, Keycloak), Argo CD can delegate the entire authentication process to the provider. By using this method, many of the same configurations that have been used previously when interacting with the OIDC provider by other tools can be reused for Argo CD, enabling a more native and consistent method for accessing identity details from the provider.

### SSO in action

With an understanding of the options available when leveraging the SSO capability within Argo CD, let's look at the steps involved when implementing SSO in our `kind` cluster. While there are a variety of options available for integrating users that are managed externally, we will utilize Keycloak, an open source identity and management tool. As external users, we will describe how to integrate users stored in

Keycloak. Keycloak exposes a native OIDC-compatible interface, which makes it ideal to demonstrate an SSO integration with both Dex and the native OIDC options.

The first step is to deploy Keycloak to your `kind` cluster. Tooling is available within the project Git repository to facilitate the deployment and configuration of Keycloak.

Ensure that you have the project codebase (*https://github.com/sabre1041/argocd-up-and-running-book*) cloned, then navigate to the *ch06* directory.

To simplify the deployment and configuration of Keycloak, the Keycloak Operator will be used. Execute the following script to deploy the operator to a new namespace called `keycloak`:

```
helm upgrade -i -n keycloak --create-namespace keycloak-operator charts/keycloak-operator
```

Confirm the Keycloak Operator is running by listing the pods within the `keycloak` namespace:

```
kubectl -n keycloak get pods
```

With the Operator running, let's work on deploying Keycloak itself. While the Operator provides the capabilities to manage the majority of concerns related to the deployment and configuration of Keycloak, it does not have the functionality to generate an SSL certificate to secure Ingress communication.

Use the OpenSSL tool to generate a self-signed certificate for Keycloak and place the generated certificates within the file folder of the Keycloak Helm chart. These files will be leveraged afterward when the chart is installed. Execute the following command to generate the certificate:

```
openssl req -subj "/CN=keycloak.upandrunning.local/O=O'Reilly Media/C=US" -newkey \
rsa:2048 -nodes -keyout charts/keycloak/files/key.pem -x509 -days 365 \
-out charts/keycloak/files/certificate.pem
```

As you might have noticed, the generated certificate uses the hostname `keycloak.upandrunning.local`. Using a similar process that was utilized in Chapter 3, add the following value to the `/etc/hosts` file so that requests are made against the `kind` environment:

```
127.0.0.1 keycloak.upandrunning.local
```

Now, install the Helm chart to configure the supporting components, including a PostgreSQL database backend, TLS certificates previously generated, and the `keycloak` custom resource. The Keycloak Operator in turn deploys and configures Keycloak:

```
helm upgrade -i -n keycloak keycloak charts/keycloak
```

In a few moments, an Argo CD pod will be created. This can be seen by querying the pods in the `keycloak` namespace:

```
kubectl get pods -n keycloak
```

Once the pod is up, navigate to the Keycloak interface at *https://keycloak.upandrunning.local*. Accept the self-signed certificate, and you will be presented with a dashboard, as shown in Figure 6-1.

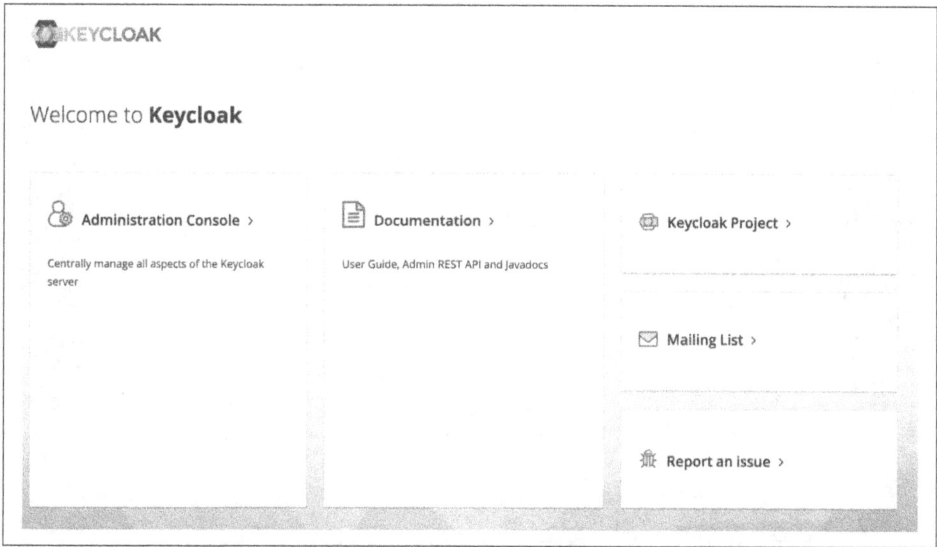


*Figure 6-1. Keycloak dashboard*

Of the available options to choose from, select Administration Console. This will take you to the sign-in page (see Figure 6-2).

The password for the default administrator account is automatically created in a secret called `keycloak-initial-admin` and stored within the `keycloak` namespace by the Keycloak Operator.

Figure 6-2. Keycloak sign-in page

Extract the value by executing the following command:

```
kubectl get secret -n keycloak keycloak-initial-admin \
-o jsonpath='{ .data.password }' | base64 -d
```

Use the retrieved password, and log in with the username "admin." Once authenticated, you will be presented with the Keycloak dashboard within the argocd *realm*. A realm in Keycloak is where you define and manage resources, including users, clients, and other entities.

"master" is the name of the default realm in Keycloak, and to emphasize a separation of duties, another realm called "argocd" will be used to define the integration with Argo CD. The Helm chart that we installed previously created a new realm called "argocd" and populated the instance with a baseline set of resources for us to start. Let's explore the argocd realm to see what was created for us.

First, ensure that you are using the argocd realm. The active realm the UI is displaying is located on the upper lefthand portion of the page. A dropdown of available realms is also available if there is more than the default master realm. If the dropdown does not display "argocd" currently, go ahead and click the dropdown and select "argocd" so that you are focusing on the appropriate realm (see Figure 6-3).

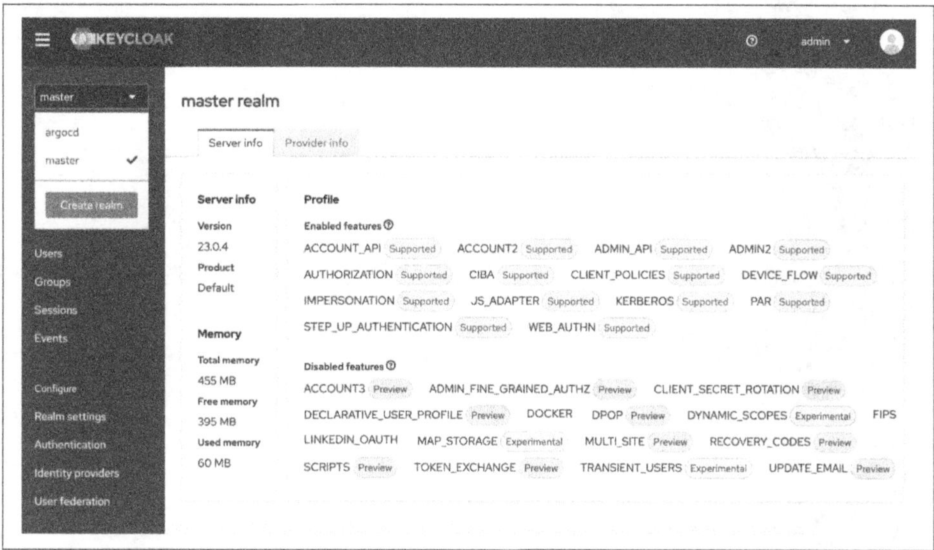


*Figure 6-3. Keycloak realm selection*

Two users were also created: John, who represents an Argo CD administrator and Mary, a senior software developer. They can be seen by selecting the Users button on the lefthand navigation pane, as shown in Figure 6-4.

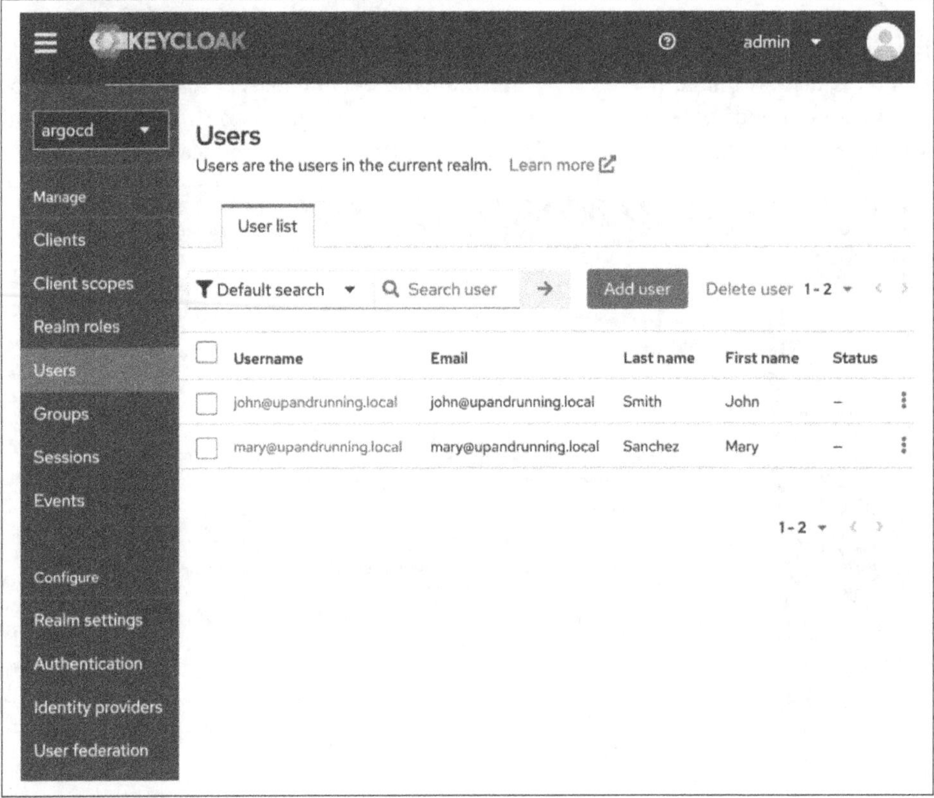


*Figure 6-4. Keycloak Argo CD realm user page*

Two Keycloak groups have also been defined: ArgoCDAdmins, which represent Argo CD administrators, and Developers, which represent members of the software development team. John is a member of the admins group and Mary is a member of the developers group. Group definition and the membership can be seen by selecting the Groups button on the lefthand navigation pane, as shown in Figure 6-5.

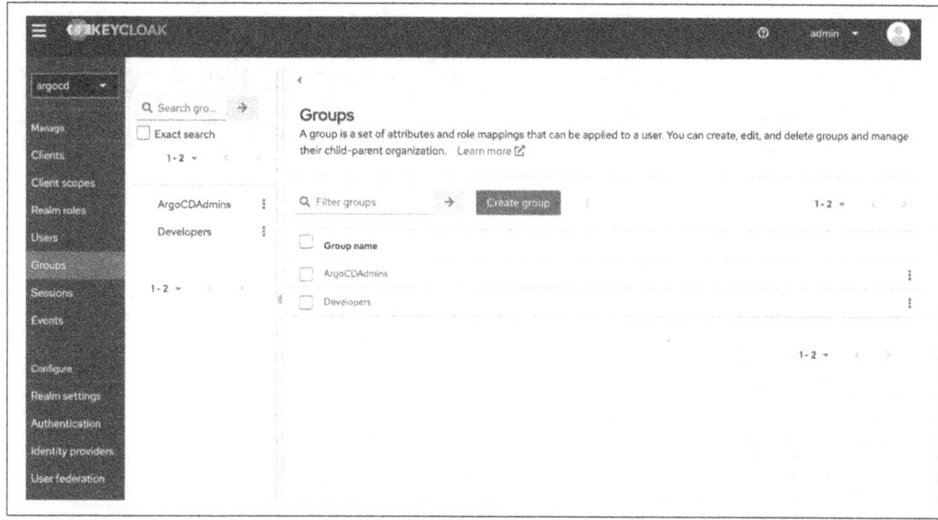


*Figure 6-5. Keycloak Argo CD realm group page*

Now, let's complete the necessary configuration to enable Argo CD to integrate with Keycloak. Create a new Keycloak client by selecting the Clients button on the lefthand navigation pane and then selecting the "Create client" button at the top, as shown in Figure 6-6.

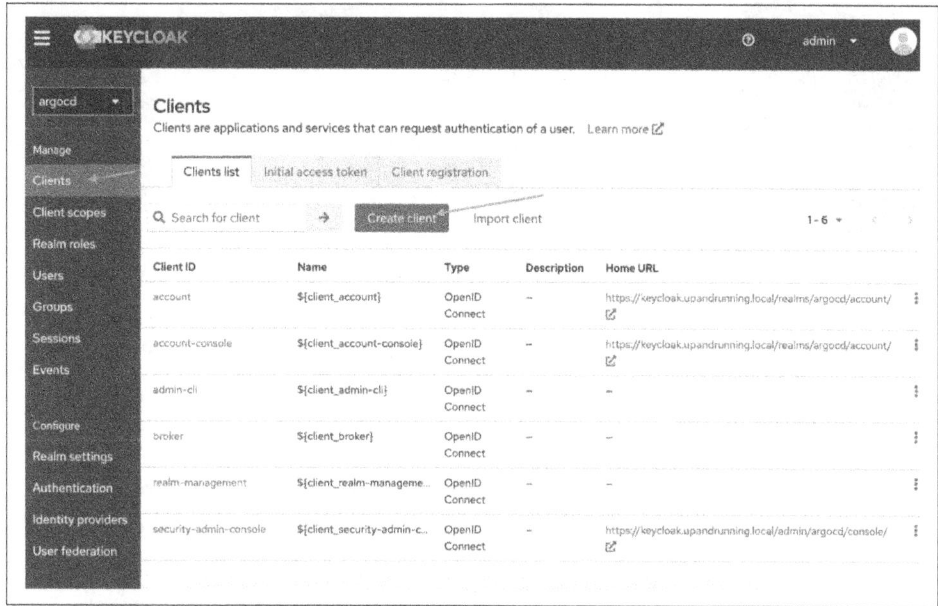


*Figure 6-6. Keycloak Argo CD client creation*

Enter "argocd" as the Client ID and "Argo CD" as the Client Name (see Figure 6-7).

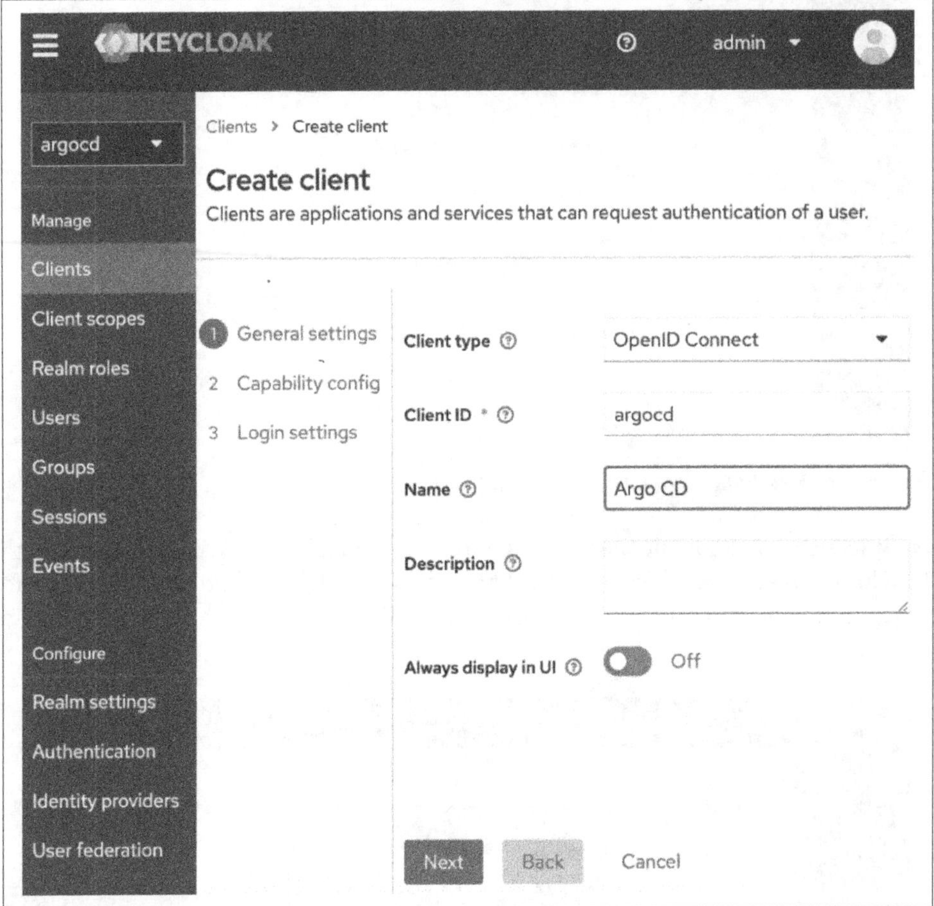


*Figure 6-7. Keycloak Argo CD client setup*

After setting these, click Next.

Enable "Client authentication" by switching the toggle to the enabled position and leaving the remaining values in their default positions (see Figure 6-8).

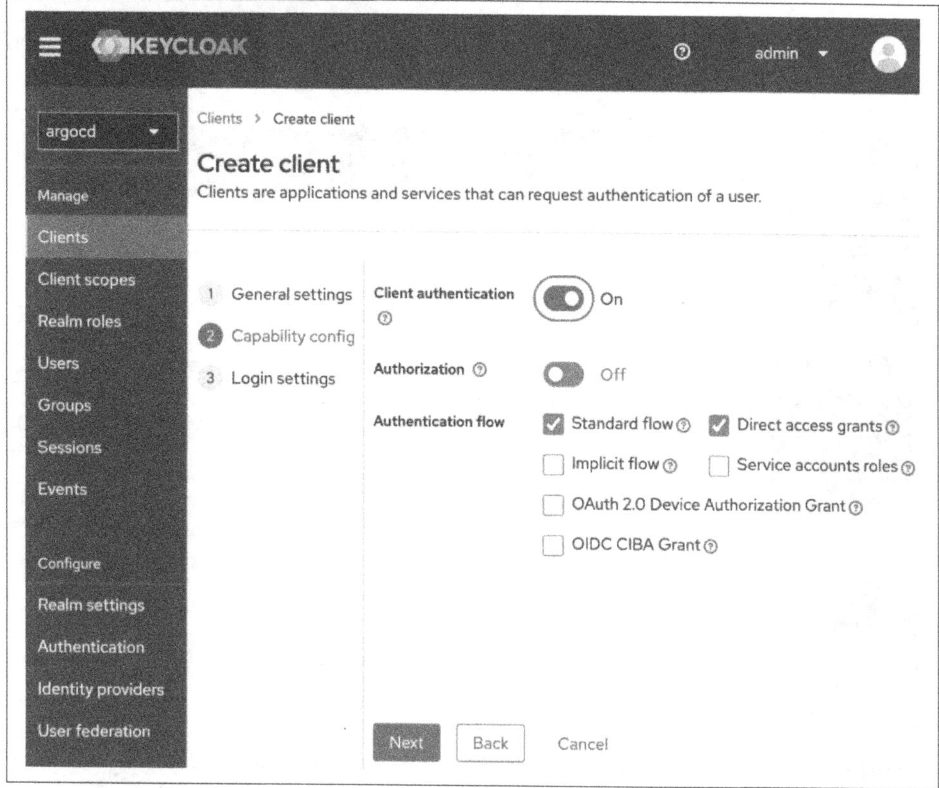


*Figure 6-8. Keycloak Argo CD enable client authentication*

After you set "Client authentication," click Next.

Set the Root URL and "Web origins" to the URL of the Argo CD instance: "https://argocd.upandrunning.local."

Argo CD exposes callback URLs for requests to invoke once the authentication process is successful for each of the SSO types at the context paths */api/dex/callback* for Dex and */auth/callback* for direct OIDC. As a result, enter the following values in the "Valid redirect URIs" field. Click the "Add valid redirect URIs" link to add the second value:

- *https://argocd.upandrunning.local/auth/callback*
- *https://argocd.upandrunning.local/api/dex/callback*

We can then set the default page within the console that a user is directed to upon a successful authentication. Set the Home URL to "/applications" so that they will be sent to the page displaying all of the applications they are allowed to view.

Finally, enter **https://argocd.upandrunning.local** into the text box next to "Valid post logout redirect URIs" (see Figure 6-9).

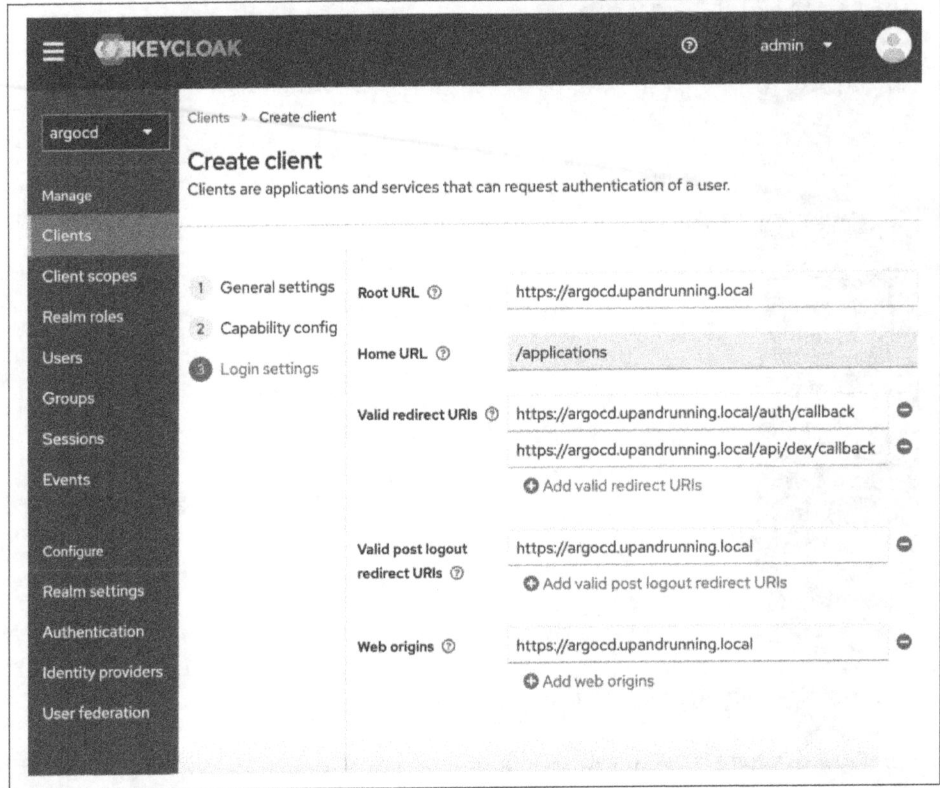


*Figure 6-9. Keycloak Argo CD client settings*

Click Save to create the Keycloak client. This brings you to the "Client details" page (see Figure 6-10).

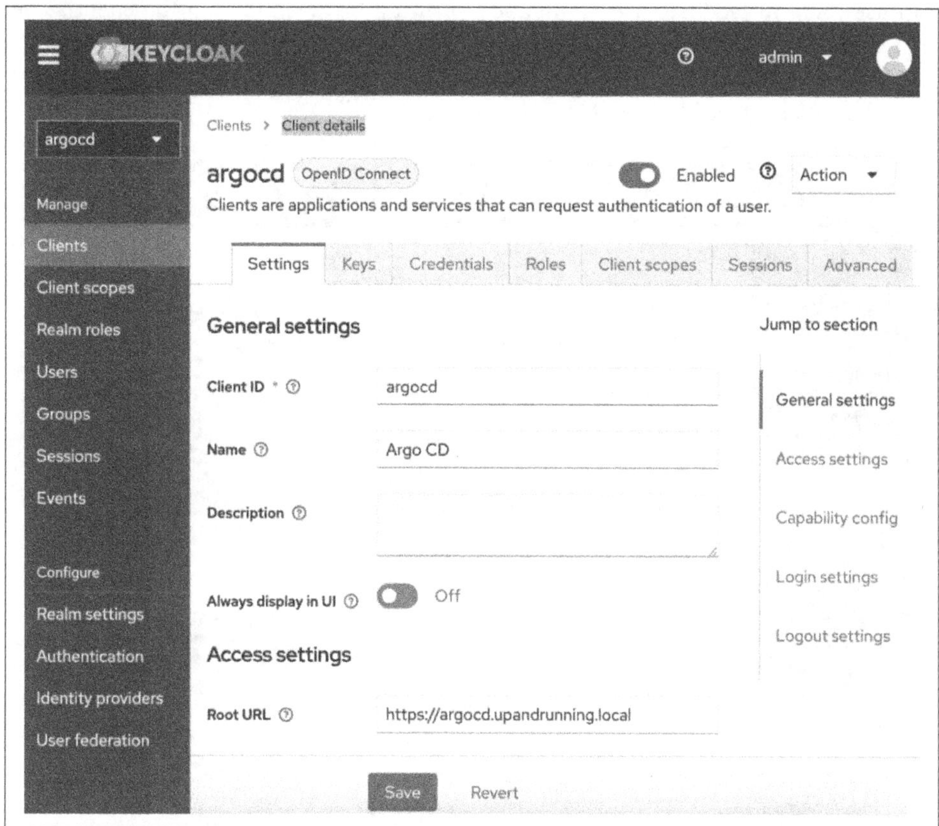


*Figure 6-10. Keycloak Argo CD "Client details" page*

Since the "Client authentication" option was selected, the OIDC confidential access type was enabled. As a result, a set of credentials were generated so that Argo CD can use them to facilitate user authentication via a browser. Obtain the client secret by selecting the Credentials tab for the argocd client and select the Copy button to capture the value to the clipboard. Feel free to select the eyeball icon, which will display the value (see Figure 6-11).

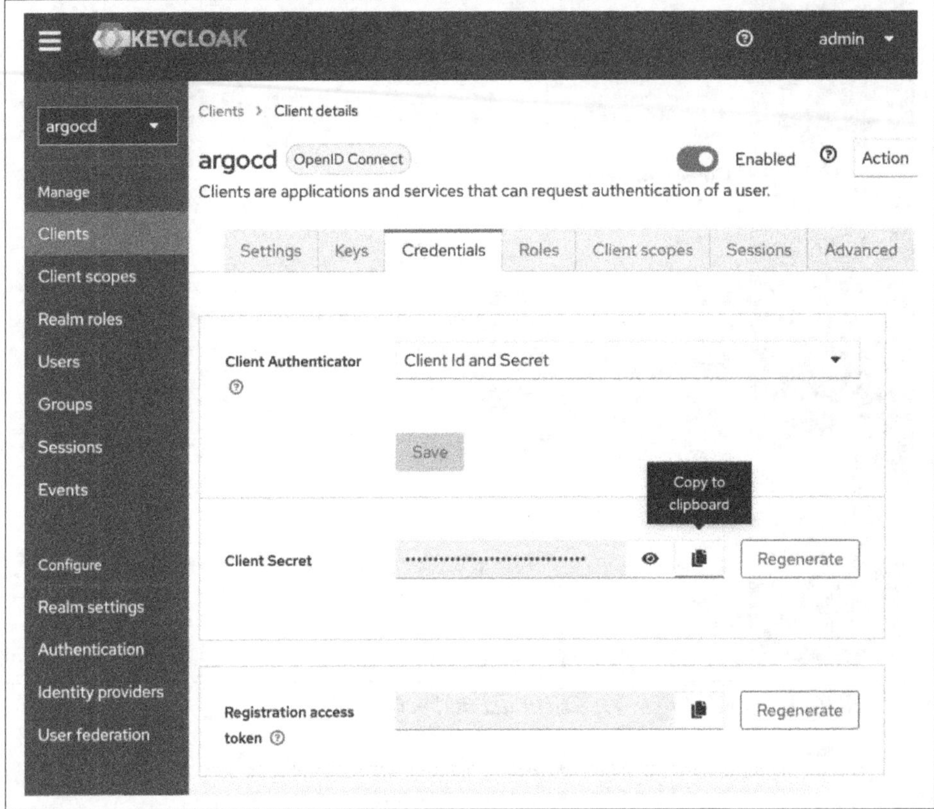


*Figure 6-11. Keycloak Argo CD client credentials*

To enable the groups that a user is a member of to be included as part of the JWT, create a new client scope by selecting "Client scopes" on the lefthand navigation pane and then select "Create client scope," as shown in Figure 6-12.

Enter "groups" as the name of the client scope and then click Save, as shown in Figure 6-13.

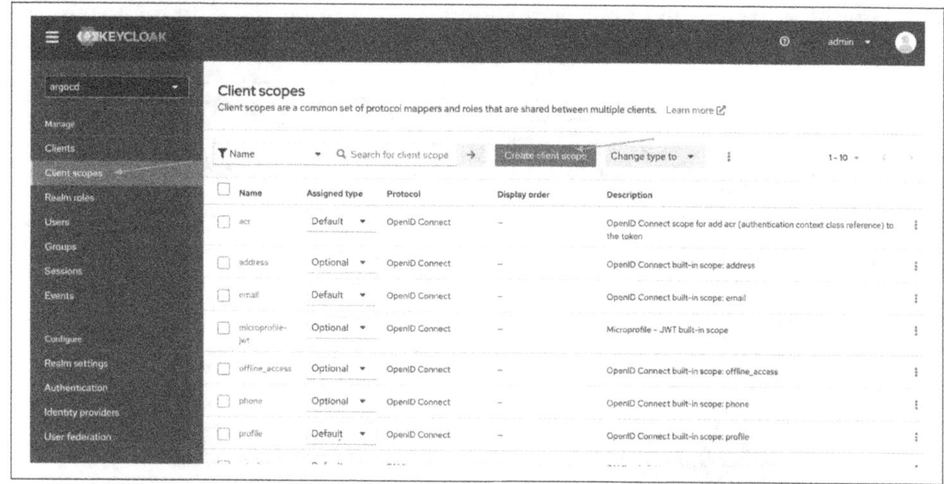


*Figure 6-12. Keycloak Argo CD client scope creation*



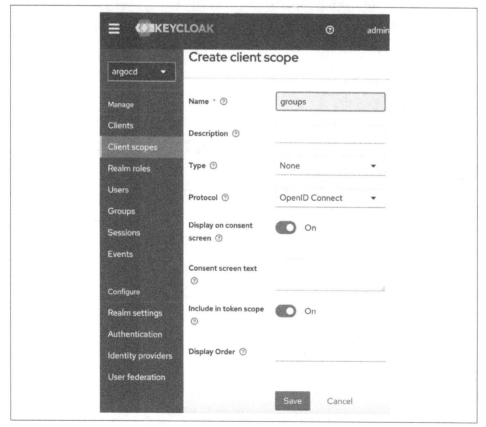

*Figure 6-13. Keycloak Argo CD client scope groups creation*

Click on the Mappers tab to enable the groups claim to be added to the token (see Figure 6-14).

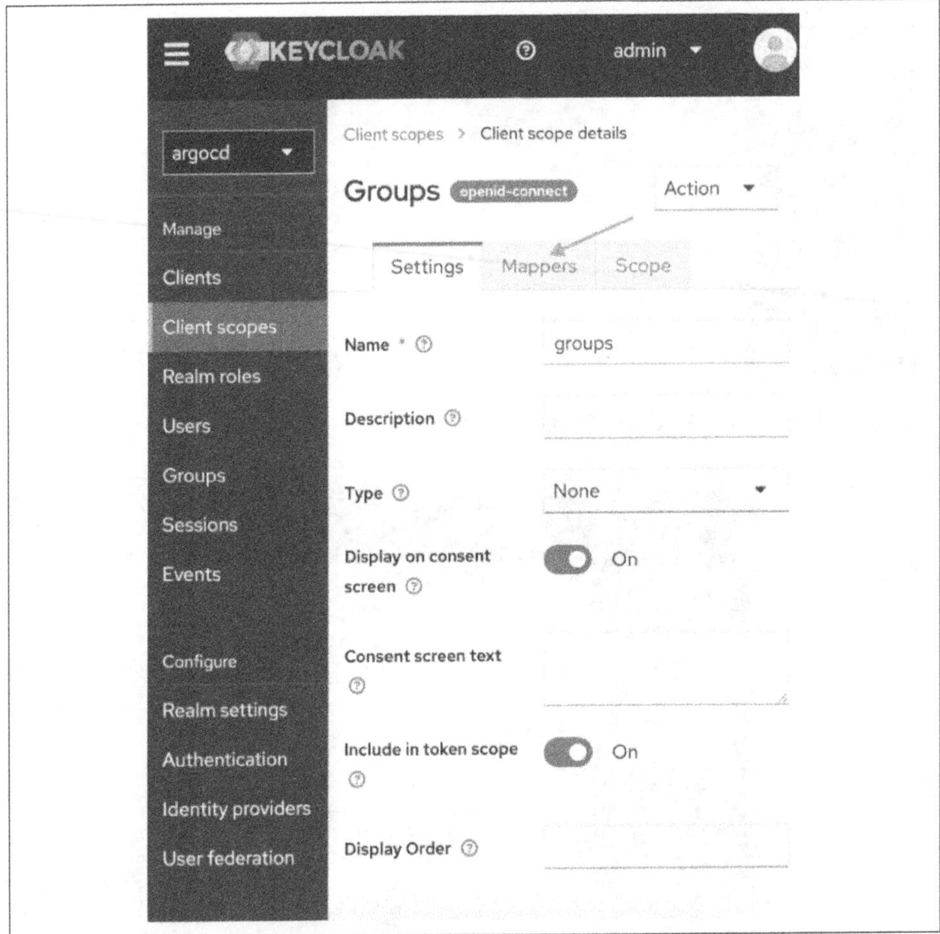


*Figure 6-14. Keycloak Argo CD group mappers*

Select "Configure a new mapper" (see Figure 6-15).

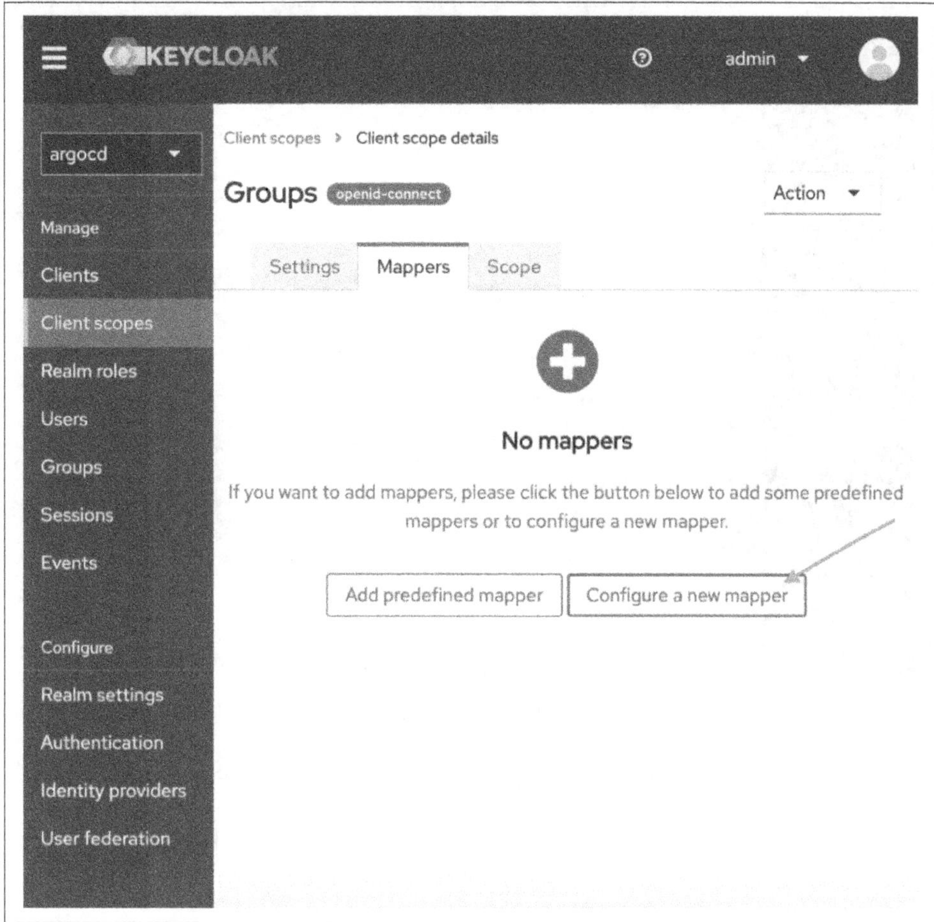


*Figure 6-15. Keycloak Argo CD configure mappers*

Select Group Membership (see Figure 6-16).

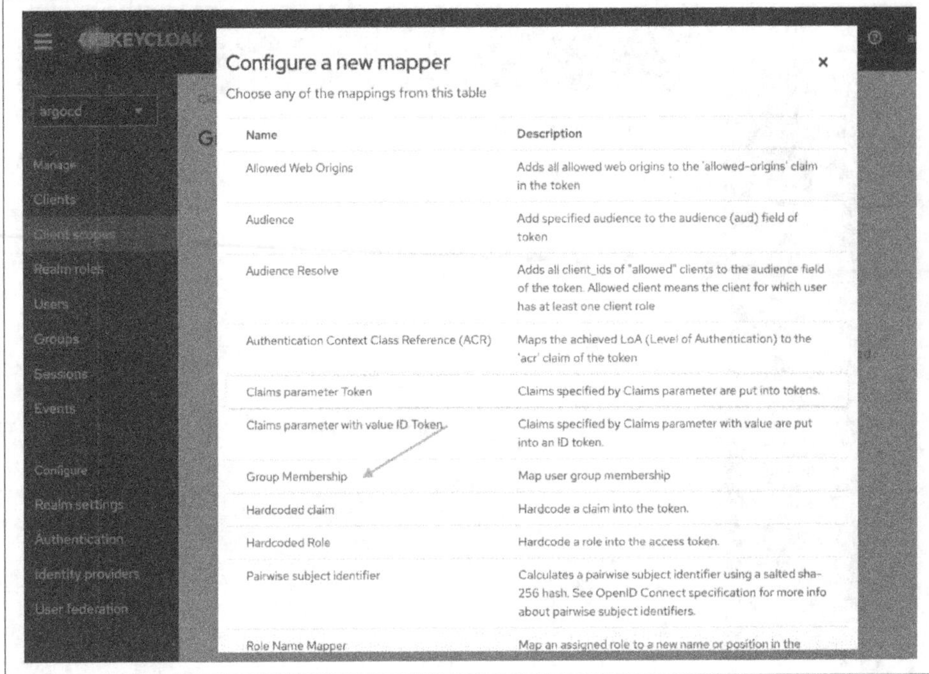


*Figure 6-16. Keycloak Argo CD Group Membership*

Enter "groups" for the Name and Token Claim Name. Deselect "Full group path" and leave the remaining options enabled (see Figure 6-17).

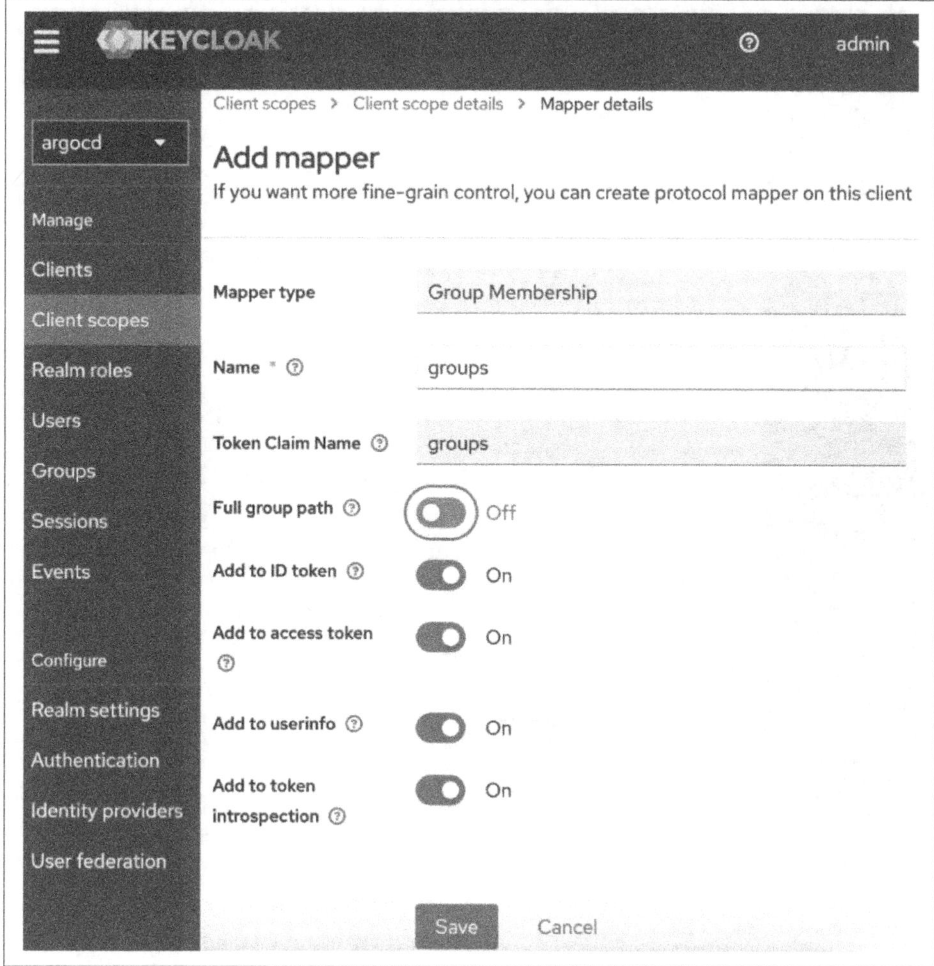


*Figure 6-17. Keycloak Argo CD Group Membership configuration*

Click Save to apply the configuration.

Finally, add the new client scope to the argocd client by once again selecting Clients on the lefthand menu and then "argocd."

On the "argocd" client configuration page, select the "Client scopes" tab (see Figure 6-18).

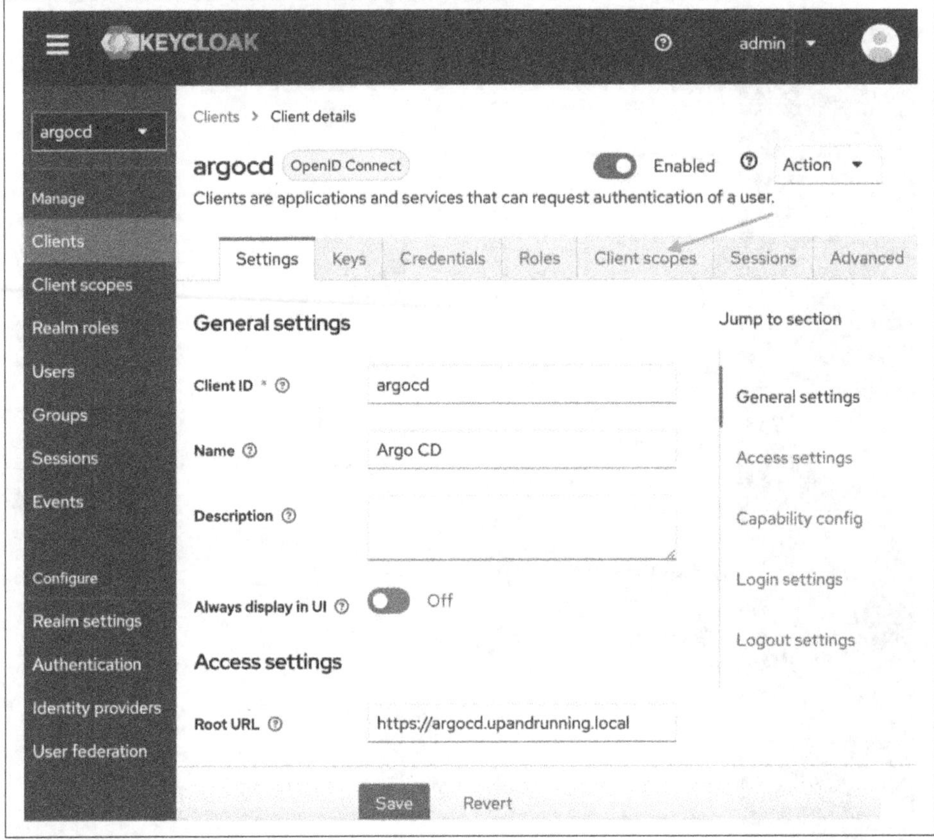


*Figure 6-18. Keycloak Argo CD "Client scopes" selection*

Then select the "Add client scope" button.

Select the checkbox next to "groups." Select the Add button, and then from the options provided, select Default so that the groups claim will always be included in the token without needing to be explicitly requested (see Figure 6-19).

At this point, Keycloak has been configured to support the integration with Argo CD. Before we can focus on the Argo CD configuration itself, there needs to be an adjustment made within our `kind` cluster. Recall that we updated the `/etc/hosts` file on our machine with the URLs for both Argo CD and Keycloak so that they would resolve and route appropriately to our `kind` cluster.

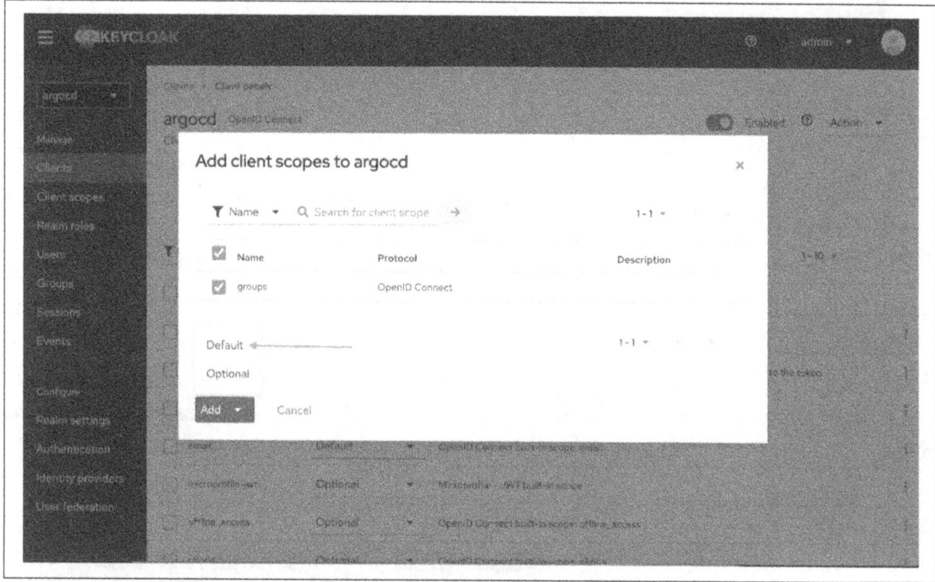


*Figure 6-19. Keycloak Argo CD adding client scopes*

Since Argo CD will need to access Keycloak to complete the authentication process, it too will need some assistance resolving the Keycloak server. `kind` makes use of CoreDNS for intra-cluster DNS resolution. We can perform a similar pattern where requests made against any address with the `*.upandrunning.local` domain (which includes the Keycloak endpoint) are rewritten to an internal Kubernetes service for NGINX that was deployed previously.

Edit the CoreDNS configuration file stored in `coredns` ConfigMap within the `kube-system` namespace:

```
kubectl edit cm coredns -n kube-system
```

Add the following bolded content to the configuration file, which will add in the rewrite rule:

```
apiVersion: v1
kind: ConfigMap
data:
  Corefile: >-
      .:53 {
      rewrite name regex (.*)\.upandrunning\.local
      ingress-nginx-controller.ingress-nginx.svc.cluster.local.
      answer auto
          errors
          health {
             lameduck 5s
          }
```

Delete the CoreDNS pods so that the changes are picked up:

```
kubectl delete pod -n kube-system -l=k8s-app=kube-dns
```

Verify that applications running within the `kind` cluster can resolve Keycloak now that the rewrite rule has been configured in CoreDNS:

```
kubectl exec -n ingress-nginx \
svc/ingress-nginx-controller -- curl -skLI https://keycloak.upandrunning.local | head -1
```

If the response returned `HTTP/2 200`, DNS resolution is working correctly.

Regardless of the type of SSO backend Argo CD communicates with or the type of SSO integration that is selected, one property must be set within the `argocd-cm` ConfigMap, the URL of the Argo CD server as defined by the `url` key. This is so that the callback function works for SSO. Execute the following command to patch the `argocd-cm` ConfigMap:

```
kubectl patch -n argocd cm argocd-cm \
-p '{"data":{"url": "https://argocd.upandrunning.local"}}'
```

Now let's shift our attention to the necessary configurations within Argo CD.

The Client ID and Secret need to be included within the SSO configuration so that Argo CD can authenticate with Keycloak. Since the client secret is a sensitive asset, instead of explicitly specifying the value, it can be stored in a Secret and then referenced from the configuration file. Secrets can be referenced from two locations:

- The global `argocd-secret` secret
- A separate secret in the same namespace where Argo CD is deployed

To avoid mixing default Argo CD and user-provided content, create a separate secret called `keycloak-secret` within the `argo` namespace and specify the Client ID and Client Secret from the argocd client previously defined using the following command:

```
kubectl create secret generic -n argocd keycloak-secret \
--from-literal=clientSecret=<keycloak_argocd_clientSecret>
```

In order for Argo CD to make use of the secret for use, it must include the label `app.kubernetes.io/part-of: argocd`. Execute the following command to add the label to the `keycloak-secret` secret:

```
kubectl label secret -n argocd keycloak-secret app.kubernetes.io/part-of=argocd
```

Sensitive data stored within Secrets can then be referenced within Argo CD configuration files. Values beginning with a $ look for keys within a Secret matching the value. If the value takes the form `$<secret>:a.key.in.k8s.secret`, Argo CD will look for the value within the Secret `<secret>` and the key which follows the colon (`:`).

For example, if the following was declared within a ConfigMap:

```
myProperty: $foo:bar
```

the referenced sensitive value would be sourced from a secret called `foo` and the key `bar`.

Alternatively, sensitive values can also be stored within the global `argocd-secret` secret instead of a dedicated Secret. The only difference when referencing the value within a configuration is that the name of the secret that the content would be placed within and the colon (`:`) separator is omitted. So, when replicating the prior example, the following would reference the `bar` key within the `argocd-secret` global secret:

```
myProperty: $bar
```

With an understanding of how sensitive resources can be accessed, in the case of the client secret that was previously stored in the `keycloak-secret` Secret, the value can be referenced within Argo CD configurations using the form `$keycloak-secret:clientSecret`.

Now that we have the insights and the necessary supporting components to enable SSO in Argo CD complete, let's walk through how to configure Argo CD to leverage Keycloak using both Dex and Direct OIDC integrations.

Either option is enabled by updating the content of the `argocd-cm` ConfigMap. It is important to note that Dex and Direct OIDC integration cannot be enabled at the same time.

**SSO using Dex.** SSO for Argo CD using Dex can be enabled by specifying the `dex.config` property of the `argocd-cm` ConfigMap. This property is an inline representation of the standard Dex configuration file that would be used in standalone deployments of Dex. Argo CD manages most of the boilerplate content, and the end user is responsible for defining the connectors (the strategy to authenticate against another identity provider) that will be leveraged. Since Dex does not contain a connector specifically engineered for Keycloak, we will leverage the generic OIDC connector.

Aside from the Client ID and Client Secret, the only other property that we will need to provide within Dex is the location of the OIDC issuer (the base URL for OIDC resources). This address can be accessed from the "Realm settings" of the argocd realm in the Keycloak UI.

Locate the OpenID Endpoint Configuration link under the *endpoints* section on the "Realm settings" page. Clicking on this link brings up the OIDC discovery document, which contains all of the OIDC metadata required to understand how to interact with this endpoint. Since the issuer URL is just the base URL, we can omit `.well-known/openid-configuration`, leaving us with an issuer URL of `https://keycloak.upandrunning.local/realms/argocd`.

Update the `argocd-cm` ConfigMap with the following content:

```
dex.config: |
  connectors:
    - type: oidc
      id: keycloak
      name: Keycloak Dex
      config:
        issuer: https://keycloak.upandrunning.local/realms/argocd
        clientID: argocd
        clientSecret: $keycloak-secret:clientSecret
        insecureSkipVerify: true
        insecureEnableGroups: true
```

The ConfigMap can be modified interactively by executing the following command:

```
kubectl edit cm -n argocd argocd-cm
```

Several items of note from the configurations from the previous `dex.config` property:

- The `clientSecret` property is making use of the Keycloak client secret that was configured in the `keycloak-secret` secret.
- Since Keycloak uses a self-signed certificate to enable TLS communication, the `insecureSkipVerify` property ignores verification errors.
- The `insecureEnableGroups` property allows Dex to process groups defined within Keycloak from the `groups` claim.

Once the configuration has been applied, launch the Argo CD UI. If you were previously authenticated and still have an active session, go ahead and log out.

On the login page itself, notice how there is a new button, Log In Via Keycloak, in addition to the username and password option that was used previously. Click on the Log In Via Keycloak button and you will be transferred to the Keycloak instance in order to authenticate.

If the Log In Via Keycloak button does not appear (if it's not working), you may need to forcibly trigger a reload of the configuration by deleting all of the pods in the argo namespace using the command `kubectl delete pods -n argocd --all`.

Recall two users were defined in Keycloak. Go ahead and authenticate as the Argo CD Administrator John using the username "john@upandrunning.local" and password "argocdAdmin123". Upon a successful authentication, you will be transferred back to the Argo CD instance, and as defined within Keycloak, the Applications page.

Select the User Info link on the lefthand navigation pane to view details related to the current user. Notice how the username matches the user we authenticated as, and the issuer matches the value we obtained from Keycloak and configured within the `dex.config` property. Most importantly, the list of groups that John is a member of is also displayed, confirming that Dex was able to retrieve the values from the groups claim (see Figure 6-20).

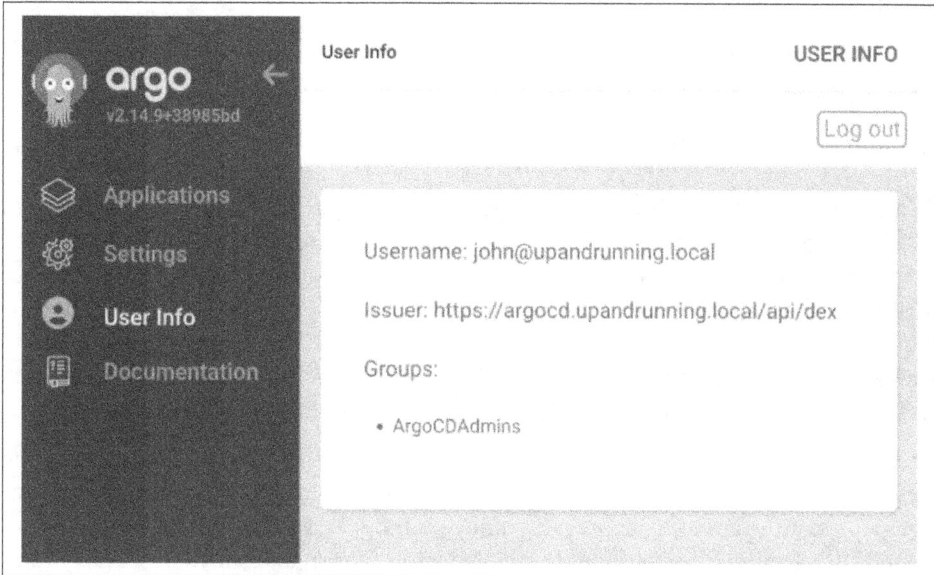


*Figure 6-20. Argo CD User Info*

Now that we have validated SSO user authentication using Dex, let's see how we can enable Argo CD SSO integration to Keycloak using the direct OIDC approach.

**SSO using direct OIDC.** Configuring Argo CD to communicate directly with the OIDC provider offers greater simplicity as well as eliminates a component (Dex) from being deployed and managed. The process for enabling direct OIDC integration mirrors the steps as described in the previous section.

First, remove the `dex.config` property, as both Dex and direct OIDC integration cannot be enabled concurrently. Direct OIDC integration is defined within the `oidc.config` property within the `argocd-cm` ConfigMap. Specify the following contents to enable direct OIDC integration with the Keycloak instance:

```
oidc.config: |
  name: Keycloak
  issuer: https://keycloak.upandrunning.local/realms/argocd
  clientID: argocd
  clientSecret: $keycloak-secret:clientSecret
  logoutURL: "https://keycloak.upandrunning.local/realms/argocd/protocol/openid-connect/log
out?client_id=argocd&id_token_hint={{token}}&post_logout_redirect_uri={{logoutRedirectURL}}"
```

As you can see, the contents are almost identical. The final step is to configure Argo CD to ignore verification errors to the OIDC endpoint. Instead of this property being defined within the OIDC config, it is instead a top-level property within the `argocd-cm` ConfigMap. Add the following to the `argocd-cm` ConfigMap to disable OIDC SSL verification:

```
oidc.tls.insecure.skip.verify: "true"
```

This property can also be set by executing the following command:

```
kubectl patch -n argocd cm argocd-cm --type='merge' \
-p='{"data": {"oidc.tls.insecure.skip.verify": "true"}}'
```

With the configurations for direct OIDC integration in place, navigate to the Argo CD web console at *https://argocd.upandrunning.local*. You should be greeted once again with the option to authenticate using a local account or using Keycloak SSO. Log in as the Argo CD Administrator John using the username "john@upandrunning.local" and password "argocdAdmin123". Select the User Info link on the lefthand navigation pane and confirm all of the properties align to the expected values, as well as those that were present previously when Dex was enabled as the provider.

Indeed, from an end user point of view, there is no difference when authenticating against Dex or direct OIDC integration for Argo CD SSO. By offloading user management to an external, purpose-built utility, Argo CD administrators and users can benefit from a simplified experience while reducing the management overhead within Argo CD itself.

**SSO using the Argo CD CLI.** In addition to being able to access the Argo CD UI with an SSO user, the same user can also leverage the Argo CD CLI to be able to take advantage of the capabilities provided by the tool. To authenticate as an SSO user from the Argo CD CLI, the `--sso` flag can be specified, which will trigger the authentication process with the configured SSO solution.

To enable SSO users to authenticate with the Argo CD CLI, several additional configurations must be implemented within the SSO solution. In our environment, this involves modifications within Keycloak.

Navigate once again to the Keycloak administration console at *https://keycloak.upandrunning.local/admin* and authenticate as the admin user.

Two modifications need to be made within the argocd Keycloak client:

- An additional callback URL
- Disable client authentication

When the CLI initiates the SSO authentication process, it starts a small web server on port 8085. The primary function of this component is to receive the callback after a user authenticates successfully.

Within the Keycloak administration console, navigate to the argocd realm, select Clients on the lefthand navigation, and select the argocd client. Locate the "Valid redirect URIs" option and click "Add valid redirect URIs" to make available an additional textbox entry. Enter **http://localhost:8085/auth/callback** into the textbox to allow Keycloak to trust the CLI endpoint, and click Save (see Figure 6-21).

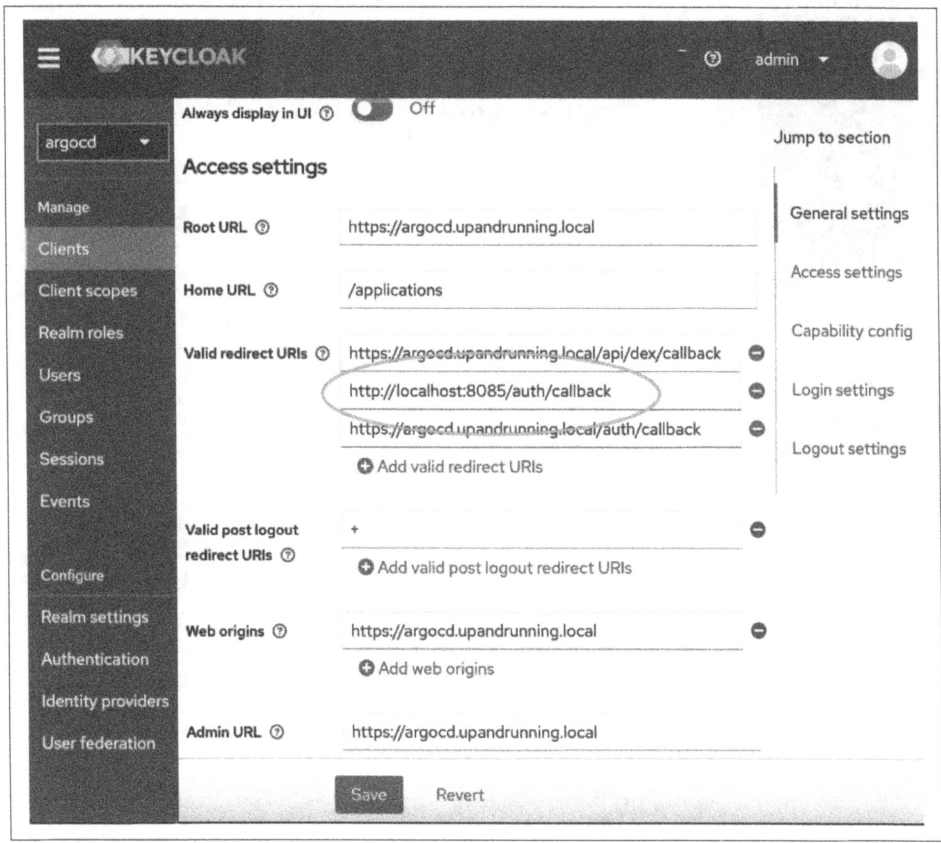


*Figure 6-21. Keycloak adding localhost callback*

Since the CLI operates in a similar fashion to a client-side web application, it is unable to manage the client credential associated with the Keycloak client. As a result, the access type for the client must be changed from "confidential" to "public," which removes the requirement to provide a client secret. Change the access type within the argocd Keycloak client by locating the "Capability config" section and deselecting "Client authentication." Click Save to apply the change (see Figure 6-22).

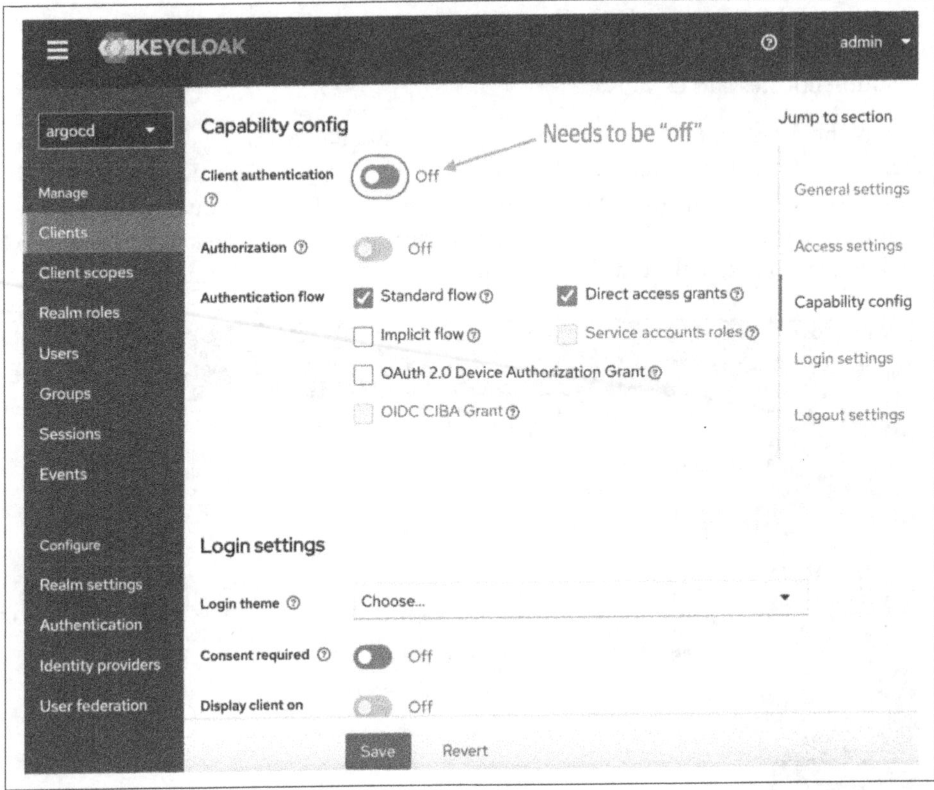


*Figure 6-22. Keycloak disabling client authentication*

One final modification needs to be made, and this change is specific to the `kind` cluster we are operating within. The CLI sends a set of HTTP headers as it authenticates. However, the content being transmitted is larger than the defaults that are configured within the NGINX ingress controller. Fortunately, this issue can be mitigated by setting the `proxy-buffer-size` parameter within the NGINX configuration, which is stored within a ConfigMap in the `ingress-nginx` namespace.

Update the NGINX configuration by setting the `proxy-buffer-size` value to `100k` using the following command:

```
kubectl patch -n ingress-nginx cm ingress-nginx-controller --type='merge' \
-p='{"data": {"proxy-buffer-size": "100k"}}'
```

With the required changes applied, log in to the Argo CD CLI using the SSO user John (`john@upandrunning.local`) with the following command:

```
argocd login --sso --insecure --grpc-web argocd.upandrunning.local
```

Once authenticated, the same user details that are found within the User Info page of the Argo CD UI can be seen within the CLI by executing the following command:

```
argocd account get-user-info

Logged In: true
Username: john@upandrunning.local
Issuer: https://keycloak.upandrunning.local/realms/argocd
Groups: ArgoCDAdmins
```

# Role-Based Access Control

Once a user has authenticated successfully to Argo CD—whether it be via the CLI or the UI, they are not granted unrestricted access to resources by default and must be granted permissions to perform certain actions. These controls are managed by Argo CD's included RBAC capability, which governs the actions that entities can perform against Argo CD resources. In the prior section, we not only established John, the acting Argo CD administrator, within Keycloak, our user management system, but also provided him the ability to log in to Argo CD. However, even though he represents an Argo CD administrator, without explicit permissions being granted to his user account, his ability to perform certain actions is restricted.

See this in practice for yourself. Using the Argo CD CLI, which has established an authenticated session for John, attempt to list all of the registered certificates and known hosts by executing the following command:

```
argocd cert list
```

Instead of returning the desired result, you will be presented with an error message similar to the following:

```
FATA[0015] rpc error: code = PermissionDenied desc = permission denied: certificates, ...
```

A similar message is displayed within the Argo CD UI when performing the same operation and can be seen by clicking on Settings on the lefthand navigation pane and selecting "Repository certificates and known hosts."

Since John is acting as an Argo CD administrator, he should be given the ability to manage all aspects of the Argo CD server. Let's work toward providing him the access that he needs by first reviewing the architecture of the Argo CD RBAC system.

## Argo CD RBAC Basics

Argo CD makes use of the Casbin authentication system (which is a library to manage authorization) to define and enforce RBAC rules.

More information about Casbin can be found at *https://casbin.org*.

Only two roles are included by default:

`role:admin`
: Unrestricted access to all resources

`role:readonly`
: View, but not modify, all resources

These roles, and the rules behind them, take the form of comma-separated values (CSV) and provide a way to define both policies, which can then be applied to users and groups.

At a high level, there are two definition structures to define RBAC within Argo CD:

- All resources except application-related permissions:

  ```
  p, <role/user/group>, <resource>, <action>, <object>, <effect>
  ```

- Applications, ApplicationSets, logs, and exec (which belong to an AppProject):

  ```
  p, <role/user/group>, <resource>, <action>, <appproject>/<object>, <effect>
  ```

Resources represents the following:

```
clusters, projects, applications, applicationsets, repositories, certificates, accounts,
gpgkeys, logs, exec, extensions
```

While an action includes:

```
get, create, update, delete, sync, override, action/<group/kind/action-name>
```

Once a policy is created, it can then be assigned to a user, group, or even another role using the following form:

```
g, <user/group/role>, <role>
```

Since the goal is to provide not only John but all users who are members of the ArgoCDAdmins group the ability to manage Argo CD fully, there is no need to create a new policy. Instead, the existing `role:admin` role can be applied to the group. To do so, the following role mapping policy can be specified:

```
g, ArgoCDAdmins, role:admin
```

RBAC definitions and configurations are specified within a ConfigMap with the name `argocd-rbac-cm` within the namespace Argo CD is deployed within. Policy definitions are contained, by default, within the `policy.csv` key.

While we could modify the `argocd-rbac-cm` ConfigMap manually or perform an inline patch of the resource, it is easier to manage policy definitions in a separate CSV file.

Create a CSV file called *policy.csv*, which includes the following content:

```
g, ArgoCDAdmins, role:admin
```

Since there is no *policy.csv* content defined initially within the `argocd-rbac-cm` ConfigMap, there are no concerns as they relate to overwriting any content that may have been defined.

Execute the following command, which will generate a ConfigMap resource containing the `policy.csv` file and merge it with the existing ConfigMap within the cluster:

```
kubectl create configmap \
-n argocd argocd-rbac-cm \
--from-file=policy.csv=policy.csv --dry-run=client \
-o yaml | kubectl patch configmap -n argocd argocd-rbac-cm \
--type merge --patch-file /dev/stdin
```

If you inspect the contents of the `argocd-rbac-cm` ConfigMap, you will see that the `policy.csv` within the ConfigMap matches the content of our local `policy.csv` file.

Now that members of the ArgoCDAdmins group have been granted the `role:admin` role, confirm that John now has the ability to access and manage all Argo CD resources by once again attempting to list all of the repository certificates and known hosts that have been defined:

```
argocd cert list
```

This time, the full result list should be returned, confirming the policy was configured and applied appropriately.

## Custom Role Creation

Argo CD includes two roles, `role:admin` and `role:readonly`, that can be designated to users and groups as necessary. However, as more users and groups adopt Argo CD, there is need for a separate role to be created that encompasses the specific permissions desired. In the prior section, we covered the basic structure of a role and how it can be applied. In this section, we will define a new role that is targeted at developers and their use case for deploying applications into Kubernetes using Argo CD.

If you recall the setup of Keycloak, two users and groups were defined. We covered John in detail, who represents an Argo CD administrator. Mary, the other user defined, is a software developer and is looking to leverage Keycloak, but as a developer, needs to be able to modify certain resources (so the `role:readonly` role does not apply) but does not need full access to Argo CD (disqualifying the `role:admin` role).

Developers require access to perform the following actions:

- Deploy and manage applications
- View a list of clusters for which they could deploy their applications
- View and access repositories containing their source code
- View and access certificates and known hosts associated with repositories

Based on the parameters that should be associated with this role, the following policy can be constructed:

```
# Define Policies for a new role called role:developers
p, role:developers, applications, *, */*, allow
p, role:developers, applicationsets, *, */*, allow
p, role:developers, clusters, get, *, allow
p, role:developers, repositories, get, *, allow
p, role:developers, certificates, get, *, allow

# Apply the role:developers role to Developers group
g, Developers, role:developers
```

Breaking down the policies, we first allow developers unrestricted access to Applications and ApplicationSets within all projects. Recall that application-related permissions have a slightly different scheme, which includes the name of the project and the resources within them. To fulfill our requirements, the pattern `*/*` is used, which allows for access to all projects and their resources.

The other two policy permissions enable access to view all cluster and repository definitions. Finally, the role is assigned to the developers group that is defined within Keycloak.

This policy definition could be appended to the previous *policy.csv* file, which was used in the prior section to grant administrator access to the ArgoCDAdmins group. However, Argo CD does include the functionality to separate policy definitions to allow them to be composed (a common use case when using the Kustomize templating tool).

Separate policy files must make use of the format `policy.<any_string>.csv`. With this in mind, create a new file called *policy.developers.csv* with the policy content provided previously.

With the new policy file created, we could patch the contents to the `argocd-cm` ConfigMap using a similar approach as the `policy.csv`. However, creating policies can be a complex process, and introducing a syntactical error is a common occurrence (such as a missing comma). Applying a misconfigured policy could potentially risk the stability of the Argo CD server.

To mitigate these concerns, options are available to perform validation prior to the resource being included within the `argocd-cm` ConfigMap by using the `argocd admin settings rbac validate` command and specifying the desired policy file to validate using the `--policy-file` parameter.

Execute the following command to validate the `policy.developers.csv` policy file:

```
argocd admin settings rbac validate --policy-file=policy.developers.csv
```

If the contents of the policy file do not contain any errors, the message `Policy is valid` will be displayed. Otherwise, an error will be thrown.

First, before applying the policy, authenticate to the Argo CD UI as Mary, our resident software developer, using the username "mary@upandrunning.local" and password "argocdDeveloper123".

Once authenticated, navigate to the list of repository certificates by selecting Settings on the lefthand navigation pane and then selecting "Repository certificates and known hosts."

As expected, a permission error should be displayed.

Apply the `policy.developers.csv` policy by patching the `argocd-cm` ConfigMap using the following command:

```
kubectl create configmap \
-n argocd argocd-rbac-cm \
--from-file=policy.developers.csv=policy.developers.csv \
--dry-run=client \
-o yaml | kubectl patch configmap -n argocd argocd-rbac-cm \
--type merge --patch-file /dev/stdin
```

Attempt to once again view the repository certificates and known hosts page within the Argo CD settings, and since the `role:developers` role has been associated with the developers group, of which Mary is a member, she is now able to view all of the defined certificates and known hosts.

Feel free to validate the remainder of the policies associated with the `role:developers` role including creating, synchronizing, and finally, deleting an application.

## RBAC Defaults

The RBAC capability provides several different methods for customizing the level of access that users and groups have against Argo CD resources. These assets build upon the default role and their associated policies employed by Argo CD as specified by the `policy.default` property within the `argocd-cm-rbac` ConfigMap. When Argo CD is installed, this property is empty—meaning that no level of access will be granted against any resource. While errors may not be returned when querying resources, no values will be returned.

To enable a specific role to be used when authenticating against Argo CD, the following command can be used to set the `policy.default` property:

```
kubectl patch -n argocd cm argocd-cm-rbac --type='merge' \
-p='{"data": {"policy.default": "role:<name_of_role>"}}'
```

## Anonymous Access

Argo CD, by default, requires that a user authenticate before being able to access the UI or make queries using the CLI. However, there are capabilities available to enable anonymous access to any entity to access Argo CD resources without needing to authenticate (for example, if you're setting up a read-only account to view statuses in the UI).

Anonymous access can be enabled by setting the `users.anonymous.enabled` property within the `argocd-cm` ConfigMap with a value of `true`. Once enabled, users are granted the level of access as specified by the value in the `policy.default` property.

## Summary

This chapter provided an overview of how users and groups can be defined and managed along with how RBAC policies can be defined and configured in Argo CD, resulting in a more secure and productive platform for all.

One of the biggest differentiators as it relates to GitOps tools that Argo CD possesses is the included UI and the associated integrations—whether it be the command line interface or API. Understanding how these assets can be accessed using Argo CD's included local users facility or integrating an external user management system through the SSO functionality enables productivity from day one.

In addition, by using the RBAC capabilities provided by Argo CD, policies can be constructed into roles and applied to users and groups to govern the level of access that these entities have when interacting with the platform.

CHAPTER 7

# Cluster Management

Argo CD can deploy applications to the Kubernetes cluster that Argo CD is installed to without further configuration from administrators. This out-of-the-box default setting makes it easy for administrators to get up and running and reap the benefits of Argo CD immediately. Whether you are just starting off in your GitOps journey or if you are a seasoned DevOps practitioner, this default setting helps administrators implement their solutions.

The simplicity of the Argo CD deployment can accelerate adoption beyond just a single team, to the point where management of additional clusters is needed and desired. Although you can deploy Argo CD instances to these additional clusters, Argo CD has the ability to add, manage, and deploy resources to additional clusters using a "hub-and-spoke" design. The "hub" is the instance of Argo CD itself and is colloquially known as the "Argo CD Control Plane" in larger installations.

In this chapter, we will explore how clusters are managed in Argo CD, including how and where they are defined in the control plane, the ways in which they can be managed, and how we can set up different role-based access control (RBAC) policies to control their access in a multi-tenant situation.

## Cluster Architecture

The cluster architecture of Argo CD is fairly straightforward; upon initial deployment, Argo CD has access to the local Kubernetes cluster (i.e., the Kubernetes cluster Argo CD was installed within). This access, as discussed previously, is enabled by default and can be referenced in an Argo CD Application deployment as `https://kubernetes.default.svc` (if using the server key in the configuration file) or `in-cluster` (if using the name key in the configuration file). The creators of Argo CD realized that administrators would like to manage more than just the local Kubernetes clusters but also deploy to and manage other clusters concurrently—most administrators would like a single pane of glass view of all their clusters.

Let's take a look at how clusters are defined and managed in Argo CD.

## Local Versus Remote Clusters

When it comes to clusters, Argo CD doesn't treat the local `in-cluster` any differently than remote clusters. To Argo CD, it sees the `in-cluster` as just another deployment target defined in the Argo CD Application manifest. As we went over in Chapter 4, this is denoted under `.spec.destination` in the Argo CD Application manifest. The following is a snippet of how the target server is defined with an Argo CD Application:

```
spec:
  destination:
    server: https://kubernetes.default.svc
    ## Can also use the following instead of "server"
    # name: in-cluster
    namespace: bgd
```

Remote clusters are referenced the same way. Again, Argo CD treats every cluster the same way—so deploying to a remote cluster is accomplished by merely changing the destination configuration to the desired target cluster. For example:

```
spec:
  destination:
    server: https://cluster1.mydomain.tld:8443
    ## Can also use the following instead of "server"
    ## the following name comes from the cluster secret
    # name: cluster1
    namespace: bgd
```

The namespace in this section refers to the destination namespace where the manifest will be applied to. It's also worth noting that the namespace value will only be set for namespace-scoped resources that have not set a value for the `.metadata.namespace` field.

How are clusters defined? How does Argo CD know what certificate authority (CA) to use to connect to that cluster's Kubernetes API endpoint? Or which endpoint to communicate with when specifying `name` instead of `server` within the destination of an application? What if you want to use a specific ServiceAccount when connecting to the remote cluster? In the next section, we will go deeper into how clusters are defined and how you can further refine how Argo CD connects to these clusters.

## Hub-and-Spoke Design

Before we get into how clusters are defined, it's important to understand that when Argo CD manages clusters, it does so in a hub-and-spoke design. See Figure 7-1 for a high-level view into what this architecture entails.

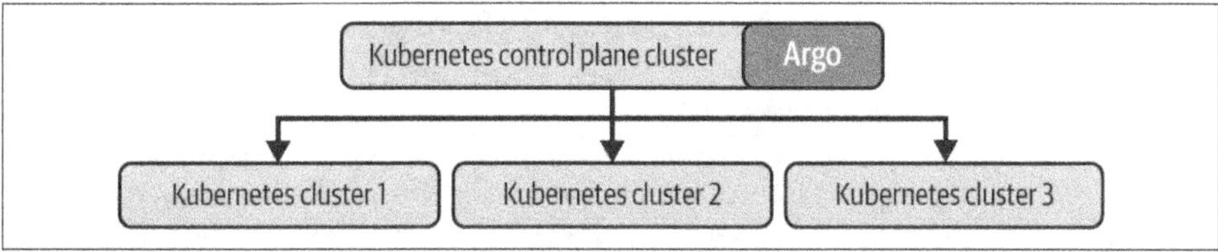


*Figure 7-1. Argo CD hub-and-spoke design*

Argo CD "reaches out" in order to perform actions on the target cluster. This is often referred to as the "push model." This means that configurations are obtained and cached on the control plane cluster (where Argo CD is running), and they are "pushed" to the desired destination cluster. It's important to keep this in mind when architecting your installation as considerations, such as firewall rules and accessing the managed cluster's Kubernetes API endpoint need to be taken into account.

## How Clusters Are Defined

Now that we've established an understanding in how Argo CD sees clusters (whether it is the local cluster or a remote cluster) as just Kubernetes API endpoints (or "destinations"), where does Argo CD retrieve the needed information for this API endpoint? Since the Kubernetes API endpoint has already been established as a means to a connection, Argo CD now needs the credentials for that Kubernetes API endpoint.

From a security point of view, ensure the credentials that Argo CD uses to connect to your managed clusters are up to your organization's security standards. Security with Argo CD will be discussed in Chapter 9.

Cluster credentials are stored in a Kubernetes Secret in the same namespace as Argo CD is installed within (in our case, this is the `argocd` namespace). To that end, you can surmise that Argo CD clusters are defined via a Kubernetes Secret. The Secret has the following fields, shown in Table 7-1.

*Table 7-1. Properties of an Argo CD cluster secret*

| Field | Description |
|---|---|
| `name` | The name given for the cluster. This value is what is referenced when using the name property within the destination section of the Argo CD Application manifest. |
| `server` | The Kubernetes cluster's API server URL. This value is what is referenced when using the server property in the destination section of the Argo CD Application manifest. |
| `namespaces` | *(Optional)* A comma-separated list of namespaces accessible in the cluster. Cluster-level resources are ignored if this field is not empty. |
| `clusterResources` | *(Optional)* A boolean string ("true" or "false") that determines whether Argo CD can deploy cluster-level resources on this cluster. Used only if the namespace field is not empty. |
| `project` | *(Optional)* A string to designate this cluster as available only to the specified Argo CD project name. |
| `config` | Written in JSON; represents the connection configuration. |

You can only have one secret per cluster, so it's imperative that you take into consideration what resources Argo CD will be managing and what level of access Argo CD needs.

Here is an example of a minimal configuration of the secret representing a cluster:

```
apiVersion: v1
kind: Secret
metadata:
  name: prod-cluster
  namespace: argocd
  labels:
    argocd.argoproj.io/secret-type: cluster
type: Opaque
stringData:
  name: prod-cluster
  server: https://prod.k8s.example.com:6443
  config: |
    {
      "bearerToken": "<ServiceAccount token should NOT be encoded>",
      "tlsClientConfig": {
        "insecure": false,
        "caData": "<base64 encoded certificate>"
      }
    }
```

For a more in-depth explanation about all available options, please consult the official documentation (*https://oreil.ly/8U95s*).

It's worth noting that the `bearerToken` section in the `config` field should *not* be base64 encoded and is represented in plain text, while the `caData` section in the `config` field *should* be encoded. Also, the label defines that the content contained in this secret contains cluster-related properties.

As mentioned earlier, the Argo CD control plane (typically referred to as *in-cluster*) is the cluster that Argo CD is installed on. There is no need to define this cluster. However, there are use cases where you might need to further refine the settings. By default, this cluster has no secret associated with it. You can confirm this assessment with the following command:

```
$ kubectl get secrets -n argocd -l argocd.argoproj.io/secret-type=cluster
No resources found in argocd namespace.
```

This is because Argo CD attempts to have working defaults for easy deployment. The assumption that Argo CD makes is that it uses the default Kubernetes Service address (`https://kubernetes.default.svc`) for the API endpoint, the default Kubernetes CA certificate for that endpoint, and the token for the `argocd-application-controller` ServiceAccount. So, if there is a desire to make updates to the `in-cluster` configuration, how could that be accomplished? Fortunately, the solution is simple.

Let's take the use case where only users who have access to the `sysadmin` Argo CD project should be able to deploy to the `in-cluster` cluster. To facilitate this requirement, a new Secret that defines the in-cluster configuration needs to be created, and within that Secret, the `project` field must grant the sysadmin Argo CD project access. First, create the Kubernetes Secret with the name in-cluster along with the secret type label indicating that the configuration contains an Argo CD cluster definition. Take note that the values specified are the default values with the addition of the `project` field.

The following example is a cluster Secret in a file called *in-cluster.yaml*:

```
apiVersion: v1
kind: Secret
metadata:
  name: in-cluster
  namespace: argocd
  labels:
    argocd.argoproj.io/secret-type: cluster
type: Opaque
stringData:
  name: in-cluster
  server: https://kubernetes.default.svc
  project: sysadmin # what we're adding
  config: |
    {
      "tlsClientConfig": {
        "insecure": false
      }
    }
```

Once the file has been created, you can apply it to your cluster by running the following (see Figure 7-2):

```
$ kubectl apply -f in-cluster-secret.yaml
```

You can also update cluster settings in the Argo CD UI under the Settings section.

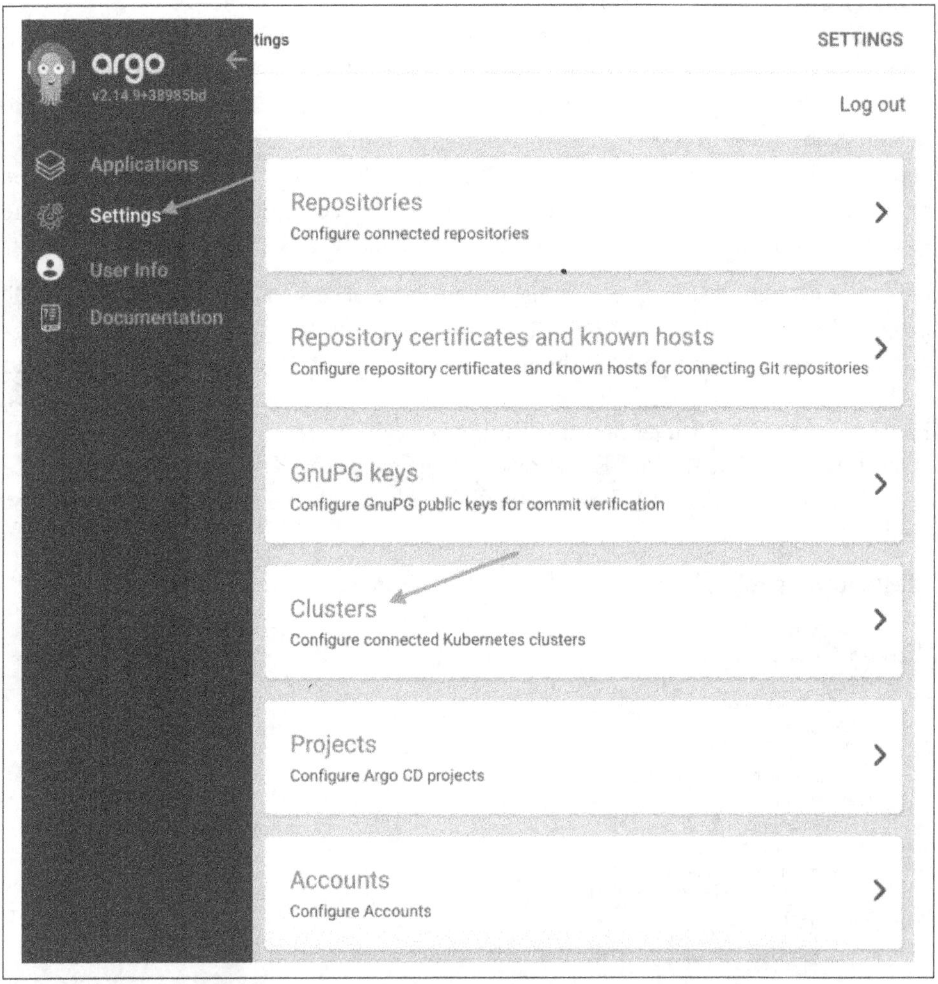

*Figure 7-2. Argo CD Clusters Settings page*

Not only are you able to now see the `in-cluster` configuration listed as a Secret, but it also has been scoped to only be available to users who have access to the `sysadmin` Argo CD Project:

```
$ kubectl get secrets -n argocd -l argocd.argoproj.io/secret-type=cluster
NAME         TYPE     DATA   AGE
in-cluster   Opaque   4      74s
```

You will need to also set the appropriate RBAC in order to scope the in-cluster to only be available to the supplied project. See Chapter 8 for more information about Argo CD RBAC and Projects.

You can also see the configuration using the `argocd` CLI:

```
$ argocd cluster get in-cluster -o json | jq -r .project
sysadmin
```

We've added a project in this configuration for demonstration purposes. We will go over Projects in depth in Chapter 8.

# Adding Remote Clusters

There are two methods to add remote clusters to Argo CD: using the `argocd` CLI and declaratively within a Kubernetes Secret. We'll explore each of these methods, but first, let's go over the basics of creating a cluster.

## Creating a Cluster

In order to demonstrate how to add a remote cluster, we are going to create another cluster using `kind`. In order for both `argocd` CLI and Kubernetes Secret to work, we must expose the Kubernetes API endpoint. For this to function properly, the environment variable of the IP address of the host that `kind` is running on must be set.

Set an environment variable called `REMOTE_CLUSTER_IP` with the IP address of the host `kind` is running on:

```
$ export REMOTE_CLUSTER_IP=192.168.4.134
```

The IP address in your environment will differ.

Given that we are going to be creating a new `kind` cluster, we should manage the `kubeconfig` file separately, export the `KUBECONFIG` environment variable to reference a file located at `~/remote-cluster.config`, which will be populated when the cluster is created:

```
$ export KUBECONFIG=~/remote-cluster.config
```

Next, create the `kind` cluster using the name `remote` with the IP address exported previously:

```
$ kind create cluster --name remote --config - <<EOF
kind: Cluster
apiVersion: kind.x-k8s.io/v1alpha4
networking:
  apiServerAddress: "${REMOTE_CLUSTER_IP}"
EOF
```

You should *take caution* when exposing your Kubernetes API endpoint on a public network.

At this point, two `kind` clusters should be running: the one we've been working with has Argo CD installed, and a new one called `remote` that was created now:

```
$ kind get clusters
kind
remote
```

Your output may differ.

To return to being able to work with the Argo CD cluster, unset the `KUBECONFIG` environment variable:

```
$ unset KUBECONFIG
```

At this point, we are ready to add the `remote` cluster to our Argo CD instance.

## Adding a Cluster with the CLI

As mentioned earlier, the `argocd` CLI utility can be used to interact with the Argo CD instance—when accessing the Kubernetes API via `kubectl` is not accessible or is not allowed. To that end, we can use this Argo CD CLI tool to add a cluster using the `kubeconfig` file that was just created. Before the cluster can be added, ensure that you are logged in to your Argo CD instance. If you haven't already, you can log in using the following command:

```
$ argocd login --insecure --grpc-web --username admin \
--password \
$(kubectl -n argocd get secret argocd-initial-admin-secret \
-o jsonpath="{.data.password}" | base64 -d) argocd.upandrunning.local
```

If you changed your admin password, use that password instead of obtaining the initial admin password.

Once authenticated, the list of currently registered clusters can be listed:

```
$ argocd cluster list
SERVER                          NAME        VERSION  STATUS      MESSAGE  PROJECT
https://kubernetes.default.svc  in-cluster  1.29     Successful
```

Now, let's add the `kind remote` cluster we just created with the `argocd cluster add` subcommand, while providing the location of the Kubeconfig path:

```
$ argocd cluster add kind-remote --yes \
--kubeconfig ~/remote-cluster.config --name remote
```

The output should look something like the following:

```
INFO[0000] ServiceAccount "argocd-manager" created in namespace "kube-system"
INFO[0000] ClusterRole "argocd-manager-role" created
INFO[0000] ClusterRoleBinding "argocd-manager-role-binding" created
INFO[0005] Created bearer token secret for ServiceAccount "argocd-manager"
Cluster 'https://192.168.1.254:38187' added
```

A few things to note about the options from this command:

- `kind-remote` is the name of the Kubernetes context inside the `kubeconfig`. To find the name of the context, we ran `kubectl config get-contexts --kubeconfig ~/remote-cluster.config`.
- `--yes` confirms adding the cluster (without prompting).
- `--name` sets the name of the cluster in Argo CD.

Argo CD uses the `kubeconfig` file to connect to the remote cluster and creates a ServiceAccount called `argocd-manager` with a corresponding RBAC in the `kube-system` namespace. This `argocd-manager` ServiceAccount is used by Argo CD to manage the remote cluster.

Once the cluster has been added, it will be visible when executing the `argocd cluster list` command once again:

```
$ argocd cluster list
SERVER                          NAME        VERSION  STATUS      MESSAGE
https://192.168.1.254:38187     remote               Unknown     Cluster has no app...
https://kubernetes.default.svc  in-cluster  1.29     Successful
```

The state will be `Unknown` until something is deployed to the cluster.

The remote cluster is now ready to be deployed to. You can reference this cluster by the name, `remote`, or by the server address, `https://192.168.1.254:38187`, as indicated in the output from the prior command in the Argo CD Application manifest. For example:

```
spec:
  destination:
    ## "name" can be used instead of "server"
    # name: remote
    server: https://kubernetes.default.svc
    namespace: demo
```

Deleting a cluster with the CLI is fairly straightforward. Either the name of the cluster or the server address should be specified.

You should remove this cluster if you want to try out the declarative approach in the next section. If you're not planning on trying it out declaratively, don't delete the cluster. We'll be using this cluster later in this chapter.

Remove the cluster using the `argocd cluster rm` command:

```
$ argocd cluster rm --yes remote
Cluster 'remote' removed
```

Confirm the remote cluster is no longer displayed in the list of registered clusters:

```
$ argocd cluster list
SERVER                          NAME        VERSION  STATUS      MESSAGE  PROJECT
https://kubernetes.default.svc  in-cluster  1.29     Successful
```

## Adding a Cluster Declaratively

The Argo CD CLI utility is a great way to work with Argo CD, as it lowers the barriers of entry. One of the big advantages is that the Argo CD CLI falls under the governance of the Argo CD RBAC. So, administrators can freely give CLI access to the platform without having to give them access to the Kubernetes API (via CLI or other methods).

Still, administrators following the GitOps principles would like a more declarative way to define and manage clusters. To support this approach, Argo CD administrators can opt to (as discussed earlier in this chapter) define clusters via a Kubernetes Secret.

Storing Kubernetes Secrets in plain text on source code is *not* recommended, and it is a security risk! It is recommended that an appropriate Secrets management solution should be utilized. Integrations with various Secrets management solutions can be brokered with operators, like the External Secret Operator that supports many Secret management backends.

Before creating the Secret representing an Argo CD cluster, make sure you are using the correct Kubernetes context (the instance that Argo CD is running within):

```
$ kubectl config get-contexts
CURRENT   NAME        CLUSTER     AUTHINFO    NAMESPACE
*         kind-kind   kind-kind   kind-kind
```

The `kubectl` CLI will be used to create the Secret representing the remote cluster. The Secret needs to be in the format that was described earlier in this chapter, and the necessary information will be extracted from the `kubeconfig` file using the `kubectl config` command. Before we do that, we need to create a ServiceAccount for Argo CD to use in the `remote` cluster. In addition, RBAC-related resources need to be created and associated with the newly created ServiceAccount in the remote cluster. These steps parallel the process that is facilitated by the Argo CD CLI, which we will emulate.

If you are following along and you did the example using the Argo CD CLI, you don't need to create the ServiceAccount or the ClusterRoleBinding. You can skip to the creation of the token.

First, create a ServiceAccount called `argocd-manager` in the `kube-system` on the `remote` cluster:

```
$ kubectl create --kubeconfig ~/remote-cluster.config sa -n kube-system argocd-manager
```

Next, create a ClusterRoleBinding for that `argocd-manager` ServiceAccount, assigning it the built-in `cluster-admin` role:

```
$ kubectl create --kubeconfig ~/remote-cluster.config \
clusterrolebinding argocd-manager-role-binding \
--clusterrole=cluster-admin --serviceaccount=kube-system:argocd-manager
```

Now, generate a token that is associated with the `argocd-manager` ServiceAccount for Argo CD to use. The token is obtained after executing the command. As a result, we will store it in a variable called `TOKEN` for later use:

```
$ kubectl apply --kubeconfig ~/remote-cluster.config -f - <<EOF
apiVersion: v1
kind: Secret
metadata:
  name: argocd-manager-token
  namespace: kube-system
  annotations:
    kubernetes.io/service-account.name: argocd-manager
type: kubernetes.io/service-account-token
EOF

$ TOKEN=$(kubectl get secret --kubeconfig ~/remote-cluster.config -n \
kube-system argocd-manager-token -o jsonpath='{.data.token}' | base64 -d)
```

Verify that the `TOKEN` variable is set:

```
$ echo $TOKEN
```

Using this information, and information that will be extracted from the `kubectl config` command, create the Secret for Argo CD to use:

```
$ cat <<EOF | kubectl apply -n argocd -f -
apiVersion: v1
kind: Secret
metadata:
  name: remote
  labels:
    argocd.argoproj.io/secret-type: cluster
type: Opaque
stringData:
  name: remote
  server: $(kubectl config view --kubeconfig ~/remote-cluster.config \
  -o jsonpath='{.clusters[?(@.name == "kind-remote")].cluster.server}')
  config: |
    {
      "bearerToken": "${TOKEN}",
      "tlsClientConfig": {
        "insecure": false,
        "caData": "$(kubectl config view --raw \
--kubeconfig ~/remote-cluster.config \
-o jsonpath='{.clusters[?(@.name == "kind-remote")].cluster.certificate-authority-data}')"
      }
    }
EOF
```

For more information about the options available when using the `kubectl config` command, consult the Kubernetes documentation (*https://oreil.ly/ohnox*).

This result from the prior command is a Secret in the `argocd` namespace:

```
$ kubectl get secret remote -n argocd --show-labels
NAME     TYPE     DATA   AGE   LABELS
remote   Opaque   3      2m    argocd.argoproj.io/secret-type=cluster
```

The newly added cluster can now be seen using the Argo CD CLI tool:

```
$ argocd cluster list
SERVER                           NAME         VERSION  STATUS       MESSAGE
https://192.168.1.254:38187      remote                Unknown      Cluster has no app...
https://kubernetes.default.svc   in-cluster   1.29     Successful
```

Updating clusters managed by Argo CD can be done via the CLI (by using `argocd cluster set`) or by updating the corresponding Secret (by using `kubectl patch` or `kubectl edit`). Both methods produce the same result and are useful when there is a need to update cluster configurations, such as ServiceAccount tokens or CA certificates.

Taking a look from a GitOps point of view, since managed clusters are defined in Secrets, then it is recommended that you use a Secret management system. The aforementioned External Secrets Operator has support for a lot of backends to help in this case.

# Deploying Applications to Multiple Clusters

As we're going through these steps, you can get the sense that Argo CD has the capability to not only manage multiple clusters, but also the ability to deploy resources to multiple clusters as well. However, you may have noticed when going through the Argo CD Application specification page (*https://oreil.ly/KLtqG*) on the official documentation, that only a single cluster can be defined with an Argo CD Application manifest. In a way, you can think of Argo CD Applications as having a 1:1 relationship with the cluster that application is being deployed to. Effectively, an Argo CD Application can be seen as an instance of your running application.

So, how can we effectively deploy our applications to multiple cluster destinations? Fortunately, several patterns are available to achieve this goal.

## App-of-Apps Pattern

The *App-of-Apps pattern* first appeared as a method of bootstrapping Argo CD instances and can also be used as a method of recovery from a catastrophic failure or major outage. This method is also flexible where organizations have a desire for creating a logical deployment across many clusters. Another advantage is that you can use other Argo CD features, like sync waves and sync phases, to orchestrate (order) Argo CD Application deployments.

As the name suggests, the App-of-Apps pattern is an Argo CD Application that just contains other Argo CD Applications. Since Argo CD Applications are just Kubernetes resources, the Argo CD Application paradigm can be used with other Argo CD Applications. Take a look at Figure 7-3 to see how this approach is depicted in the Argo CD UI.

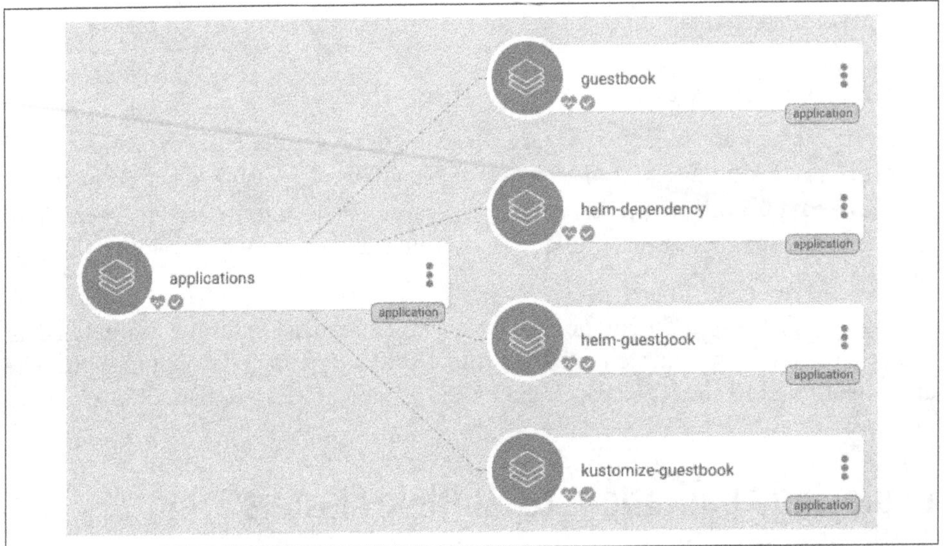


*Figure 7-3. App-of-Apps taken from the Argo CD documentation*

The following example can be found in this book's accompanying repository (*https://github.com/sabre1041/argocd-up-and-running-book*). You can apply the "parent" Argo CD Application by running the following:

```
$ kubectl apply -n argocd -f ch07/pricelist-app-of-apps.yaml
```

This Argo CD Application manifest included multiple Application manifests, which created several Argo CD Applications:

```
$ kubectl get applications -n argocd
NAME                 SYNC STATUS   HEALTH STATUS
pricelist-app        Synced        Healthy
pricelist-config     Synced        Healthy
pricelist-database   Synced        Healthy
pricelist-frontend   Synced        Healthy
```

Each of these Argo CD Applications represents the same application, with the difference being they target a different destination cluster.

## Using Helm

Several challenges are introduced when starting to consider Argo CD Applications to multiple destination clusters. First, you may be thinking, "That's a lot of YAML to write just for one small delta (changing the destination cluster). While on the other side, I have to change a lot for my application to run successfully on each cluster." As a result, many Argo CD administrators have started utilizing Helm to parameterize the deployment of Argo CD Applications.

Let's take a quick look at the example from the official Argo CD documentation page for using Helm (*https://oreil.ly/SxhKs*):

```
apiVersion: argoproj.io/v1alpha1
kind: Application
metadata:
  name: guestbook
  namespace: argocd
  finalizers:
  - resources-finalizer.argocd.argoproj.io
spec:
  destination:
    namespace: argocd
    server: {{ .Values.spec.destination.server }}
  project: default
  source:
    path: guestbook
    repoURL: https://github.com/argoproj/argocd-example-apps
    targetRevision: HEAD
```

As depicted in the previous manifest, certain properties from the Argo CD Application can be parameterized and can be injected using a Helm values file. Here's an example:

```
spec:
  destination:
    server: https://kubernetes.default.svc
```

While this is still a valid (and fully supported) way of deploying your Argo CD Applications, this pattern of using Helm was first implemented in a time before Argo CD Applications could natively be templated. It is recommended that those who can, migrate to ApplicationSets. That being said, the App-of-Apps pattern is still valuable and, in a lot of cases, you will use both.

## ApplicationSets

An Argo CD ApplicationSet (*https://oreil.ly/8hmsC*) is a Kubernetes CRD that can be seen as a templating engine for Argo CD Applications. This templating engine is fed parameters, known as *generators*, which produces *N* number of Argo CD Applications based on those provided configurations (which can also include business logic depending on the generator selected). The original author of the Argo CD

ApplicationSet controller described ApplicationSets as a "factory that produces Argo CD Applications."

The aforementioned generators are a method for producing the necessary information for an Argo CD Application. These generators range from simple key/value pairs to structures based on your Git repository organization layout. Here is a list of generators at the time of this writing:

*List generator*
: The List generator allows you to target Argo CD Applications to clusters based on a fixed list of any chosen key/value element pairs. This is normally where people start, since it's basic key/value pairs.

*Cluster generator*
: The Cluster generator allows you to target Argo CD Applications to clusters, based on the list of clusters defined in Argo CD. This also includes the ability to automatically respond to cluster addition/removal in Argo CD.

*Git generator*
: The Git generator allows you to create Applications based on a configuration file found within a Git repository or based on the directory structure of a Git repository.

*Matrix generator*
: The Matrix generator may be used to combine the generated parameters of two separate generators. This is generally used if you need to mix and match generators.

*Merge generator*
: The Merge generator may be used to merge the generated parameters of two or more generators. It basically "flattens" the configuration of the generators used (in contrast to the Matrix generator that combines). Additional generators can override the values of the base generator.

*SCM Provider generator*
: The SCM (source code management) Provider generator uses the API of an SCM provider (for example, GitHub) to automatically discover repositories within an organization. This is normally used if you have many Applications in an organization that you'd like to deploy.

*Pull Request generator*
: The Pull Request generator is used to automatically discover open pull requests within a repository. This is used typically for previewing environments or changes.

*Cluster Decision Resource generator*
: The Cluster Decision Resource generator is used to interface with Kubernetes custom resources that use custom resource-specific logic to decide which set of Argo CD clusters to deploy to.

*Plugin generator*
: The Plugin generator gives you the ability to create your own generator where the other generators don't quite fit your particular use case. Generally speaking, if none of the built-in generators fits your use case, the Plugin generator is the way to go.

For most organizations, starting off with the List generator, Cluster generator, or one of the Git generators (there are two subgenerators) is the easiest way to get started with Argo CD ApplicationSets. Let's take another example from the accompanying repository, where an Application is deployed using different settings to separate clusters based on the content originating in different repositories:

```
$ kubectl apply -n argocd -f ch07/appset-bgd.yaml
```

With this one manifest, you can see that the ApplicationSet generated Argo CD Applications based on the parameters of the List generator:

```
$ kubectl get applicationsets -n argocd
NAME   AGE
bgd    29s

$ kubectl  get applications -n argocd
NAME        SYNC STATUS   HEALTH STATUS
bgd-blue    Synced        Healthy
bgd-green   Synced        Healthy
```

One thing to note about Argo CD ApplicationSets is that functionality, such as sync waves and sync phases between Applications, are not fully supported. If there is a need to leverage such functionality, it is recommended that the standard App-of-Apps pattern be used for the time being. That being said, there is an *alpha* feature (i.e., not ready for production) called Progressive Syncs that you can read about in the official documentation site (*https://oreil.ly/7Dtv4*). We will go over Progressive Syncs in Chapter 10.

# Summary

In this chapter, you learned how clusters are defined in Argo CD and how Argo CD is architected in a hub-and-spoke design. You also explored how to add, delete, and manage the lifecycle of the managed cluster. Finally, several patterns for deploying Argo CD Applications to different clusters were introduced. In the next chapter, you will learn how to handle multi-tenant-based deployments of Argo CD, including considerations that should be taken under consideration when architecting for multi-tenancy, along with several patterns and examples.

CHAPTER 8

# Multi-Tenancy

Multi-tenancy in tech refers to an architecture where a single instance of software (or infrastructure) serves multiple tenants. A tenant is typically a group of users who share common access and privileges within the software—for example, a company using a SaaS app or a team using a shared Kubernetes cluster.

Argo CD extends multi-tenancy beyond just basic RBAC. It has the ability to granularly set access controls based on the actor performing the action (user, group, or automated service account), which resource is being accessed, and what action is being performed.

In Chapter 6, you learned about RBAC and its various uses. In this chapter, we are going to extend that knowledge by introducing the Argo CD AppProject concept and how to manage RBAC configurations on a per-project basis. We'll start off by demonstrating different Argo CD deployment models. Then, we will explore, in detail, what Argo CD AppProjects are and how to effectively use them in a multi-tenant system. Finally, we will explore how to perform resource management using Projects.

## Argo CD Installation Modes

There are two primary ways to install Argo CD, and each includes a set of capabilities for achieving multi-tenancy. As one might expect, there are advantages and disadvantages, depending on the chosen deployment mode. Additional considerations as it relates to multi-tenancy need to be taken into account depending on how your organization is laid out, how your release process is handled, and/or if you have to meet certain criteria for regulation purposes.

## Cluster Scoped

The most common and default model for deploying Argo CD is the *cluster-scoped* method.

This is also the deployment method that we have been using thus far during our exploration of Argo CD.

This method is used, specifically, for installations that require Argo CD to act in a multi-tenant when a hub-and-spoke design is desired. This provides all the tooling and features needed (like RBAC, AppProjects [more on that later], and roles/groups) for Argo CD administrators to create a GitOps platform that can support many applications, users, teams, and groups within their organization. From the point of view of Argo CD, it now becomes the interface on how to interact with all managed Kubernetes clusters.

The biggest challenge of a cluster-scoped deployment of Argo CD is that, by default, the service accounts associated with Argo CD, effectively, have `cluster-admin` privileges on all managed clusters. The elevated permissions might be excessive in some scenarios, posing potential security risks. This was a design decision to enable Argo CD to fully manage the cluster. The permissions, however, can be scoped down using standard Kubernetes RBAC by adjusting the `ClusterRole/ClusterRoleBinding` for the Argo CD service account.

## Namespace Scoped

The alternate method for deploying Argo CD as it relates to multi-tenancy is the namespace-scoped method. This installation method requires only privileges against a single namespace, allowing cluster administrators the ability to install different instances of Argo CD on the same cluster and then delegate the control over to individual teams. Since these installations do not have privileges outside of their own namespace, it is an attractive solution for security-conscious Argo CD administrators to achieve multi-tenancy and an increased security posture.

There are a few drawbacks to this type of installation. First, instead of being able to use the `in-cluster` cluster (the default in a cluster-scoped deployment of Argo CD), additional steps must be taken to configure the local cluster for use by Argo CD, including setting up the associated service accounts and RBAC policies. Another drawback is that the installation assumes no privileges outside the namespace, so tasks requiring elevated permissions (e.g., installing CRDs) must be coordinated with cluster administrators. It's also worth noting that there will be operational overhead in managing multiple Argo CD instances.

Given the number of steps involved for deploying Argo CD using the namespace method, this book will instead continue to focus on the cluster-scoped method, and this chapter will show you how to utilize the included tools and capabilities needed to set up a multi-tenant system using this installation method.

## Projects

Argo CD has a concept of a Project (which is controlled via the `AppProject` CRD). An Argo CD Project provides a grouping of applications, and it is a point of RBAC/demarcation for Argo CD. This logical grouping of Argo CD components is paramount for Argo CD administrators that are setting up their installation to support multi-tenancy.

With an Argo CD Project, administrators can:

- Restrict the sources of content that can be used (Git, Helm, etc.)
- Restrict where Argo CD Applications can be deployed to (clusters and namespaces)
- Restrict which Kubernetes objects *can* be deployed (Deployments, services, CRDs, NetworkPolicies, etc.)
- Restrict who has access to which resources based on Group/User membership.

Argo CD includes a Project called `default`. This Project allows the deployment of any resource to any cluster by anyone. While you can't delete the `default` Project, you can lock it down to the point where no one can use it. When Argo CD is initially installed, it has the following permissions for the `default` project, which are the most permissive:

```
spec:
  sourceRepos:
  - '*'
  destinations:
  - namespace: '*'
    server: '*'
  clusterResourceWhitelist:
  - group: '*'
    kind: '*'
```

It's important to note that an Argo CD Application can only ever belong to one Project. When the `AppProject` isn't specified, the `default` Project is used.

## Resource Management

Resource management is at the heart of an Argo CD Project and it is what allows Argo CD administrators to set up the platform to support multi-tenancy. It follows the "allow/deny" model where the first matching rule takes precedence. The following are some examples of how this works.

Let's review how you manage Git repositories within an Argo CD Project under the `.spec.sourceRepos` of an `AppProject` manifest:

```
spec:
  sourceRepos:
    - '!ssh://git@github.com:argoproj/test'
    - '!https://gitlab.com/group/**'
    - '*'
```

Note the use of the `!` symbol to indicate an explicit "deny" against the associated repositories. In the prior example, users would not be allowed to deploy from the *git@github.com:argoproj/test* repository in the argoproj GitHub organization; nor would users be allowed to deploy any repository from GitLab that's part of the "group" organization. However, any other repository would be allowed.

Similarly, you can accomplish the same goal for managing the clusters and namespaces that can be deployed to under the `.spec.destinations` property:

```
spec:
  destinations:
  - namespace: '!kube-system'
    server: '*'
  - namespace: '*'
    server: '!https://team1-*'
  - namespace: '*'
    server: '*'
```

Again, note the use of the ! symbol to indicate an explicit "deny" against those destinations. In this case, users will be able to deploy to any namespace, except the namespace `kube-system` or any cluster with the URL that matches `team1-*`. Any other namespace/server combination would be allowed.

The first matching rule takes precedence, so deny rules must appear before the allow rules to be effective.

You can also limit what Kubernetes objects may or may not be created. This is for both namespaced and cluster-scoped objects. For example, to allow all namespaced-scoped resources to be created, except for `ResourceQuota`, `LimitRange`, and `NetworkPolicy`; you can set the associated policy in the `.spec.namespaceResourceBlacklist` property. For example:

```
spec:
  namespaceResourceBlacklist:
  - group: ''
    kind: ResourceQuota
  - group: ''
    kind: LimitRange
  - group: ''
    kind: NetworkPolicy
```

Conversely, you can deny all namespaced-scoped resources from being created, except for those specified within the `.spec.namespaceResourceWhitelist` property. This has the same format as `namespaceResourceBlacklist` shown previously.

Cluster-scoped resources can be constrained in a similar fashion using the `.spec.clusterResourceWhitelist` and `.spec.clusterResourceBlacklist` properties as their namespace-scoped counterpart. For example, the following example can be used to deny all cluster-scoped resources from being created, except for a `Namespace`:

```
spec:
  clusterResourceWhitelist:
  - group: ''
    kind: Namespace
```

In Chapter 6, you learned the basics of RBAC and how it can be configured at the Argo CD platform level. You can also configure RBAC at the Argo CD Project level as well. For example, the following configuration illustrates how to set a policy that only enables those users with the `role:dev` permission the ability to `view` and `sync` on the `pricelist` Argo CD Project:

```
spec:
  roles:
  - description: Developers get view and sync
    name: developer
    policies:
    - p, proj:myproj:role:dev, applications, get, pricelist/*, allow
    - p, proj:myproj:role:dev, applications, sync, pricelist/*, allow
    - p, proj:myproj:role:dev, projects, get, pricelist, allow
```

As we've reviewed here, you can see how granular you can get with resource management with Argo CD. While this example focuses on applications and projects as resources, other resource types (repositories, clusters, logs, exec) can also be controlled via RBAC. You can even apply these policies to specific users and/or groups. In the following section, we will go over a use case to see how AppProjects can be used in your environment.

## Use Case: GitOps Dashboard

When working through Chapter 6, you got some experience working with RBAC. In this section we'll see the level of granularity that can be achieved at the Project level. This enables Argo CD administrators to grant permission ranging from "read only" to delegating complete control to specific Argo CD Applications.

The most common pattern Argo CD administrators seem to start with when implementing RBAC at a project level is to grant groups/end users the ability to see Applications within a Project, perform syncs on demand, but not modify or delete anything. This provides a sort of "developer portal" where end users can see and perform issue triage and also do on-demand syncs when needed.

In order to complete this section, you must have set up SSO as described in Chapter 6, as the users and groups will be reused.

### Create Project

We will first create the project using the Argo CD CLI, which will allow us to deploy an Application that is Project scoped. First, make sure that you are logged in as the `"admin"` user, which provides the necessary permissions to create a Project:

```
$ argocd account get-user-info -o json | jq .username
"admin"
```

Retrieve the list of currently defined Projects:

```
$ argocd proj list -o name
default
```

Only a single Project, `default`, will be returned since this is our first opportunity to manage Projects. Create a new Project called `golist` using the following command:

```
$ argocd proj create golist \
--src '*' --dest '*,*' --allow-cluster-resource '*/*'
```

This new project should now be present when listing Projects:

```
$ argocd proj list -o name
default
golist
```

With the `golist` Project created, it can be associated with newly created Applications. We will configure more granular RBAC for this Project in a later section.

## Deploy Applications

Now that the Project `golist` has been created, review the Application manifests in the repository accompanying this book under the *ch08/argocd/applications/* directory:

```
spec:
  # ...omitted for brevity
  project: golist
```

Note that each Application will be deployed into the `golist` Project as denoted under the `.spec.project` section of each manifest. Create each Application using either `kubectl` or the `argocd` CLI (the following example shows use of the `argocd` CLI):

```
$ argocd app create --file ch08/argocd/applications/golist-db.yaml
$ argocd app create --file ch08/argocd/applications/golist-api.yaml
$ argocd app create --file ch08/argocd/applications/golist-frontend.yaml
```

List the Applications, confirming that they were added to the project:

```
$ argocd app list -o name --project=golist
argocd/golist-api
argocd/golist-db
argocd/golist-frontend
```

The Applications that were deployed are part of an application stack, which includes a frontend service, a backend service, and a database. At this point, the workloads managed by the Applications should be running:

```
$ kubectl get pods -n golist
NAME                               READY   STATUS    RESTARTS        AGE
golist-api-764879758b-bs57q        1/1     Running   5 (9m59s ago)   11m
golist-db-mariadb-0                1/1     Running   0               10m
golist-frontend-7647cb44d4-g7kvx   1/1     Running   0               10m
```

The database may take some time to become ready. During this time, you may notice other `Pods` in a `CrashLoopBackOff` state. This is expected and should correct itself after some time since the restarts occur due to the database not being available.

Now that the Application has been deployed to the Project, the next step is to configure RBAC policies within the Project to grant access to a particular SSO group.

## Configure Project

In the previous section, we created the Project imperatively using the `argocd` CLI. While a completely valid way of configuring the Project, the most effective way is to do it declaratively. This allows us to take full advantage of the GitOps framework that Argo CD provides.

Take a look in the *ch08/argocd/projects/* directory and you will see a *golist.yaml* Project file. Reviewing the file reveals the following contents:

```
spec:
  # ...omitted for brevity
  roles:
  - description: Developers get view and sync
    name: golist-developer
    policies:
    - p, proj:golist:golist-developer, applications, get, golist/*, allow
    - p, proj:golist:golist-developer, applications, sync, golist/*, allow
    groups:
    - Developers
```

In the `polices` section, notice that "get" and "sync" are allowed for all Applications in the Project. All other actions are disallowed since there is an implicit "deny" associated with the RBAC model of Argo CD. Under the `groups` section there is a list of SSO groups for which the policies will be applied against. This group name originates from the OIDC configuration that was completed in Chapter 6.

For more information on RBAC and its use, please refer to Chapter 6.

Apply this Argo CD Project manifest in order to set these configurations:

```
$ argocd proj create --upsert --file ch08/argocd/projects/golist.yaml
```

## Test Setup

With the configuration of the `golist` Project complete, including the deployment of Applications and policies to grant permissions for a specific group, let's confirm the expected results.

Log in to your Argo CD instance as *mary@upandrunning.local* (since this user is part of the Developer group), and you should see the aforementioned Applications in the Argo CD overview page, as depicted in Figure 8-1.

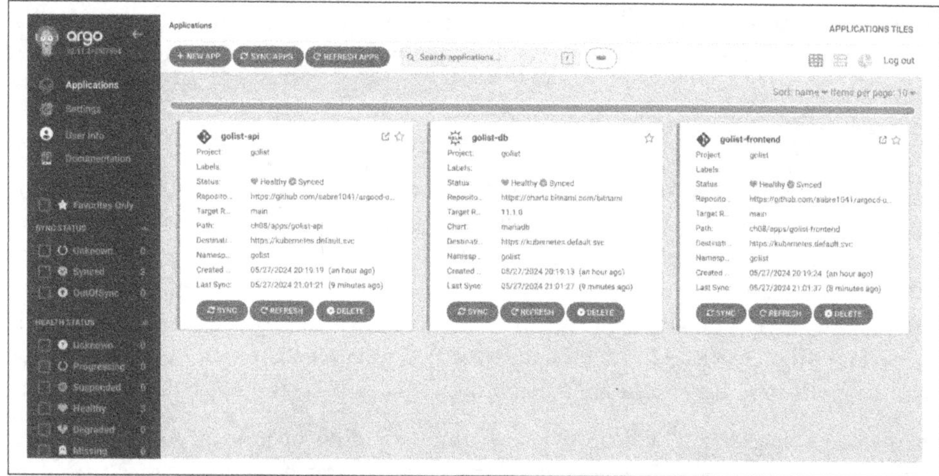

Figure 8-1. Applications overview

On the overview page, click on SYNC APPS, select all Applications, and click on SYNC. You should see all Applications sync, with the status of Complete, which will appear similar to Figure 8-2.

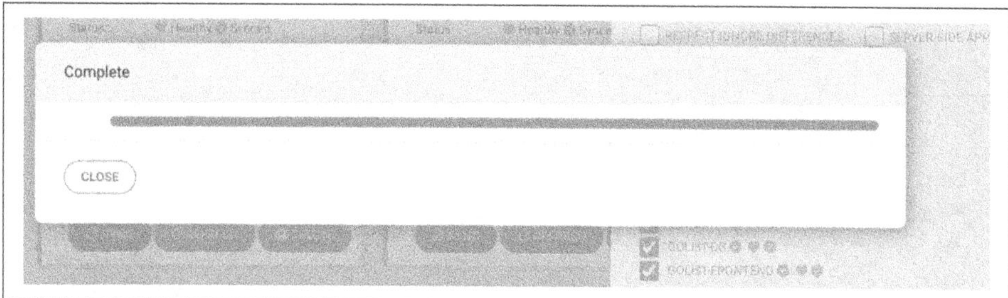

Figure 8-2. Sync complete

Now, click on the golist-db "card," click on DELETE, and in the pop-up prompt, type in **golist-db** (leaving the rest of the default values), and click OK. An error similar to Figure 8-3 will be displayed.

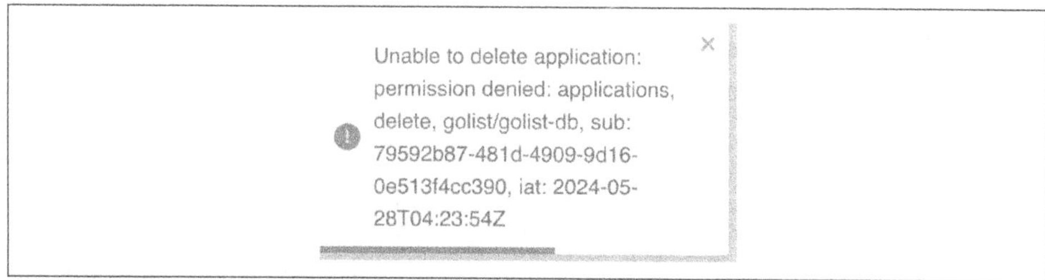

Figure 8-3. Error when deleting

The ability to delete this Application is disallowed since the configuration of the golist Project doesn't allow users in the Developers group to delete Applications.

# Summary

In this chapter, you learned about the two models for how Argo CD implements multi-tenancy and became familiar with Argo CD AppProjects. You investigated how to manage resources using Projects and how to have fine-grained permissions for not only deploying resources but also the actions that users can perform once they are deployed. Finally, you put this knowledge to use by creating an Argo CD Project, configuring RBAC policies, and verifying that certain actions could only be performed by members of the specified group.

In the next chapter, we will deepen our understanding of how Argo CD manages security. In particular, we will explore the different methods that can be used to harden the security level of Argo CD and how to communicate securely with target systems. In addition, we will also discuss how sensitive content that is used at various points within the Argo CD lifecycle can be handled to avoid being discovered by others.

CHAPTER 9

# Security

One of the top technology concerns, whether from the perspective of an individual developer or enterprise organization, is security. Ensuring that systems are protected in a manner that reduces compromise while communicating using secure mechanisms are just some of the steps that can be taken to increase the overall level of security in an environment. Argo CD includes a number of native capabilities that support conducting secure operations and enforces certain requirements for use when operating and interacting with the platform.

In this chapter, we will explore the different methods that can be implemented to harden the security level of Argo CD and how to communicate securely with target systems. In addition, we will also discuss how sensitive content that is used at various points within the Argo CD lifecycle can be handled to avoid being discovered by individuals and systems that should not be granted access.

## Securing Argo CD

One of the key areas where security hardening can be employed in Argo CD is within the Argo CD server component, as it represents the location where the REST API and UI is exposed to end users. Considerations should be made whenever there are any externally facing resources, as there is an increased potential where attackers could gain unauthorized access to Argo CD.

The admin user gives users the ability to simplify initial setup and onboarding for Argo CD. However, this user also presents a potential risk for the misuse by an attacker. First, whenever Argo CD is deployed, a secret called `argocd-initial-admin-secret` is created within the namespace where Argo CD is deployed.

One of the first steps that an Argo CD administrator should take is to change the default password for the admin user. Otherwise, anyone with access to read Secrets within the Argo CD namespace can readily decode the password and gain elevated access to Argo CD. Fortunately, Chapter 6 covered the steps in detail for changing the admin password as well as deleting the Secret containing the initial password, as the contents are no longer valid. Of course, if the admin user is no longer being used or needed, the account can be disabled entirely to completely eliminate the potential risk. Steps to accomplish this task are also described in Chapter 6.

Beyond managing user access, securing communications with the Argo CD server at the transport level is critical. This involves ensuring that all interactions with the API and UI occur over encrypted channels. When Argo CD was deployed, the `--insecure` extra argument was added within the Helm values file. By specifying this parameter, the Argo CD server starts without TLS enabled, allowing the communication with the server to occur without any form of encryption.

Encrypting network traffic using TLS certificates is almost a must these days, as it guarantees that the communication with Argo CD cannot be easily observed as it is being transferred. Implementing TLS often involves creating, managing, and renewing certificates, which can be a barrier for some users. We saw some of these steps firsthand when configuring Keycloak as an OIDC server in Chapter 6.

Fortunately, Argo CD simplifies the process for enabling TLS by automatically generating a set of self-signed certificates at server startup, eliminating the need to communicate insecurely whenever the `--insecure` option is not enabled. Let's update the configuration of Argo CD by removing the use of the `--insecure` extra argument.

While we could update the `argo-cd-argocd-server` deployment manually, let's use Helm to deploy a new release of the Argo CD chart and remove the `--insecure` property from the Helm values file.

The updated values file can be found in the *ch09/helm/values* directory of the repository accompanying this book. Execute the following command to enable TLS within the Argo CD server:

```
helm upgrade -i argo-cd argo/argo-cd --namespace argocd --create-namespace \
-f ch09/helm/values/values-argocd-secure.yaml
```

You can wait for the rollout of the new settings by checking the status of the Argo CD API server deployment by running the following:

```
kubectl rollout status -n argocd deployment/argo-cd-argocd-server
```

With the new release rolled out, launch a web browser and navigate to the Argo CD UI at *https://argocd.upandrunning.local.*

What you quickly observed by attempting to navigate to the Argo CD UI is that something is not configured correctly. Your browser most likely reported an error with too many redirects being the cause (see Figure 9-1).

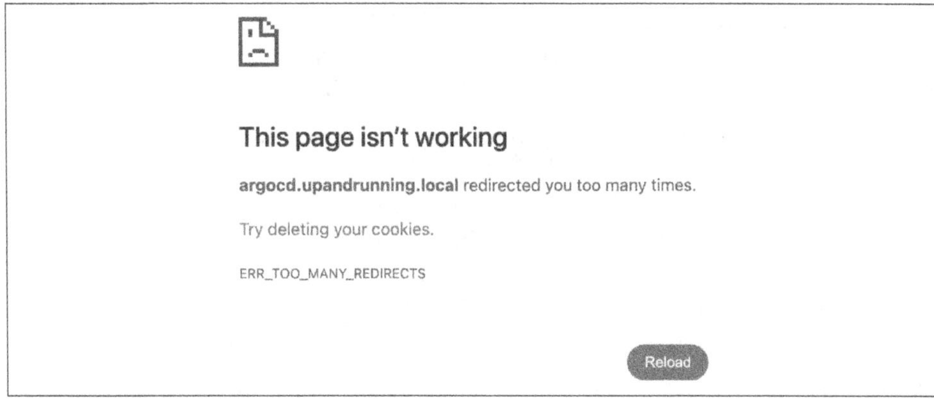


*Figure 9-1. Too many redirects*

So, what could be the issue?

By default, when the Argo CD Helm chart configures the Ingress resource, it performs what is known as edge termination, resulting in TLS traffic being terminated at the NGINX ingress controller. Traffic is then sent to Argo CD unencrypted. When removing the `--insecure` argument from the Argo CD server, we effectively closed the method of communication that the NGINX was expecting to be able to use. Argo CD responds to the request, redirecting to the secure channel, but the subsequent request from NGINX still attempts to connect insecurely. This cyclical loop continues until the browser's maximum redirect limit is reached, resulting in the error.

There are several ways that this issue can be solved, including establishing a new TLS connection from NGINX to communicate with Argo CD. However, the simplest method is to offload the management of certificates entirely and pass through the connection to the Argo CD backend without any form of TLS termination within the NGINX controller. To accomplish this task, two changes need to be made:

- Set the `nginx.ingress.kubernetes.io/ssl-passthrough` annotation on the Ingress resource; this informs the NGINX ingress controller to forward encrypted traffic directly to the backend.
- Enable SSL passthrough support within the NGINX ingress controller by specifying the `--enable-ssl-passthrough` CLI argument at startup, as this feature is disabled by default.

CLI arguments for the NGINX controller can be defined within the `controller.extraArgs` Helm value and by specifying `controller.extraArgs.enable-ssl-passthrough=true`; SSL passthrough support will be enabled.

Enable SSL passthrough support within the NGINX ingress controller by updating the Helm chart using the `values-ingress-nginx-ssl-passthrough.yaml` values file in the *ch09/helm/values* directory by executing the following command:

```
helm upgrade -n ingress-nginx ingress-nginx ingress-nginx/ingress-nginx \
-f ch09/helm/values/values-ingress-nginx-ssl-passthrough.yaml
```

Finally, specify both the `nginx.ingress.kubernetes.io/ssl-passthrough: "true"` and `nginx.ingress.kubernetes.io/force-ssl-redirect: "true"` annotations on the Ingress resource of Argo CD within the Helm values file to not only enable SSL passthrough support on requests made against this Ingress resource but to automatically redirect insecure connections (HTTP) to their secure counterparts (HTTPS).

Upgrade the Argo CD Helm chart using the `values-argocd-secure.yaml` values file within the *ch09/helm/values* directory by specifying the following command:

```
helm upgrade -i argo-cd argo/argo-cd --namespace argocd --create-namespace \
-f ch09/helm/values/values-argocd-secure.yaml
```

With SSL passthrough support enabled on both the NGINX ingress controller and within the Ingress resource for the Argo CD server, once again navigate to *http://argocd.upandrunning.local* in a web browser. Accept the self-signed certificate warning that is presented within the browser from the automatically generated Argo CD certificate to confirm the Argo CD server is once again accessible, now with end-to-end TLS support.

## Configuring TLS Certificates

The automatic generation of TLS certificates by Argo CD enables the ability to securely communicate without any additional effort by the Argo CD administrator. However, complications are introduced when relying on this feature, as any external system that communicates with the Argo CD server will struggle to fully trust the certificate, as it is always generated when the instance starts up. Instead of relying on the automatic certificate generation feature within Argo CD, it is recommended that static certificates be provided by the Argo CD administrator so that secure and reliable communication can be achieved when communicating with Argo CD components.

While TLS certificates can be configured within each Argo CD component (including Dex and the repo server) to avoid the automatic TLS certification generation feature, since end users will directly communicate with the Argo CD server, we will limit our discussion to only this component.

## Generating Argo CD TLS Certificates

TLS certificates can be created for the purpose of securely communicating with the Argo CD server. The process for generating certificates was covered briefly in Chapter 6 when Keycloak was deployed to support SSO-based authentication. The key difference in this case is that two sets of certificates, a root certificate and another for the Argo CD server, will be generated to enable the creation of a certificate chain. By creating the Argo CD server TLS certificate on top of a root certificate, only the root certificate will be needed to trust an array of certificates that could be created in the future to serve other purposes or components.

Generate the root certificate by executing the following command:

```
openssl req -nodes -x509 -sha256 -newkey rsa:4096 \
  -keyout root.key \
  -out root.crt \
  -days 365 \
  -subj "/O=O'Reilly Media/CN=Argo CD: Up and Running Root CA" \
  -extensions v3_ca \
  -config <( \
  echo '[req]'; \
  echo 'distinguished_name=req'; \
  echo 'extensions=v3_ca'; \
  echo 'req_extensions=v3_ca'; \
  echo '[v3_ca]'; \
  echo 'keyUsage=critical,keyCertSign,digitalSignature,keyEncipherment'; \
  echo 'basicConstraints=CA:TRUE')
```

Next, generate the TLS certificate for Argo CD based on the root certificate stored in the `root.crt` and `root.key` files:

```
openssl req -nodes -x509 -sha256 -newkey rsa:4096 \
-keyout argocd.key \
-out argocd.crt \
-days 365 \
-subj "/O=O'Reilly Media/CN=argocd.upandrunning.local" \
-extensions v3_ca \
-CA root.crt \
-CAkey root.key \
-config <( \
echo '[req]'; \
echo 'distinguished_name=req'; \
echo 'extensions=v3_ca'; \
echo 'req_extensions=v3_ca'; \
echo '[v3_ca]'; \
echo 'keyUsage=critical,digitalSignature,keyEncipherment'; \
echo 'subjectAltName=DNS:argocd.upandrunning.local'; \
echo 'extendedKeyUsage=serverAuth'; \
echo 'basicConstraints=CA:FALSE')
```

TLS certificates for the Argo CD server are defined in a Secret called `argocd-server-tls` within the namespace containing Argo CD. Since a root certificate was also generated in addition to the certificate for the Argo server, combine the two certificates into a single file called `argocd-fullchain.crt` containing the entire certificate chain:

```
cat argocd.crt root.crt > argocd-fullchain.crt
```

Now create the `argocd-server-tls` secret:

```
kubectl create -n argocd secret tls argocd-server-tls \
  --cert=argocd-fullchain.crt \
  --key=argocd.key
```

The Argo CD server automatically detects the creation of the `argocd-server-tls` Secret and will load the newly provided certificate. Navigate to the Argo CD UI and confirm that the newly generated certificate chain is being used. You will once again be greeted with a warning related to trusting the provided certificate. By inspecting the certificate, you can confirm that it matches the instance created previously, as shown in Figure 9-2.

Your connection is not private
Attackers might be trying to steal your information from **argocd.upandrunning.local** (for example, passwords, messages, or credit cards). Learn more
NET::ERR_CERT_AUTHORITY_INVALID
**Subject:** argocd.upandrunning.local
**Issuer:** Argo CD: Up and Running Root CA
**Expires on:** Jun 13, 2025
**Current date:** Jun 13, 2024
**PEM encoded chain:**
-----BEGIN CERTIFICATE-----



*Figure 9-2. Web browser displaying the contents of the provided TLS certificate*

Accept the self-signed certificate to proceed to the Argo CD UI.

The root certificate can be configured at an operating system level to avoid the warnings related to untrusted connections. Since the configurations are operating system dependent, the steps will not be covered in detail.

The Argo CD server, including how external resources communicate with the REST API and UI, is just one of the areas for which TLS certificates can be configured. In the following sections, we will explore some of other ways the TLS certificates play a role within Argo CD.

## Repository Access

Argo CD, as a tool that implements GitOps practices, interacts with a variety of externally facing resources to source content that can be applied to one or more Kubernetes clusters. These interactions can be configured to communicate in a secure fashion, such as requiring the use of TLS certificates.

Thus far, we have sourced all of the exercise content from the Git repository that corresponds to this publication. This repository is hosted in publicly hosted Git service, and while this service greatly simplifies how anyone can easily access the content, it does limit the type of configurations that can be applied to demonstrate the capabilities of Argo CD. In order to avoid these limitations, we will deploy a Git server of our own to demonstrate some of the ways that Argo CD can be configured to securely communicate with Git repositories.

Given the popularity of Git, there are a multitude of options available when looking to operate a self-hosted Git server, ranging from an instance that exposes just the Git protocol to fully functional collaboration suites. Gitea is an open source Git platform that offers a good middle ground as it includes a number of useful features, such as source code and project management capabilities, but is also lightweight compared to other options in the market.

Much like how Argo CD and the rest of the supplemental tools that have been deployed throughout this book, Gitea will be installed using a Helm chart. To simplify the interaction with the Gitea instance, it will be initialized with a set of content that we will use throughout this chapter and contained within a wrapper chart located in the *ch09/helm/charts/gitea* directory.

Before the wrapper chart can be used, first, add the upstream Gitea Helm repository:

```
helm repo add gitea-charts https://dl.gitea.com/charts/
helm repo update
```

A custom Helm values file is located in the *ch09/helm/values* directory of the repository of this book. Take a moment and inspect the `values-gitea.yaml` file within this directory containing the Helm values. Notice within the `ingress` property, details related to `tls` configuration are provided, including the name of a Secret containing TLS certificates. Unlike how Argo CD was configured, TLS termination will not occur at the Gitea instance and will instead take place within the NGINX ingress controller. By including the reference to the Secret containing TLS certificates, these assets will automatically be picked by and configured by the NGINX ingress controller.

The creation of the TLS Secret is an "out-of-band" action and occurs before the installation of the Helm chart. Let's now create a TLS certificate using the same TLS root certificate that was used for Argo CD. Execute the following command to generate a new certificate pair for Gitea:

```
openssl req -nodes -x509 -sha256 -newkey rsa:4096 \
-keyout git.key \
-out git.crt \
-days 365 \
-subj "/O=O'Reilly Media/CN=git.upandrunning.local" \
-extensions v3_ca \
-CA root.crt \
-CAkey root.key \
-config <( \
echo '[req]'; \
echo 'distinguished_name=req'; \
echo 'extensions=v3_ca'; \
echo 'req_extensions=v3_ca'; \
echo '[v3_ca]'; \
echo 'keyUsage=critical,digitalSignature,keyEncipherment'; \
echo 'subjectAltName=DNS:git.upandrunning.local'; \
echo 'extendedKeyUsage=serverAuth'; \
echo 'basicConstraints=CA:FALSE')
```

Next, create a new namespace called `gitea` that will be used to create the Secret containing the TLS certificates and the Gitea instance:

```
kubectl create namespace gitea
```

Now, add the previously generated TLS certificate to the namespace within a Secret called `git-server-certificate`. Similar to the Argo CD server, the Gitea and root certificate must be combined into a single file so that they can be added to the Secret:

```
cat git.crt root.crt > git-fullchain.crt
```

Create the Secret containing the combined certificate and private key:

```
kubectl create secret tls -n gitea git-server-certificate \
--cert=git-fullchain.crt --key=git.key
```

Finally, deploy the Gitea instance by installing the wrapper Helm chart with the corresponding values file. Prepare the wrapper chart by updating the dependencies to pull down the upstream Gitea chart and then install the wrapper chart:

```
helm dependency update ch09/helm/charts/gitea
helm upgrade -i --create-namespace -n gitea gitea ch09/helm/charts/gitea \
-f ch09/helm/values/values-gitea.yaml
```

Once the chart has been deployed successfully, launch a web browser and navigate to *https://git.upandrunning.local*. Accept the use of the self-signed certificate, which will then direct you to the Gitea home page, depicted in Figure 9-3.

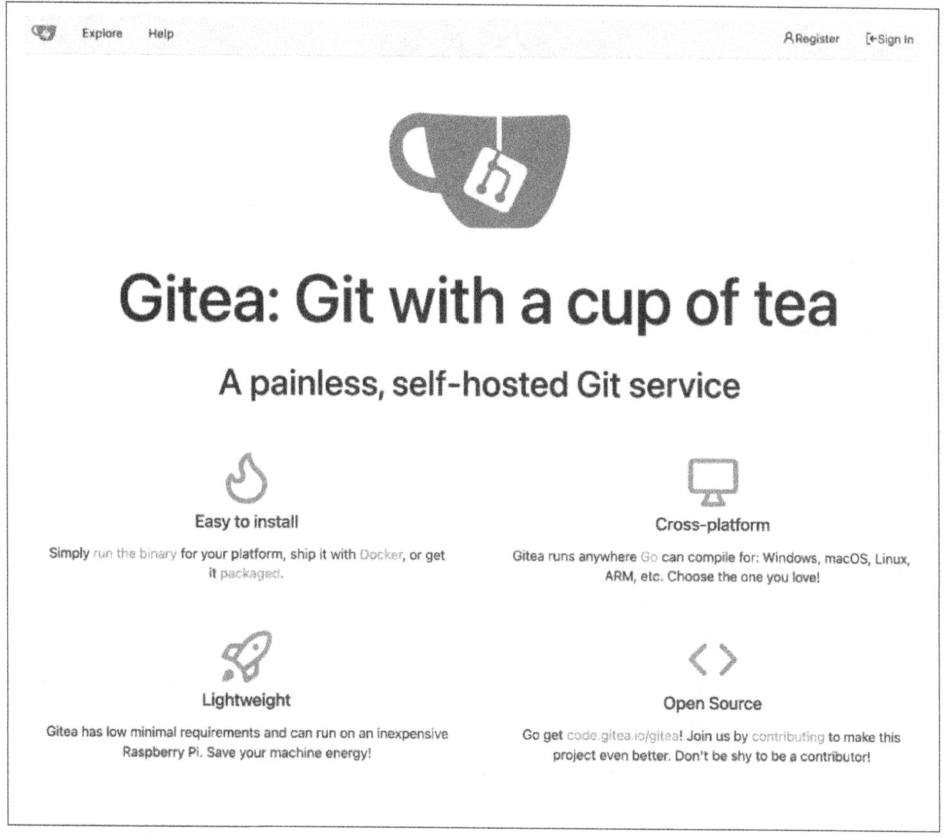


*Figure 9-3. The Gitea UI*

On the top right corner of the page, click the Sign In link and use the following credentials:

- Username: gitea_admin
- Password: Argocdupandrunning1234@

Once logged in, you will be redirected to the Gitea landing page (see Figure 9-4).

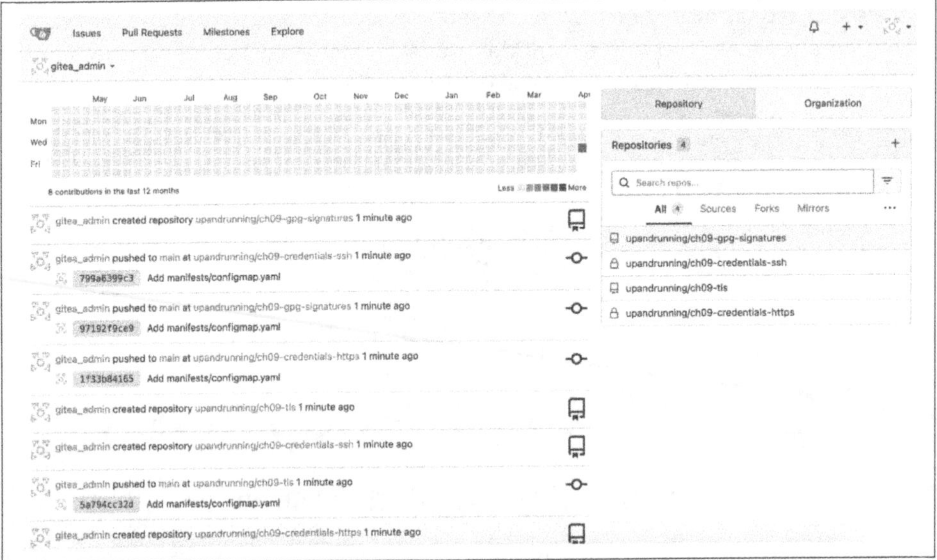


*Figure 9-4. The Gitea landing page*

Let's take a moment and review the content that has been automatically populated within the Gitea instance. An organization called *upandrunning* was created and contains a set of Git repositories that will be used throughout this chapter as different concepts are introduced.

On the right side of the page within the *Repository* box, locate and select the "upand running/ch09-tls" repository (see Figure 9-5).

The repository includes a directory called *manifests*, which contains the Kubernetes resources that will be synchronized by Argo CD.

To make use of this repository as a source of content in Argo CD, an application called `ch09-tls` is found within the *ch09/argocd* directory in the accompanying book repository in a file called `ch09-tls-application.yaml`.

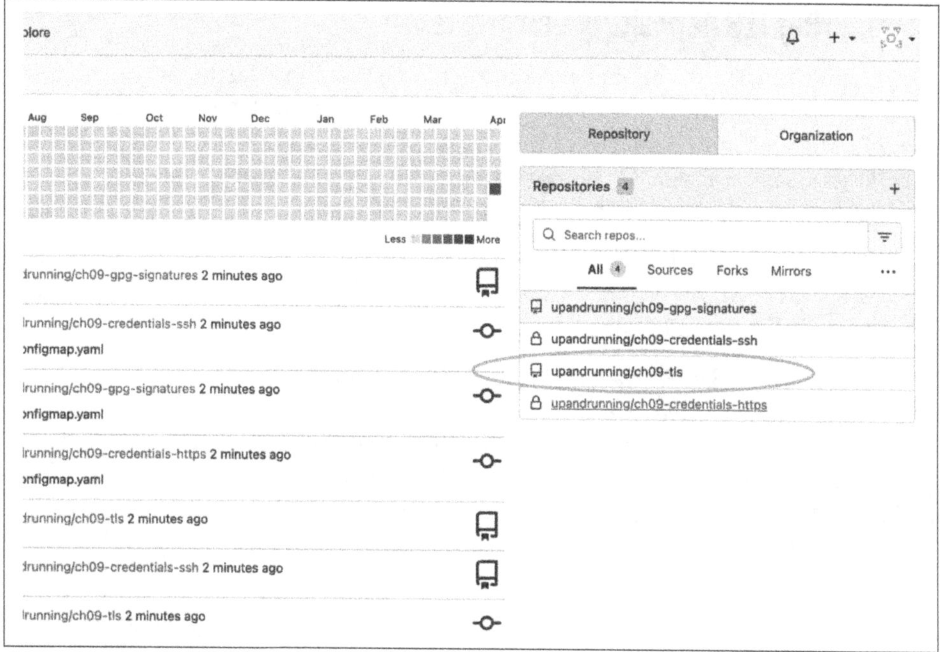


*Figure 9-5. The TLS repository*

Apply the manifest to the Kubernetes cluster by executing the following command:

```
kubectl apply -f ch09/argocd/ch09-tls-application.yaml
```

Check the status of the Application using the `argocd` CLI:

```
argocd app get ch09-tls
```

Upon inspecting the output, you will notice that the sync was not successful, and the cause (which is also displayed) is noted:

```
Failed to load target state: failed to generate manifest for source 1 of 1: rpc error: ...
```

Similar to the message that was presented when the Gitea instance was accessed for the first time in a web browser, trust could not be established between the Argo CD repository pod and Gitea. Since a custom certificate authority (root certificate) was created for these exercises, Argo CD is unaware of the authenticity and will, by default, deny all communication.

Fortunately, Argo CD provides several options for managing trust when communicating with remote repositories.

## Configuring TLS Repository Certificates

TLS certificates can be configured within Argo CD to allow for the secure communication with remote repositories. These configurations can be applied using either the UI, CLI, or native Kubernetes resources. Let's use the Argo CD UI to add the certificate associated with Gitea so that Argo CD will be able to interact with the remote repository in a secure fashion.

Launch the Argo CD UI at *https://argocd.upandrunning.local*. Click on Settings and then select "Repository certificates and known hosts." Click on Add TLS Certificate to launch the dialog for adding the Gitea certificate.

In the Repository Server Name, enter **git.upandrunning.local**. Copy the contents of the combined *git-fullchain.crt* file that was created in the prior section when deploying the Gitea instance in the TLS Certificate (PEM Format) text area. Click the Create button, and the newly added certificates will be displayed in the list of known and trusted TLS certificates, as shown in Figure 9-6.

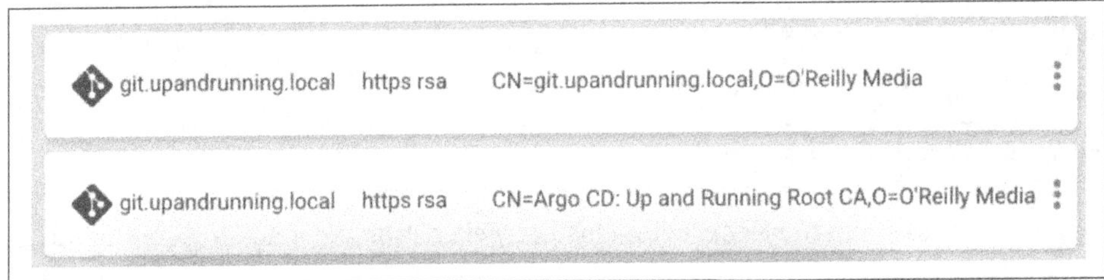


*Figure 9-6. TLS repository certificates within the Argo CD UI*

Now that the TLS certificates associated with Gitea have been configured in Argo CD, display the configured applications by clicking on the Applications button and then select the `ch09-tls` Application. Check the status of the application to determine if the resources stored in the Git repository were applied to the Kubernetes cluster now that Argo CD has been configured to trust the Gitea instance. If the application is still in an errored state, click the Refresh button to manually trigger Argo CD, which will allow the application to attain a healthy and synchronized state.

TLS certificates associated with repositories can also be managed using the Argo CD CLI using the `argocd cert` subcommand. List the configured repository using the `argocd cert list` command:

```
argocd cert list
```

What you may have noticed in both the results from the preceding command and the page in the Argo CD UI is that it contains more than the list of TLS repository certificates. Also present is the list of known SSH hosts, which will be covered in a later section.

TLS repository certificates can be removed using the `argocd cert rm` command. To remove the previously added certificates associated with the Gitea instance, execute the following command:

```
argocd cert rm git.upandrunning.local
```

To add the Gitea certificate back to Argo CD, use the `argocd cert add-tls` command with the hostname to associate with the certificate and the location of the certificate using the `--from flag` on the local machine:

```
argocd cert add-tls git.upandrunning.local --from git-fullchain.crt
```

Of course, since Argo CD defines its configurations in a fully declarative fashion, TLS repository configurations can be managed directly within the `argocd-tls-certs-cm` ConfigMap, the same resource that both the CLI and UI interact with.

The ConfigMap is structured in a straightforward manner, where the key represents the hostname associated with the certificate and the value being the certificate itself:

```
apiVersion: v1
kind: ConfigMap
metadata:
  name: argocd-tls-certs-cm
  namespace: argocd
data:
  <hostname>: |
    <certificates>
```

## Protected Repositories

Thus far, all interactions with remote repositories (whether they be from a Git or Helm source) have been with resources that are readily available and accessible and do not enforce any form of access restrictions. Since the content that is managed by Argo CD can contain either sensitive information or relate to the configuration of the Kubernetes clusters or applications, it is important that appropriate controls are applied to restrict access to only the individuals and systems that require it.

Argo CD includes support for communicating with remote repositories using either HTTPS- or SSH-based credentials. Both of these credential types and their associated configuration will be described in detail against resources stored within the Gitea instance previously deployed.

### HTTPS Credentials

The deployment of the Gitea instance automatically created a set of repositories that require credentials be provided to access the content. They are denoted within the Gitea UI with the word "Private" next to the repository. Several options are available when authenticating with Gitea using an HTTPS-based credential and include a username and password combination or an access token.

The *ch09-credentials-https* repository within the Gitea instance and in the *upandrunning* organization will be used to integrate Argo CD using HTTPS-based credentials.

First, let's explore how Argo CD reacts when it attempts to fetch resources that it does not have access to. Apply the `ch09-credentials-https` application located within the `ch09/argocd/ch09-credentials-https-application.yaml` file:

```
kubectl apply -f ch09/argocd/ch09-credentials-https-application.yaml
```

Check the status of the `ch09-credentials-https` application using the Argo CD CLI:

```
argocd app get ch09-credentials-https
```

As expected, the application is failing since the content cannot be accessed, as authentication is required:

```
Failed to load target state: failed to generate manifest for source 1 of 1: rpc error:
code = Unknown desc = authentication required
```

Similar to TLS certificates, repository credentials can be managed by either using the Argo CD UI or CLI, and the configurations that are made using either of these tools are realized as a Kubernetes Secret.

First, use the Argo CD UI to define the credentials to access the *ch09-credentials-https* repository by navigating to the Settings page and selecting Repositories in a web browser. Click the Connect Repo button to begin the process for defining repository configuration.

Enter the following into the dialog:

- Connection method: https
- Project: default
- Repository URL: *https://git.upandrunning.local/upandrunning/ch09-credentials-https.git*
- Username: gitea_admin
- Password: Argocdupandrunning1234@

Additional options are available for configuring TLS client certificates to enable mutual authentication as well as ignoring TLS verification when connecting to remote repositories.

Since mutual authentication was not configured, and the Argo CD server has been configured to trust the certificates exposed by the Gitea instance, those options will not be used.

Click the Connect button to create the repository configuration.

Confirm the connection status has a checkmark indicating that verification of the connectivity between Argo CD and the remote repository was successful, as shown in Figure 9-7.

*Figure 9-7. Successful connection to the Git repository*

With the repository configured and confirmed, navigate to the Applications page, select the `ch09-credentials-https` application, and click the Refresh button, which will make use of the repository configuration created previously to enable the successful synchronization of the application.

Configuring repository credentials can also be accomplished using the Argo CD CLI with the `argocd repo` subcommand. Using a similar flow that was accomplished in the previous section when managing TLS certificates, first list the defined repository configurations using `argocd repo list`:

```
argocd repo list

TYPE  NAME  REPO                                                              ...
git         https://git.upandrunning.local/upandrunning/ch09-credentials-https.git  ...
```

Remove the previously configured repository using the `argocd repo rm` command and include the name associated with the repository (`https://git.upandrunning.local/upandrunning/ch09-credentials-https.git` as in the previous example):

```
argocd repo rm https://git.upandrunning.local/upandrunning/ch09-credentials-https.git
```

Add the repository configuration back to Argo CD using the `argocd repo add` command while specifying the Git repository URL, username, and password:

```
argocd repo add https://git.upandrunning.local/upandrunning/ch09-credentials-https.git \
--username=gitea_admin --password=Argocdupandrunning1234@
```

One of the benefits of the CLI over the UI when adding repository configurations is that connectivity against the remote repository is validated in real time before it is added, and an appropriate error is presented. The UI will add the repository regardless of whether the connection to the remote repository was successful.

When a new repository configuration is added, a Secret is created within the namespace Argo CD is deployed within containing the provided properties. In Chapter 7, you saw how Argo CD clusters are also defined as Kubernetes Secrets and use the `argocd.argoproj.io/secret-type=cluster` label to denote that the contents contain properties defining an Argo CD cluster.

An Argo CD repository configuration is defined in a similar fashion, but utilizes the value of the `argocd.argoproj.io/secret-type` label as `repository`. The following is how the *ch09-credentials-https* repository configuration would be represented as a `Secret`:

```
apiVersion: v1
kind: Secret
metadata:
  annotations:
    managed-by: argocd.argoproj.io
  labels:
    argocd.argoproj.io/secret-type: repository
  name: ch09-credentials-https
  namespace: argocd
stringData:
  password: Argocdupandrunning1234@
  type: git
  url: https://git.upandrunning.local/upandrunning/ch09-credentials-https.git
  username: gitea_admin
type: Opaque
```

Aside from a username and password, both Argo CD and Gitea support the use of tokens as a form of authentication. A token can be thought of as a password that typically has a separate lifecycle than a standard user account password. Most Git-based solutions include support for some form of token-based authentication. Tokens also have the benefit of being scoped to specific resources or functions, such as access to only certain repositories or the ability to perform certain functions within those repositories (read versus write).

Credentials associated with repositories can be updated using either the Argo CD UI or using the `argo repo add` command. To update an existing repository configuration, include the `--upsert` flag when invoking the CLI to apply the desired changes.

## SSH-Based Authentication

The other primary option for authenticating against remote repositories is to use SSH keys. SSH-based authentication involves a cryptographic keypair, a public key, and a private key. The public key is broadly shared and used to determine whether trust should be established, while the private key is proof of the user's identity. Let's illustrate how Argo CD can authenticate with the remote Gitea instance to retrieve manifests using SSH-based credentials.

The first step is to generate an SSH keypair using the `ssh-keygen` command. Create a new keypair in the current directory using the following command:

```
ssh-keygen -t ed25519 -f argocd_ssh -C "argocd@upandrunning.local" -q -N ""
```

A private key was generated in the file `argocd_ssh`, while the associated public key was generated in the file `argocd_ssh.pub`. It is important to note that SSH keys with passphrases are not currently supported in Argo CD.

Next, add the public key to Gitea so that it will be able to trust the Argo CD instance when it attempts to communicate using the private key. Gitea supports associating SSH keys with either a user or with individual repositories. To limit the level of access that Argo CD has against the Gitea instance, the previously generated SSH key will be associated with only a single repository within Gitea using a facility called "Deploy Keys."

Navigate to the Gitea instance (*https://git.upandrunning.local*) and locate the *upandrunning/ch09-credentials-ssh* link within the box denoted by Repositories on the right-hand side of the page. Click on Settings and then Deploy Keys. Select the Add Deploy Key to define the key that should be trusted for the repository.

Enter **argocd** in the Title textbox and paste the contents of `argocd_ssh.pub` file from the generated SSH keypair. Click the Add Deploy Key to add the public SSH key to the repository.

Now that Gitea has been configured, the next step is to configure Argo CD. Navigate to the Argo CD instance (*https://argocd.upandrunning.local*) and once again revisit the Repository configuration page by clicking on the Settings button and then selecting Repositories.

Adding an SSH repository follows a very similar process that was described previously using TLS certificates (https). Click the Connect Repo button. Enter the following into the fields in the dialog:

- Connection method: ssh
- Project: default
- Repository URL: *git@gitea-ssh.gitea:upandrunning/ch09-credentials-ssh.git*

In the "SSH private key data" field, enter the contents of the SSH private key stored in the *argocd_ssh* file.

Click the Connect button to verify the connection.

Argo CD is taking a slightly different path when communicating with the Gitea instance over SSH. Traffic is leveraging the internal Kubernetes Service network, as the NGINX ingress controller is only exposing HTTP/S-based traffic (80/443). While this configuration does limit direct connectivity over SSH, alternate methods, like `kubectl port-forward`, can be used to connect to Gitea via SSH if needed.

Unfortunately, adding the repository will result in a failed connection state. Even though the SSH key that is being used to communicate with the Gitea has been configured at a repository level, an additional step needs to take place for Argo CD to trust connecting to the Gitea instance via SSH.

The SSH protocol includes a series of verification steps to enforce that connections to remote sources are trusted prior to allowing the connection being established. This process of requiring trust is similar to how TLS-based connections require that certificates are trusted and verified. SSH clients maintain a list of the public keys that they trust and reference these entries at connection initiation.

To enable Argo CD to connect to Gitea, the public key exposed by the Gitea instance needs to be added to the list of known SSH hosts that Argo CD maintains within the *argocd-ssh-known-hosts-cm* ConfigMap. These entries can be managed on the "Repository certificates and known hosts" page within the Settings section of the Argo CD UI or with the `argocd cert add-ssh` CLI subcommand.

`ssh-keyscan` is one of the tools that can be used to obtain the public key from remote servers. Since SSH access is not exposed outside of the Kubernetes clusters, `kubectl exec` will be used to execute the `ssh-keyscan` command to communicate with Gitea. The output of the command will be redirected to the `argocd cert add-ssh` command, which will add the public key to the list of known hosts in Argo CD.

Execute the following command to obtain and add the public key to Argo CD:

```
kubectl -n argocd exec -c repo-server \
$(kubectl get pods \
-l=app.kubernetes.io/component=repo-server \
-n argocd \
-o jsonpath='{ .items[*].metadata.name }') \
-- ssh-keyscan gitea-ssh.gitea | argocd cert add-ssh --batch
```

Confirm the public key was added to Argo CD by navigating to the "Repository certificates and known hosts" page within the Settings section of the Argo CD UI, as shown in Figure 9-8.

*Figure 9-8. The SSH key present within the Argo CD UI*

With the Gitea instance added to the list of known SSH hosts, return to the Repositories page within the Settings section and confirm the *ch09-credentials-ssh* repository is displaying a successful status. If the status remains in a Failed state, disconnect the repository by selecting the kabob menu icon and clicking Disconnect. The repository can then be added once again using the values described earlier in this chapter. Once again, confirm that the repository is reporting a successful connection to Gitea.

With the connection to the repository established, create an application that synchronizes the contents into the Kubernetes cluster. Execute the following command from the *ch09* directory of the accompanying project repository:

```
kubectl apply -f ch09/argocd/ch09-credentials-ssh-application.yaml
```

Confirm that the `ch09-credentials-ssh` application was not only added successfully but was synchronized successfully, verifying the integration between Argo CD and Gitea using SSH-based communication.

## Enabling Reuse Through Credential Templates

One item that might have come to mind when working through this chapter and each of the steps necessary to configure the connectivity to repositories from Argo CD is the long-term management and scalability considerations. While ultimately only two repositories were configured, time and effort were dedicated to support the setup, configuration, and verification. Replicating for each repository at a large organization scale, and it becomes a nightmare to consider.

Fortunately, Argo CD includes a capability called *credential templates*, which allows for a single repository configuration to be defined that can then be reused across multiple repositories. Credential templates make use of URL prefix matching when selecting potential repositories for which the configuration should be applied to.

For example, instead of defining a configuration for each individual repository, a single credential template that utilized the URL prefix `https://git.upandrunning.local/upandrunning`, it would match all of the repositories that we have used thus far, as they are all within the same Gitea organization. However, if a repository configuration is defined at an individual repository level, it will take precedence over a credential template.

To set up a credential template from the Argo CD UI, configure the HTTPS or SSH repository configuration, as described throughout this chapter, but instead of selecting "Connect," select "Save as Credential Template."

From an Argo CD CLI perspective, the `argocd repocreds` subcommand enables the management of credential templates. The content that is ultimately persisted as a Secret specifies the label `argocd.argoproj.io/secret-type=repoc-reds`, which differentiates itself from a standard repository configuration.

While the use of credential templates will not be covered in depth, feel free to experiment by removing the existing repository configurations and defining a single repository configuration that would match all of the private repositories in the *upandrunning* Gitea organization.

## Enforcing Signature Verification

Argo CD plays a key role in the overall delivery of software. By managing how and when applications are deployed, it is important to ensure that nothing has unwillingly compromised the integrity of the system. Recent attacks on the software supply chain have caused both organizations and government entities to take a closer look at how they deliver software. One method for ensuring that no malicious activities have occurred during the normal course of how software is built and delivered is to apply cryptographic signatures at various steps throughout this process. By enabling the use of signatures, not only is there a mechanism to understand the origin of the content, but there is an assurance that no unwanted or unexpected actions occurred after the signature was applied.

Support for signature verification is available in Argo CD, and, once enabled, the synchronization of resources can be achieved when the referenced Git repository has a revision that has a GNU Privacy Guard (GnuPG or GPG) signature present, and the keys used to sign the content have been trusted by Argo CD.

The enforcement that content be signed is applied at a Project level and when configured, it applies to every application associated with the project.

Signature verification is enabled by performing the following steps:

- Import the public key that was used to sign the content.
- Configure a project and associate one or more of the public keys that Argo CD trusts.

Since signature verification applies against commits in a Git repository, at the time of this publication, signature verification is not supported for Helm repositories.

### Enable Signature Verification

In order to begin enforcing signatures, a GnuPG-formatted public key must be configured in Argo CD. An existing public key may be used, or a new keypair can be generated. If your machine does not have the GPG command-line tools installed, follow the steps on the GnuPG website (*https://oreil.ly/aizFO*) to download, install, and configure the tools on your local machine.

Once the tools have been installed, generate a keypair:

```
gpg --full-generate-key
```

When prompted, generate an RSA-formatted key with a key size of your choosing. Selecting the default size that is suggested is acceptable. When specifying your personal information, be sure to use an email address that you will remember, as it is needed later when referencing the generated key.

Once a keypair has been generated, obtain the ID of the key:

```
KEY_ID=$(gpg --list-secret-keys --keyid-format=long \
| grep sec | cut -f2 -d '/' | awk '{ print $1}')
```

Export the public key in armored format so that it can be added to Argo CD. Be sure to replace the email that was used when generating the key into the following command:

```
gpg --output public.pgp --armor --export <email>
```

GPG keys can be managed either within the *GnuPG public keys* page within the Argo CD UI or the CLI using the `argocd gpg` subcommand.

Add the exported public key using the `argocd gpg add` command:

```
argocd gpg add public.pgp
```

Confirm the key was added successfully by viewing the list of keys in the Argo CD UI or by using the `argocd gpg list` command of the CLI.

GPG public keys are stored in the `argocd-gpg-keys-cm` ConfigMap, which enables the management of this content in a declarative fashion.

Since signature verification is enforced at a Project level and to avoid affecting any of the existing applications that have been created previously, create a new Argo CD Project called `ch09-gpg` by applying the AppProject manifest stored in the `ch09-gpg-appproject.yaml` file from within the *ch09/argocd* directory of the accompanying repository:

```
kubectl apply -f ch09/argocd/ch09-gpg-appproject.yaml
```

With the new Argo CD Project created, enable signature verification by adding the ID of the GPG key that was created previously. Navigate to the Projects page from within the Settings page of the Argo CD UI.

Select the `ch09-gpg` Project and locate the GPG Signature Keys section. Click Edit and then Add Key. Select the ID of the GPG key from the dropdown and then click Save.

## Signature Verification in Action

At this point, signature verification has been enabled against the `ch09-gpg` project.

To illustrate just how Argo CD performs and enforces signature verification, create an application that references content in the *ch09-gpg-signatures* repository in the Gitea instance where commits have not been signed:

```
kubectl apply -f ch09/argocd/ch09-gpg-signatures-application.yaml
```

Inspecting the status of the application reveals a ComparisonError with a message similar to the following:

```
Target revision a9e4a971219b690e2d591605417f8cacba6ab0cf in Git is not signed,
but a signature is required
```

Argo CD has blocked the Application from syncing because the commit associated with the revision was not signed with the configured GPG key.

To resolve the error and enable the application to synchronize successfully, a signed commit must be made against the repository. Since your machine has already been configured with a set of GPG keys, and the public key has been installed in Argo CD as the method for signature verification, let's clone the repository locally, enable your Git client to use the newly created GPG key, and add a signed commit that can be pushed to the remote repository for Argo CD to use.

First, clone the contents of the *ch09-gpg-signatures* repository to your local machine and change into the repository directory:

```
git -c http.sslVerify=false clone \
https://git.upandrunning.local/upandrunning/ch09-gpg-signatures.git
cd ch09-gpg-signatures
```

Enter the username and password for Gitea if prompted.

The `http.sslVerify=false` config option was specified to ignore TLS certificate errors when communicating with the self-signed certificate exposed by the Gitea instance and will be used in each interaction with the Git server.

Next, associate the GPG key with the Git client so that it can be used to sign commits by specifying the ID of the key that was stored previously as the *KEY_ID* environment variable:

```
git config --global user.signingkey $KEY_ID
```

Now, update the content of the *README.md* file in the *ch09-gpg-signatures* repository so that a signed commit can be made:

```
echo "Now with signed commits!" >> README.md
```

Create a signed commit by specifying the `-S` flag to enable GPG signing:

```
git commit -S -am "Updated README"
```

Confirm the commit was signed by running the following command:

```
git log --show-signature
```

A commit log message with a signature applied will appear similar to the following:

```
gpg: Signature made Sun Jul 7 03:52:14 2024 UTC
gpg:                using RSA key 5CG73B102FD36W88C6F522A1B27298BS6A0E355B
gpg: Good signature from "John Doe <jdoe@upandrunning.local>" [ultimate]
```

With a signed commit being present, the content can be pushed to the remote Gitea instance:

```
git -c http.sslVerify=false push origin main
```

Return to the Argo CD UI and the `ch09-gpg-signatures` application and click Sync to synchronize the application with the content in the Git repository (see Figure 9-9).

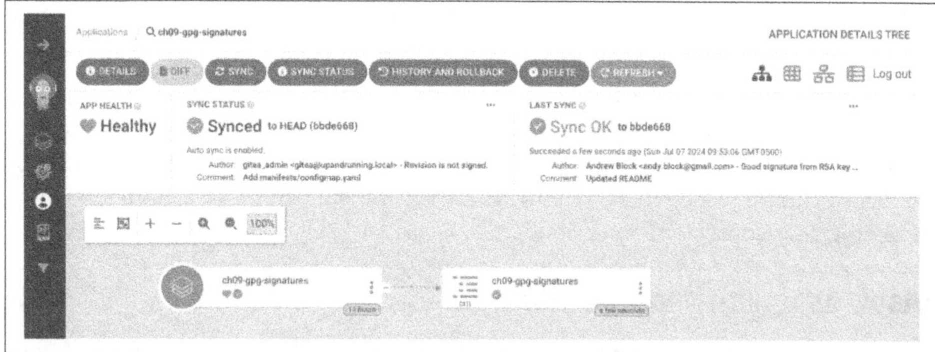


*Figure 9-9. The result of a successful app sync with signed commits*

Since the HEAD revision is signed with the public key that is configured for the Project the Application is associated with in Argo CD, the synchronization was successful and the associated manifests were added to the Kubernetes cluster, as shown in Figure 9-9.

Signature verification of Git commits is just another way that security can be applied within Argo CD. However, if there was a desire to disable the capability entirely, the `ARGOCD_GPG_ENABLED` environment variable can be added to the `argocd-server`, `argocd-repo-server`, and `argocd-application-controller` deployments.

# Application Sync Impersonation

In Argo CD, the service account used for synchronizing Application resources is the same as the one used for control plane operations. This setup allows users to decouple the service account for Application synchronization from the control plane service account. While this is effective in most scenarios, particularly in large multi-tenant environments, administrators often rely heavily on Argo CD's built-in RBAC system to manage permissions. However, there are cases where additional restrictions are required to meet regulatory requirements, adhere to organizational policies, or enhance security by adding extra layers of protection beyond RBAC.

By default, Application Sync operations in Argo CD inherit the same privileges as the control plane. In a multi-tenant environment, this means that the control plane must be provisioned with the highest level of privileges required by any application.

For instance, if an Argo CD instance manages ten applications and only one requires elevated privileges, the control plane itself must be granted the same level of access. This setup poses a security risk: malicious tenants could potentially exploit these elevated privileges to gain unauthorized access to resources in the cluster. While Argo CD's multi-tenancy model, through `AppProjects`, helps restrict what individual applications can do, it is not sufficient to fully mitigate the risk. If the Argo CD control plane were to be compromised, attackers could still gain elevated, and even cluster-admin level access.

Starting with Argo CD version 2.14, the Kubernetes Impersonation feature can be used to mitigate these concerns. By integrating this feature, Argo CD can now perform Application Sync operations using a specific service account specified by the administrator, rather than relying solely on the control plane's service account, providing an extra layer of security.

## Enable Sync with Impersonation

To enable Application Sync impersonation, the `application.sync.impersonation.enabled` option in the `data` field in the `argocd-cm` ConfigMap must be set to `"true"`:

```
apiVersion: v1
kind: ConfigMap
metadata:
  name: argocd-cm
  namespace: argocd
data:
  application.sync.impersonation.enabled: "true"
```

You can patch the running `argocd-cm` ConfigMap by using the provided patch file in the repository that accompanies this book. Apply the patch by running the following command:

```
kubectl patch cm/argocd-cm -n argocd --patch-file \
ch09/argocd/ch09-impersonation-cm-patch.yaml
```

Restart the Application controller StatefulSet by running the following:

```
kubectl rollout restart statefulset -n argocd \
-l app.kubernetes.io/component=application-controller
```

It's always good practice to wait for the application controller to become ready after the restart. This can be achieved by running the following:

```
kubectl rollout status statefulset -n argocd \
-l app.kubernetes.io/component=application-controller
```

The impersonation feature in Argo CD can only be enabled/disabled at the *system level*, meaning that once it is enabled or disabled, it is applicable to *all* applications managed by Argo CD.

## Define the Service Account to Use for Impersonation

Destination service accounts to impersonate can be configured within an `AppProject` under the `.spec.destinationServiceAccounts` field. For each target destination server and namespace, the corresponding service account to be used during the sync operation should be specified using the `defaultServiceAccount` field. Applications associated with this AppProject will automatically utilize the designated service account for their respective destinations.

During the Application Sync operation, the controller iterates through the list of defined `destinationServiceAccounts` in the AppProject. If multiple matches exist for a given destination server and namespace combination, the first valid match is selected. If no matching service account is found, the sync operation will report an error. Some administrators add a "catchall" to mitigate this potential issue. For example:

```
spec:
  destinationServiceAccounts:
    - server: in-cluster
      namespace: '*' # Doing * targets every namespace in the defined cluster
      defaultServiceAccount: default
```

However, it is not necessary to define a catchall and many administrators elect not to do so. This is on purpose to further lock down the sync by purposely failing instead of using a defined catchall service account. In our example scenario, we won't be using a catchall, so you can see how Application Sync impersonation works. Inspect the `ch09/argocd/ch09-impersonation-project.yaml` file, and you'll see the following manifest:

```
apiVersion: argoproj.io/v1alpha1
kind: AppProject
metadata:
  name: ch09-impersonation
  namespace: argocd
spec:
  description: Impersonation Example Project
  sourceRepos:
    - '*'
  clusterResourceWhitelist:
    - group: '*'
      kind: '*'
  destinations:
    - name: '*'
      namespace: '*'
      server: '*'
  destinationServiceAccounts:
    - server: https://kubernetes.default.svc
      namespace: impersonation
      defaultServiceAccount: nginx-deployer
```

Note in the `.spec.destinationServiceAccounts` we have the namespace `impersonation` with the `nginx-deployer` service account defined for syncs. Apply this manifest to create the project with impersonation:

```
kubectl apply -f ch09/argocd/ch09-impersonation-project.yaml
```

This creates the AppProject with Application Impersonation Sync set up for the namespace `impersonation`. Any Application defining this namespace will use the defined `nginx-deployer` service account.

## Deploying an Application with Impersonation

At this point, you can deploy the Application into the AppProject we just created. Inspect the `ch09/argocd/ch09-impersonation-app.yaml` file:

```
apiVersion: argoproj.io/v1alpha1
kind: Application
metadata:
  name: nginx
  namespace: argocd
spec:
  project: ch09-impersonation
  source:
    repoURL: https://github.com/sabre1041/argocd-up-and-running-book
    targetRevision: main
    path: ch09/manifests/nginx
  destination:
    namespace: impersonation
    server: https://kubernetes.default.svc
  syncPolicy:
    automated:
      prune: true
      selfHeal: true
```

Note, we defined `ch09-impersonation` under the `.spec.project` field and also the corresponding destination under the `.spec.project.destination` field that matches our AppProject configuration. Apply this Application manifest using the following command:

```
kubectl apply -f ch09/argocd/ch09-impersonation-app.yaml
```

By running `kubectl get application nginx -n argocd -o yaml`, you will notice the following message in the `.status.operationState.syncResult.resources` field:

```
deployments.apps "nginx" is forbidden: User "system:serviceaccount:impersonation:nginx...
```

In order for us to overcome this error, we need to set up not only the namespace, but also the service account and any roles and RoleBindings needed for the sync to be successful.

First, create the namespace:

```
kubectl create namespace impersonation
```

Next, create the service account in the newly created `impersonation` namespace:

```
kubectl create sa nginx-deployer -n impersonation
```

Create the role `restricted` in the `impersonation` namespace, allowing for the management of Deployments:

```
kubectl create role restricted --verb=* --resource=deployment -n impersonation
```

Next, create a `rolebinding` in the impersonation namespace, specifying the `nginx-deployer` service account from the same namespace:

```
kubectl create rolebinding restricted-binding --role=restricted \
--serviceaccount=impersonation:nginx-deployer -n impersonation
```

The steps of creating the namespace, the service account, the role, and the RoleBinding should be performed by the administrator *first*, as impersonation is considered an administrative task. These resources could also be (and is recommended) stored in Git and managed via GitOps workflows.

Now, initiate a sync using the `argocd` CLI. Upon completion, this should result in a successful deployment of the Application to the cluster:

```
argocd app sync --project=ch09-impersonation nginx
```

If you inspect the cluster by running `kubectl get deploy,pods -n impersonation`, you will see that the resources were successfully deployed:

```
NAME                    READY   UP-TO-DATE   AVAILABLE   AGE
deployment.apps/nginx   1/1     1            1           5m35s

NAME                          READY   STATUS    RESTARTS   AGE
pod/nginx-5869d7778c-6h4v8    1/1     Running   0          5m35s
```

This AppProject is now set up to use the `nginx-deployer` service account anytime an Application tries to deploy resources into the `impersonation` namespace. Since the `nginx-deployer` service account is set up to only manage Deployments, any other resource that is attempted to be deployed will fail. This provides the fine-grained control many security teams are looking for when implementing Argo CD.

# Summary

Security will continue to remain an important area of consideration for both Kubernetes developers and administrators. Users interacting with Argo CD can feel confident knowing that the platform includes several features specifically designed to enforce common security practices.

In this chapter, you first learned how to serve custom TLS certificates, enabling end-to-end encryption between the caller and Argo CD. Then, you deployed an instance of Gitea to act as a Git repository, thus allowing for more specialized configurations, which are common in many enterprise organizations, to be explored.

Once the Gitea instance was established, you extended your understanding of the benefits of operating securely with TLS certificates and configured trust within Argo CD so that resources stored in Gitea could be accessed securely.

We then transitioned to accessing content stored in protected Git repositories and the various methods that Argo CD supports for specifying credentials, including HTTPS with usernames/passwords and tokens along with SSH keys.

Finally, the integrity of content from Git repositories was hardened by enforcing that commits were signed using a GnuPG key, ensuring that no malicious actions occurred from the time the commit took place to when Argo CD accessed the content.

Also, we set up Application Sync Impersonation to provide finer-grained access to Argo CD deployments, adding an additional level of security for sync operations.

It is also important to note that while this chapter did cover quite a number of capabilities related to security, it is not a comprehensive list of features that Argo CD supports in this realm. However, the topics covered are some of the most common that apply to Argo CD administrators and users.

CHAPTER 10

# Applications at Scale

In Chapter 4, you were introduced to the Application Custom Resource Definition (CRD) object, which facilitates the logical grouping of your Kubernetes manifests. This Application object serves as the atomic unit of work in Argo CD, allowing you to manage a collection of Kubernetes objects as a single entity. Argo CD uses the Application CRD to manage the entire lifecycle of this collection of Kubernetes objects.

Argo CD Applications operate autonomously, meaning that one Application does not have awareness of the status or health of another. This autonomy can pose challenges, especially in organizations employing a microservices architecture where each component resides in its own Application custom resource. For instance, certain Applications may need to be deployed sequentially—such as a database before a backend service or a service mesh before the main application. As infrastructure scales, managing these dependencies and Argo CD Applications becomes increasingly complex.

In this chapter, we will explore various deployment patterns available in Argo CD. These include approaches like the App-of-Apps with sync waves and ApplicationSets with Progressive Sync. These patterns will assist in managing dependencies between Argo CD Applications and facilitate the deployment and management of these Applications at scale.

## Argo CD Application Drawbacks

In Chapter 5, we explored the customization of the Argo CD sync operation to accommodate the varying complexities of deployments. While not explicitly stated, the chapter implicitly conveyed the default behavior of an Argo CD Application, which applies Kubernetes manifests as is. Although this approach is effective in many scenarios, it can pose challenges when the deployment sequence of workloads is critical. To address this issue, the chapter introduced the concept of sync waves. Sync waves provide a mechanism to orchestrate the deployment of Kubernetes resources in a predetermined sequence, thereby ensuring the correct order of operations. This feature is instrumental in mitigating potential issues arising from unordered deployments, thus enhancing the reliability and predictability of the deployment process. For example, if you want to create a `Namespace` before a `Pod`, set the value of the `argocd.argoproj.io/sync-wave` annotation appropriately:

```
apiVersion: v1
kind: Namespace
metadata:
  name: web
  annotations:
    argocd.argoproj.io/sync-wave: "1"
---
apiVersion: v1
kind: Pod
metadata:
  labels:
    run: nginx
  annotations:
    argocd.argoproj.io/sync-wave: "2"
  name: nginx
  namespace: web
spec:
  containers:
  - image: nginx
    name: nginx
```

While sync waves are an effective method for ordering the manifests within a single Argo CD Application, they are limited to the resources contained within that specific application. They do not apply to the Argo CD Application itself or facilitate ordering between multiple Argo CD Applications. Additionally, Argo CD Applications are designed to be autonomous, meaning there is no inherent mechanism for establishing dependencies or relationships between individual applications.

While sync waves effectively handle the ordering of resources within a single Argo CD Application, they fall short in scenarios requiring coordination between multiple Applications. This limitation arises because of the autonomy of an Argo CD Application and the lack of built-in inter-Application dependency management. Unfortunately, there is no native feature within the Argo CD Application specification to enforce such dependencies. However, it is still possible to establish dependencies between Argo CD Applications using various tools, methods, and deployment strategies available within the Argo CD ecosystem.

To address this gap, the following strategies can be employed within the Argo CD ecosystem:

- Eventual consistency
- App-of-Apps with sync waves
- ApplicationSets Progressive Sync

Before delving into these methods, there are several important considerations to keep in mind: these will include things like resource health, Argo CD Application health checks, and Argo CD Application-specific health.

# Consideration and Best Practices

There are some important considerations that must be taken into account when implementing any of the approaches with respect to scaling and orchestrating Argo CD Applications. With that in mind, we will review these considerations before delving into any implementation details.

So before diving into how to handle Argo CD Application at scale, we'll go over some prerequisites and best practices. These include readiness/liveness probes, Argo CD Application health checks, and resource health checks.

## Set Up Probes

It's generally good practice to configure readiness and liveness probes within Kubernetes manifests. For those who aren't familiar with the concept, liveness probes assess whether a resource (like a container in your Deployment) is up and running (aka "alive"); readiness probes check to see if your resources are ready to accept connections. For more information about readiness and liveness probes, take a look at the official Kubernetes documentation (*https://oreil.ly/HQ7cY*) on the topic.

Setting up readiness and liveness probes is not only a best practice, but also paramount to an Argo CD Application. Argo CD Application health is based on the collective health of its resources being deployed. *Without proper readiness and liveness probes, Argo CD might mark resources as "healthy" and "synced" when, in fact, they might still be deploying.*

Let's take the scenario of a MySQL database. If we deploy the MySQL StatefulSet without any probes, Argo CD will mark the MySQL StatefulSet as healthy, even though it might be going through its startup process. Furthermore, it will also be marked as healthy when the StatefulSet isn't even ready to start receiving requests!

To that end, you can see how adding probes can help when deploying resources with Argo CD. Here is an example of adding probes for MySQL:

```
spec:
  template:
    spec:
      containers:
        - image: mysql:5.6.51
          name: mysql
          livenessProbe:
            tcpSocket:
              port: 3306
            initialDelaySeconds: 12 # How long to wait before probe starts
            periodSeconds: 10
          readinessProbe:
            exec:
              command: ["mysql", "-h", "127.0.0.1", "-e", "SELECT 1"]
            initialDelaySeconds: 12
            periodSeconds: 10
```

In this example, Kubernetes considers the MySQL StatefulSet as "alive" when port 3306 responds to requests, and it will consider it "ready" when a query executes successfully.

## Argo CD Health Checks

Argo CD doesn't only rely on the generic Kubernetes health status for the objects it's managing, but it also provides built-in health checks for a multitude of Kubernetes types, which are then surfaced to the overall Application health status. Health checks are written in Lua (*https://www.lua.org*), and you can see the current built-in checks in the Argo CD GitHub repo (*https://oreil.ly/R2xo9*).

There are times where there's a need to add or customize these health checks. For example, if you're working with a Kubernetes Operator (perhaps because you have either written one for your organization or because you're using a relatively new one), you might need to add these custom health checks in the `resource.customizations` field in the `argocd-cm` ConfigMap. The format looks like the following:

```
data:
  resource.customizations: |
    <group/kind>:
      health.lua: |
```

For example, here is what the health check for the cert-manager.io/Certificate object would look like in the argocd-cm ConfigMap:

```
data:
  resource.customizations: |
    cert-manager.io/Certificate:
      health.lua: |
        hs = {}
        if obj.status ~= nil then
          if obj.status.conditions ~= nil then
            for i, condition in ipairs(obj.status.conditions) do
```

```
          if condition.type == "Ready" and condition.status == "False" then
            hs.status = "Degraded"
            hs.message = condition.message
            return hs
          end
          if condition.type == "Ready" and condition.status == "True" then
            hs.status = "Healthy"
            hs.message = condition.message
            return hs
          end
        end
      end
    end

    hs.status = "Progressing"
    hs.message = "Waiting for certificate"
    return hs
```

Cert Manager is a popular addition to Kubernetes clusters, as it simplifies the creation and rotation of TLS certificates. More information can be found at the official website (*https://cert-manager.io*).

To read more about Argo CD health checks please refer to the official documentation (*https://oreil.ly/9Ifyf*).

## Application Health

Another important thing to note is that the health check for the Argo CD Application CRD has been removed in Argo CD 1.8 (see the related issue (*https://oreil.ly/lTWby*) for more information). This is an important thing to keep in mind, especially in the case of orchestrating Argo CD Application deployments that rely on each other. Since some of the patterns we're going to go through rely on the Argo CD Application health check's presence, we'll need to add it to the `argocd-cm` ConfigMap. This is easily done. Here's an example:

```
data:
  resource.customizations: |
    argoproj.io/Application:
      health.lua: |
        hs = {}
        hs.status = "Progressing"
        hs.message = ""
        if obj.status ~= nil then
          if obj.status.health ~= nil then
            hs.status = obj.status.health.status
            if obj.status.health.message ~= nil then
              hs.message = obj.status.health.message
            end
          end
        end
        return hs
```

With all these considerations (not only are they general best practices, *but they're also prerequisites for the upcoming use cases*) in place, we can start exploring different patterns on how to create Argo CD inter-Application dependencies.

## Eventual Consistency

One of the patterns worth mentioning for Argo CD Application orchestration is to rely on the fact that things will eventually be consistent with retries, which is the philosophy that Kubernetes was built on. This can easily be set up using the Argo CD Application manifest itself and also by using Argo CD Sync Option annotation. Here's an example Application manifest:

```
apiVersion: argoproj.io/v1alpha1
kind: Application
metadata:
  name: simple-go
spec:
  destination:
    name: in-cluster
    namespace: demo
  source:
    path: deploy/overlays/default
    repoURL: 'https://github.com/christianh814/simple-go'
    targetRevision: main
  project: default
  syncPolicy:
    automated:
      prune: true
      selfHeal: true
    syncOptions:
      - CreateNamespace=true
    retry:
      limit: 5
      backoff: # how long to wait before the next retry
        duration: 5s
        maxDuration: 3m0s
        factor: 2 # the factor in which the duration is increased
```

Note that there are retries set in this example to tell Argo CD to try again when an error occurs. You can (and probably should) also add the following annotation to resources that are dependent on other resources being present (like a custom resource of a CRD):

```
metadata:
  annotations:
    argocd.argoproj.io/sync-options: SkipDryRunOnMissingResource=true
```

In Kubernetes, a dry run is a simulation of an operation, like deploying a resource, that doesn't actually change the cluster. It allows users to evaluate a request through the typical stages without making persistent changes. It's important to note that Argo CD will do a "dry run" if the dependent resource is present.

These two settings, when configured together, will make Argo CD "keep retrying until success or until the retries are exhausted" (whichever comes first). In this way, Argo CD handles deployment orchestration by not handling the specific details, but instead attempting to apply resources and relying on the eventual consistency nature of Kubernetes.

# Use Case Setup

Before going through the use cases, we'll need to set up the aforementioned prerequisites in order for orchestration to work properly. This is a one-time setup that not only enables you to perform the following use cases; they are also, as stated before, best general practices when using Argo CD. We will be working out of the root directory of the Git repository that accompanies this book.

## Inspecting Probes

The manifests we will be deploying are already set up with readiness and liveness probes. You can verify these configurations by using `yq` to inspect these resources.

You can find more information about `yq` at the project website (*https://oreil.ly/3oujc*).

From the root directory, run the following commands:

```
## To view the liveness probe
$ yq .spec.template.spec.containers.0.livenessProbe \
ch10/apps/golist-api/golist-api-deployment.yaml

## To view the readiness probe
$ yq .spec.template.spec.containers.0.readinessProbe \
ch10/apps/golist-api/golist-api-deployment.yaml
```

You can verify the other deployment manifest by running the same command against the `ch10/apps/golist-frontend/golist-frontend-deployment.yaml` file.

Since we are also deploying a Helm chart, you'll need to run the Helm template to the *ch10/apps/golist-db* directory to verify the presence of those probes.

## Adding Argo CD Health Checks

As described previously in this chapter, Argo CD Applications health checks are disabled by default. You will need to enable the health checks in order to proceed with the use cases in the upcoming sections. We have added a convenient patch file to enable this configuration. From the root directory of the repository, run the following:

```
$ kubectl patch cm/argocd-cm -n argocd --type=merge --patch-file \
ch10/argocd-cm-patchfile.yaml
```

You can verify Argo CD has been updated:

```
$ kubectl get -n argocd cm/argocd-cm -o \
jsonpath='{.data.resource\.customizations\.health\.argoproj\.io_Application}'
```

The escapes on the period characters are necessary, as they're in the element name, not hierarchy indicators.

With the probes verified and Argo CD Application health check in place, you can now start with the first use case.

# Use Case: App-of-Apps with Sync Waves

Originally conceived as a method of bootstrapping Argo CD, the App-of-Apps pattern is basically an Argo CD Application that consists of other Argo CD Applications (since an Argo CD Application is nothing but a Kubernetes CRD). In Chapter 7, you were introduced to the App-of-Apps pattern and how it can be used to bootstrap Argo CD, including how to deploy Argo CD Applications using Argo CD itself.

Extending beyond just bootstrapping, users found other advantages of using this pattern thanks to also having access to other features that Argo CD provides natively (notably, Argo CD orchestration features, like sync waves and sync phases). When setting up probes and Argo CD Application health, you will now have everything you need to set up Argo CD Application deployment orchestration using App-of-Apps and sync waves.

Let's take a look at a use case of deploying a three-tiered application. We will have one Argo CD Application that deploys a frontend app, a backend app, and also a database. We want to have these managed by a "parent" Argo CD Application, and we want to deploy these in the following order:

- Database
- Backend
- Frontend

As you're going through examples, you might get some name collisions (duplicate Application names). You may delete former samples from your setup or run them on a different Kubernetes cluster.

In order to achieve this architecture, we'll have to use sync waves with our App-of-Apps. We first apply the `argocd.argoproj.io/sync-wave` annotation to the Argo CD Application that deploys the "database" application. Taking a look at the annotations for the `ch10/argocd/applications/golist-db.yaml` file, you should see the annotation set to `"1"`:

```
apiVersion: argoproj.io/v1alpha1
kind: Application
metadata:
  annotations:
    argocd.argoproj.io/sync-wave: "1"
  name: database
  namespace: argocd
```

Keep in mind that lower numbers get higher priority when working with sync waves, which include negative numbers.

Since we want the backend to become available afterward, we'll annotate that Application with a higher number. In this case, taking a look at the `ch10/argocd/applications/golist-api.yaml` file, note the annotation value is set to `"2"`:

```
apiVersion: argoproj.io/v1alpha1
kind: Application
metadata:
  annotations:
    argocd.argoproj.io/sync-wave: "2"
  name: backend
  namespace: argocd
```

Finally, we can see in the ch10/argocd/applications/golist-frontend.yaml file that the annotation for the frontend Application is set with a higher number than the database and backend so that it comes up last. In our case, it's annotated with "3":

```
apiVersion: argoproj.io/v1alpha1
kind: Application
metadata:
  annotations:
    argocd.argoproj.io/sync-wave: "3"
  name: frontend
  namespace: argocd
```

The parent Application, being just another Argo CD Application, will create the resources in the specified order. Taking a look at the ch10/argocd/applications/parent.yaml file, you'll see the following:

```
apiVersion: argoproj.io/v1alpha1
kind: Application
metadata:
  name: parent
  namespace: argocd
  finalizers:
  - resources-finalizer.argocd.argoproj.io
spec:
  source:
    path: argocd/applications
    repoURL: 'https://github.com/sabre1041/argocd-up-and-running-book'
    targetRevision: main
  destination:
    namespace: argocd
    name: in-cluster
  project: default
  syncPolicy:
    automated:
      prune: true
      selfHeal: true
    retry:
      limit: 5
      backoff:
        duration: 5s
        maxDuration: 3m0s
        factor: 2
    syncOptions:
      - CreateNamespace=true
```

Once this parent Argo CD Application is applied, Argo CD will apply the "child" Argo CD Applications in the order it was annotated with. To start the process, apply the parent Argo CD Application by running the following command:

```
$ kubectl apply -n argocd -f \
ch10/argocd/applications/parent.yaml
```

Walking through the process, you will notice some elements in the Argo CD UI dashboard.

First, the parent Argo CD Application is created and begins the sync process, which includes deploying the database Application (since it's annotated with a "1"). You can see this in Figure 10-1.

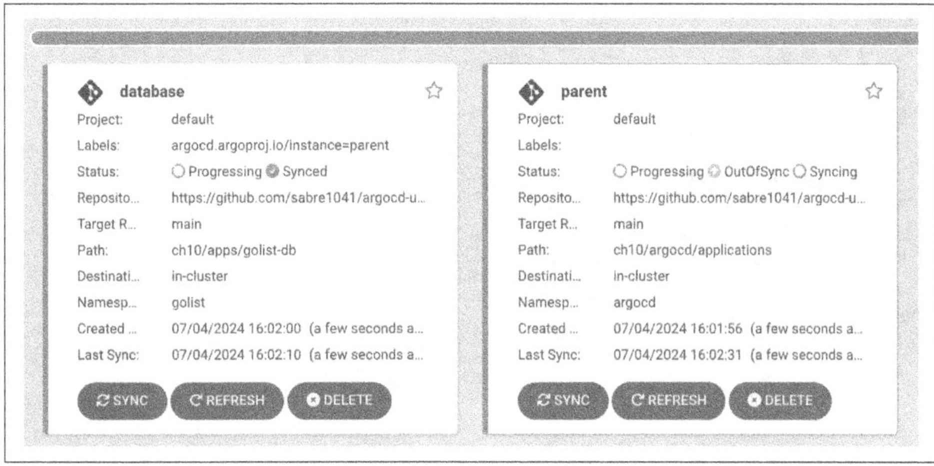


*Figure 10-1. App-of-Apps sync wave 1*

Once the database Application is synced and healthy, Argo CD will apply the backend Application (as it is annotated with a "2"). You can see this in Figure 10-2.

*Figure 10-2. App-of-Apps sync wave 2*

Once the backend Application is synced and healthy, Argo CD will finally apply the frontend Application (as it is annotated with a “3”). This is represented in Figure 10-3.

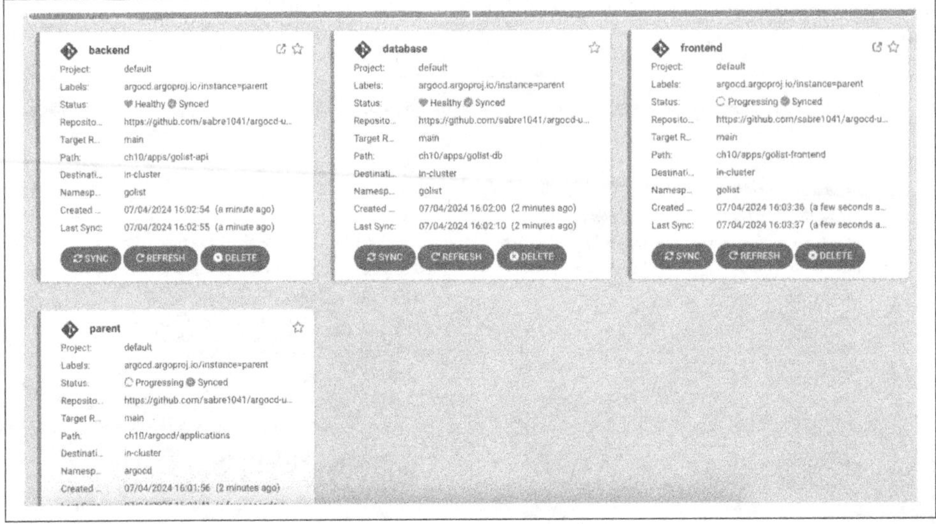


*Figure 10-3. App-of-Apps sync wave 3*

In the end, all three Applications that make up this workload, plus the parent Application, are synced and healthy.

The parent Application is now your control point of all other Applications. For example, if you delete the parent Application, all of the children will be deleted (in our example).

Figure 10-4 should represent the current state in your environment.

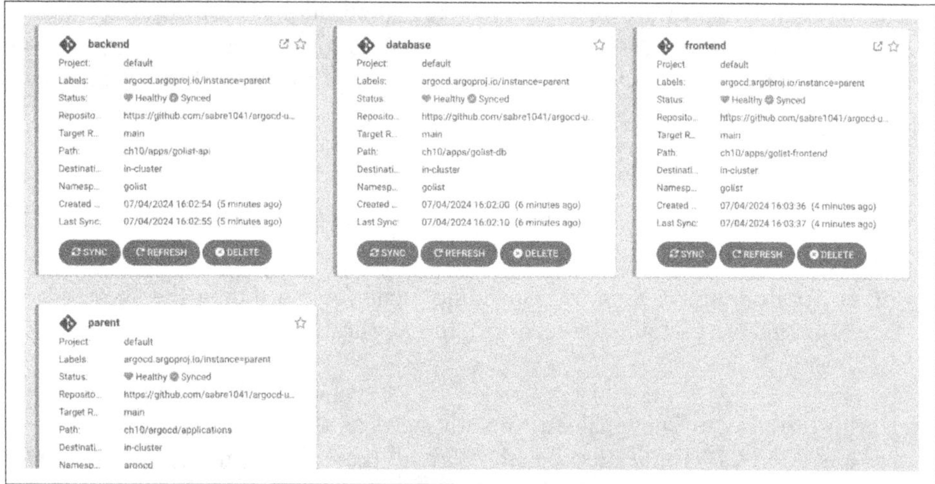


*Figure 10-4. App-of-Apps sync wave finished*

As you can see, this approach provides a powerful method of setting up Application dependencies, bootstrapping, and performing custom Application deployment orchestration, and it's currently the recommended way of doing it. *It's worth reiterating that this is all possible because all readiness/liveness probes were set up and Argo CD was configured with the proper Lua health checks.*

# ApplicationSets

With all the power that Argo CD gives you with Argo CD Applications and the App-of-Apps pattern, there was still a need to templatize the creation of Argo CD Applications. Yes, we can manage Argo CD Application deployments in a controlled manner. But we still need to create those Application manifests.

In Chapter 7, we introduced Argo CD ApplicationSets, which can be seen as an Application "factory." The sole purpose of the Argo CD ApplicationSet controller is to create Argo CD Applications. As you saw in Chapter 7, this gives us the ability to not only create multiple Applications at the same time using a single manifest, but it also allows us to deploy many applications to many destination clusters.

## Progressive Sync

One drawback of ApplicationSets is that it just generates Applications. There had been no built-in mechanism to order or have dependencies. That was until ApplicationSets Progressive Sync was introduced.

The Progressive Sync feature aims to deploy the Applications in an ApplicationSet in the specified order, while also taking Application health into consideration (meaning it won't sync Applications unless the previous one is synced and healthy). While using ApplicationSets Progressive Sync is great, there are a few things to keep in mind:

- Generated Applications will have autosync disabled.
- This is an alpha feature and will be subject to change. This also means that the feature needs to be explicitly enabled.
- If an Application has been in a "pending" state for more than the allotted progressing timeout (default 300 seconds), the ApplicationSet controller will mark it as "healthy."

Even with Progressive Sync enabled, you still need to set up your readiness/liveness probes and Argo CD Application health. With all these things in mind, let's go over the same example as was described previously, except with the Progressive Sync feature.

## Use Case: Using Progressive Sync

We can have similar behavior of Application dependency management using ApplicationSet Progressive Sync that you had with the App-of-Apps use case. The biggest advantage of using Progressive Sync over App-of-Apps is that you only need to manage one manifest.

There are other advantages of using Progressive Sync. There are features of being able to group many Applications in each deployment phase but also include things like specifying `maxUpdate`, which allows for the deployment of only a percentage of Applications at a time in each phase. This is helpful in the situation where you have thousands of applications and want to prevent a "broadcast storm" of syncs happening.

The term *broadcast storm* (*https://oreil.ly/iHQET*) here is used generally to indicate many syncs happening at the same time. It was originally coined as a networking term.

Let's take a look at the same use case of deploying the same three-tiered application. This time, we will use an Argo CD ApplicationSet that uses a Progressive Sync to deploy that frontend app, along with the backend app, and also that same database we used in the previous use case.

Before anything else, you'll need to remove the existing Applications related to the three-tier deployment. This can be easily accomplished by deleting the parent application:

```
$ kubectl delete application parent -n argocd
```

Since the parent Application controls the other Applications (via a finalizer), it will also delete the children Applications.

Next, you need to explicitly enable Progressive Sync in Argo CD. A patch file is included to simplify this process:

```
$ kubectl patch cm/argocd-cmd-params-cm -n argocd --type=json \
--patch-file ch10/argocd-cmd-params-cm-patchfile.yaml
```

Next, the ApplicationSet controller deployment must be restarted to pick up the updated configuration:

```
$ kubectl rollout restart deploy/argocd-applicationset-controller -n argocd
```

Any ApplicationSet can use Progressive Sync. The only configuration difference is the target labels that will be added and a new section under `.spec.strategy` in the ApplicationSet YAML. If you take a look at the `ch10/argocd/appsets/progressive sync.yaml` file, you'll see a List generator used with the following strategy:

```
spec:
  # ...omitted for brevity...
  strategy:
    type: RollingSync
    rollingSync:
      steps:
        - matchExpressions:
            - key: golist-component
              operator: In
              values:
                - database
        - matchExpressions:
            - key: golist-component
              operator: In
              values:
                - backend
        - matchExpressions:
            - key: golist-component
              operator: In
              values:
                - frontend
```

Take note of the `.spec.strategy` section as it includes "steps." This is how ordering is accomplished, similar to the App-of-Apps with sync waves method. This section allows you to group Applications by the labels present on the generated Application resources. When the ApplicationSet changes, the changes will be propagated to each group of Application resources sequentially. Progressive Sync uses the familiar `matchExpressions` that are found in various standard Kubernetes resources. You can potentially group together hundreds of Applications in each "step."

The next section to notice is the `.spec.template.metadata.labels` section in the same ApplicationSet manifest:

```
spec:
  # ...omitted for brevity...
  template:
    metadata:
      name: '{{srv}}'
      labels:
        golist-component: '{{srv}}'
```

This section will apply the label to the corresponding Argo CD Application that this ApplicationSet creates. Then the Progressive Sync operation will use these labels to determine which Argo CD Application gets synced in each step.

To start the process, apply the ApplicationSet in the `progressivesync.yaml` file:

```
$ kubectl apply -n argocd -f ch10/argocd/appsets/progressivesync.yaml
```

Once applied, it will create all three of the Argo CD Applications at once (in contrast to App-of-Apps pattern where they are created as they are synced); but they will remain "missing/out of sync." Then it will progress to syncing the first database Application. You can see this in the Argo CD UI, as depicted by Figure 10-5.

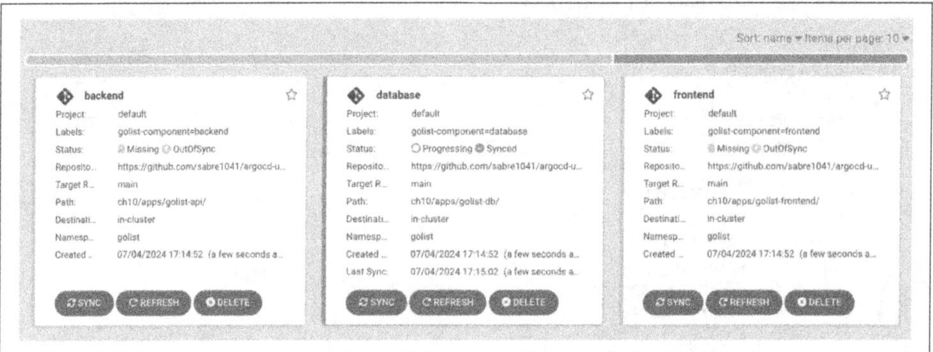


*Figure 10-5. Progressive Sync database*

Once the database is synced, the backend Application will start syncing. A similar representation appears in Figure 10-6.

When the backend Application becomes synced, the frontend Application will begin to sync. A state similar to Figure 10-7 will be present in the Argo CD UI.

In the end, it should appear similar to that of the App-of-Apps method, except there is no parent Application since we are using an ApplicationSet to deploy this workload. You will see all Applications synced and healthy in the Argo CD UI, as shown in Figure 10-8.

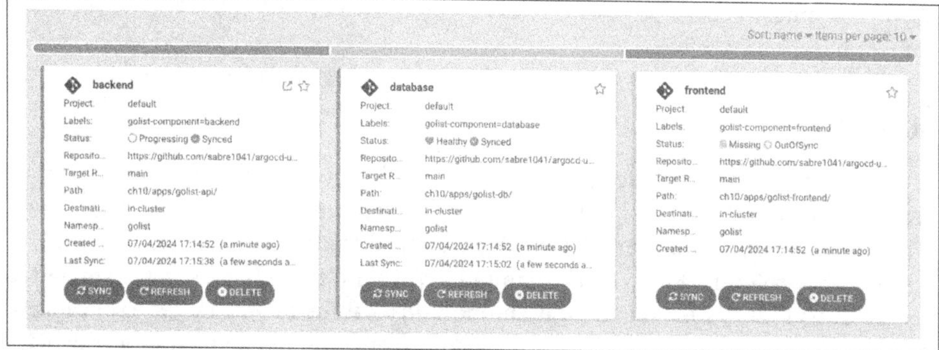


*Figure 10-6. Progressive Sync backend*

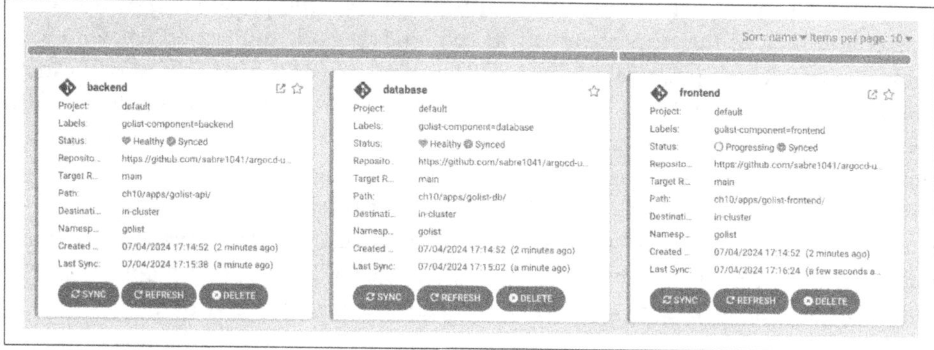


*Figure 10-7. Progressive Sync frontend*

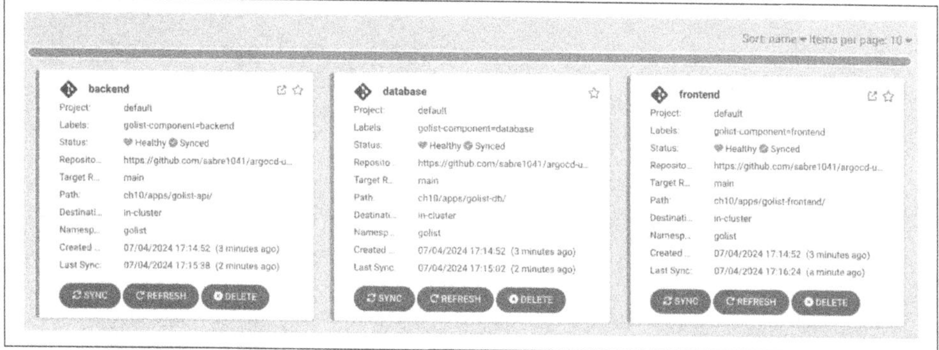


*Figure 10-8. Progressive Sync finished*

The end result is the same, except that with ProgressiveSync, there is only one manifest to create and manage.

It's important to note that it's not App-of-Apps versus Progressive Sync. There are some situations where you could use both or a combination of both, for example "App-of-ApplicationSets"—where you use a parent Argo CD Application to bootstrap your ApplicationSets.

## Summary

In this chapter, we delved into the complexities and strategies of managing large-scale deployments with Argo CD. We reviewed the foundational concept of the Application Custom Resource Definition (CRD) object, introduced in Chapter 4, which helps in logically grouping Kubernetes manifests. Also in this chapter, we highlighted the challenges that arise due to the autonomous nature of Argo CD Applications, especially in microservices architectures where sequential deployment dependencies exist.

We provided an in-depth look into various deployment patterns to tackle these challenges, such as the App-of-Apps with sync waves and ApplicationSets with Progressive Sync. These patterns are designed to manage dependencies and orchestrate the deployment of multiple Argo CD Applications effectively. Additionally, we also went through the importance of readiness and liveness probes, Argo CD Application health checks, and resource health checks as best practices to ensure the reliable and predictable deployment of Applications. All of these concepts came together to support the deployment of a multitier application using these advanced patterns, demonstrating how to set up and manage these dependencies, and highlighting the nuances and benefits of each method in a scalable deployment environment.

CHAPTER 11

# Extending Argo CD

Thus far, we have described many of the features that are included within Argo CD to not only manage resources effectively using GitOps patterns in Kubernetes, but also to provide a rich set of options for end users to interact with the platform. By offering a way to integrate tools and frameworks common to Kubernetes, complex workflows can be developed to create a robust management strategy for infrastructure and applications. However, even with all of the supported set of capabilities, there may be a need to integrate an additional set of components that are not natively included within Argo CD or to customize the platform itself to better serve the needs of end users.

In this chapter, we will introduce several different mechanisms that can be used to extend the default configuration of Argo CD, including the use of a pluggable framework to incorporate additional tools to support how Kubernetes resources are created. These options give end users the power to take Argo CD to the next level.

## Config Management Plugins

Kubernetes resources in Argo CD can be created using a variety of methods. They may be declared using standalone manifests or incorporate one of the included set of config management tools, such as Helm, Kustomize, or Jsonnet. While these tools represent some of the most common options available for managing Kubernetes resources, there became a need to provide a facility for which additional options were available to customize the generation of Kubernetes resources.

Kubernetes itself faced a similar challenge early on where it only provided a finite list of resource types and APIs for users and systems to interact with. This limitation could have reduced the impact that Kubernetes would ultimately have on the IT industry. However, it was the introduction of Custom Resource Definitions (CRDs) that enabled the ability to extend the types of resources served by Kubernetes and unleash an entirely new way to work with the platform. Argo CD provides its own solution to the configuration management tool challenge through the use of config management plugins, which offers a flexible method for enabling additional options for facilitating the creation of Kubernetes resources.

If you recall, the repo server is the component responsible for building Kubernetes resources using one of the supported configuration management tools. For alternate tools to be used, it is within this location where tasks need to be executed.

A config management plugin consists of two parts:

- A `ConfigManagementPlugin` manifest describing how and when the plugin should be used
- Tooling to enable the execution of the plugin

The use of alternate tools will typically require additional dependencies, such as binaries associated with the tool and scripts containing the logic employed by the plugin. While the repo server image could be extended to include these custom assets, the preferred approach is to package any of the necessary assets into a separate container and run this container alongside the repo server. This model is known as the *sidecar pattern* in Kubernetes, as it has a number of benefits:

- Avoids conflicts between the plugin and the repo server
- Eliminates the need to manage the lifecycle of the repo server
- Owns the entire lifecycle plugin and its components

With an understanding of the high-level set of components involved when integrating config management plugins, let's explore each of these items in depth and how they can be used to implement a plugin within Argo CD.

## The ConfigManagementPlugin Manifest

The `ConfigManagementPlugin` manifest provides instructions to the repo server so that it understands when the plugin should be invoked and how it should be invoked. The following contains the structure of the manifest:

```
apiVersion: argoproj.io/v1alpha1
kind: ConfigManagementPlugin
metadata:
  # The name of the plugin must be unique within a given Argo CD instance.
  name: my-plugin
spec:
  # The version of your plugin. Optional. If specified, the Application's
  # spec.source.plugin.name field must be <plugin name>-<plugin version>.
  version: v1.0
  # The init command runs in the Application source directory at the beginning of each
```

```
# manifest generation. The init command can output anything.
# A non-zero status code will fail manifest generation.
init:
  # Init always happens immediately before generate, but its output
  # is not treated as manifests.
  # This is a good place to, for example, download chart dependencies.
  command: [sh]
  args: [-c, 'echo "Initializing..."']
# The generate command runs in the Application source directory each time manifests
# are generated. Standard output must be ONLY valid Kubernetes Objects in either
# YAML or JSON. A non-zero exit code will fail manifest generation. To write log
# messages from the command, write them to stderr, it will always be displayed.
# Error output will be sent to the UI, so avoid printing sensitive information
# (such as secrets).
generate:
  command: [sh, -c]
  args:
    - |
      echo "{\"kind\": \"ConfigMap\", \"apiVersion\": \"v1\",
      \"metadata\": { \"name\": \"$ARGOCD_APP_NAME\",
      \"namespace\": \"$ARGOCD_APP_NAMESPACE\",
      \"annotations\": {\"Foo\": \"$ARGOCD_ENV_FOO\",
      \"KubeVersion\": \"$KUBE_VERSION\",
      \"KubeApiVersion\": \"$KUBE_API_VERSIONS\",\"Bar\": \"baz\"}}}"
# The discovery config is applied to a repository. If every configured discovery
# tool matches, then the plugin may be used to generate manifests for Applications
# using the repository. If the discovery config is omitted then the plugin will
# not match any application but can still be invoked explicitly by specifying the
# plugin name in the app spec. Only one of fileName, find.glob, or find.command
# should be specified. If multiple are specified then only the first (in that
# order) is evaluated.
discover:
    # fileName is a glob pattern (https://pkg.go.dev/path/filepath#Glob) that is
    # applied to the Application's source directory. If there is a match, this plugin
    # may be used for the Application.
  fileName: "./subdir/s*.yaml"
  find:
    # This does the same thing as fileName, but it supports double-start (nested
    # directory) glob patterns.
    glob: "**/Chart.yaml"
    # The find command runs in the repository's root directory. To match, it must
    # exit with status code 0 _and_ produce non-empty output to standard out.
    command: [sh, -c, find . -name env.yaml]
# The parameters config describes what parameters the UI should display for an
# Application. It is up to the user to actually set parameters in the Application
# manifest (in spec.source.plugin.parameters). The announcements _only_ inform the
# "Parameters" tab in the App Details page of the UI.
parameters:
  # Static parameter announcements are sent to the UI for _all_ Applications handled
  # by this plugin. Think of the `string`, `array`, and `map` values set here as
  # "defaults". It is up to the plugin author to make sure that these default values
  # actually reflect the plugin's behavior if the user doesn't explicitly set
  # different values for those parameters.
  static:
    - name: string-param
      title: Description of the string param
      tooltip: Tooltip shown when the user hovers over field in the UI
      # If this field is set, the UI will indicate to the user that they must set the
      # value.
```

```yaml
        required: false
        # itemType tells the UI how to present the parameter's value (or, for arrays
        # and maps, values). Default is "string". Examples of other types which may be
        # supported in the future are "boolean" or "number". Even if the itemType is not
        # "string", the parameter value from the Application spec will be sent to the
        # plugin as a string. It's up to the plugin to do the appropriate conversion.
        itemType: ""
        # collectionType describes what type of value this parameter accepts (string,
        # array, or map) and allows the UI to present a form to match that type. Default
        # is "string". This field must be present for non-string types. It will not be
        # inferred from the presence of an `array` or `map` field.
        collectionType: ""
        # This field communicates the parameter's default value to the UI. Setting this
        # field is optional.
        string: default-string-value
      # All the previous fields besides "string" apply to both the array and map type
      # parameter announcements.
      - name: array-param
        # This field communicates the parameter's default value to the UI. Setting this
        # field is optional
        array: [default, items]
        collectionType: array
      - name: map-param
        # This field communicates the parameter's default value to the UI. Setting this
        # field is optional.
        map:
          some: value
        collectionType: map
    # Dynamic parameter announcements are announcements specific to an Application handled
    # by this plugin. For example, the values for a Helm chart's values.yaml file could
    # be sent as parameter announcements.
    dynamic:
      # The command is run in an Application's source directory. Standard output must
      # be JSON matching the schema of the static parameter announcements list.
      command: [echo, '[{"name": "example-param", "string": "default-string-value"}]']

  # If set to `true` then the plugin receives repository files with original file
  # mode. Dangerous since the repository might have executable files. Set to true only
  # if you trust the CMP plugin authors.
  preserveFileMode: false
```

As depicted, there are a wide range of options that a `ConfigManagementPlugin` manifest supports. However, there are only a few properties that you need to be concerned with whenever developing and using a config management plugin, as they dictate how the plugin will operate. A description of each of these key properties are listed here:

`init`
: This is an optional parameter that performs any preparation steps that the plugin requires, such as downloading dependencies.

`generate`
: This performs the primary function of the plugin. This action runs within the directory associated with the Argo CD Application and can be implemented in a variety of ways, including executing a script, binary, or printing arbitrary content.

The one requirement is that the only output that is produced from this stage be a set of valid YAML- or JSON-formatted Kubernetes manifests.

`discover`
: This is a set of rules that determines whether the Application is applicable for execution. Common examples include searching for the presence of a file in the application source or executing a command to perform more complex capabilities. The exit code determines whether the plugin is applicable for the content.

They each are located directly underneath the `.spec` property and work hand in hand to determine the applicability of a plugin for the source Application and the steps necessary to produce Kubernetes manifests.

To determine whether a plugin should be executed for a given Application, two methods are available. First, the `discover` property within the `ConfigManagementPlugin` can either match the name of a file, or file based on a glob pattern in the content source, or return a 0 exit code as a result of the execution of a command. Otherwise, the name of the plugin can be explicitly defined on the Application manifest as shown here:

```
apiVersion: argoproj.io/v1alpha1
kind: Application
metadata:
  name: guestbook
spec:
  source:
    plugin:
      name: my-plugin
```

In most cases, you will want to both abstract when a plugin is executed as well as the need for the end user to define the plugin within their `Application`. A common example for determining whether a plugin should be executed using the auto-discovery capability is the presence of a particular file within the application source—such as a file called `Chart.yaml` for a Helm-based application. Here is an example of how the `discover` property can be configured to support this use case using the `fileName` option:

```
discover:
  fileName: "Chart.yaml"
```

Once a match has been made using any of the methods previously described, the next step is to perform any initialization steps that are required by the plugin. This step is optional and only executed when the `init` property has been defined. When working with Helm-based applications within the context of a config management plugin, a common initialization task may involve the need to manage any of the dependencies that the chart relies on. This way, when the chart is processed within the main logic as defined in the `generate` property, all of the necessary resources will be available. The following is an example of how Helm dependencies can be handled within the `init` property:

```
init:
  command: ["/bin/sh", "-c"]
  args: ["helm dependency build || true"]
```

Finally, after defining any of the key optional properties, the primary plugin logic as defined by the `generate` property can be specified. Instead of providing a simple code example like we demonstrated previously for the `init` and `discovery` properties, let's use this as an opportunity to look into how a config management plugin could be used and implemented in practice.

Kustomize and Helm on their own provide a powerful set of capabilities for templating Kubernetes manifests. But why choose one tool over the other when you can utilize both at the same time? Kustomize includes support for inflating Helm charts, and the two tools, working hand in hand, provide a powerful combination that provides a number of benefits, particularly when working with Argo CD. For example, a common challenge when consuming Helm charts from the community is that customizations are limited to only the options that the chart creator provides. When used with Kustomize, the rendered charts can be augmented using any of the Kustomize features, including patching and transformation.

The challenge, where a config management plugin can be beneficial, is that an additional flag (`--enable-helm`) must be provided to the underlying `kustomize` command to enable support for the Helm inflator. Argo CD does provide support for customizing the Kustomize build options. However, these configurations are enabled globally within the `argo-cd` ConfigMap, and there may be either a desire to avoid setting configurations globally or the inability to modify Argo CD configurations at a global level due to access limitations.

To enable the Helm inflator feature within the context of a config management plugin, the following can be specified in the `generate` property:

```
generate:
  command: ["/bin/sh", "-c"]
  args: ["kustomize build --enable-helm"]
```

## Registering the Plugin

With the `generate` property now defined, we have all the necessary steps to be able to utilize a `ConfigManagementPlugin` manifest. Now, while this resource may appear similar to a Kubernetes custom resource, it is just a configuration file that Argo CD understands. It is included within the plugin sidecar at a known location so that it can be discovered by the Argo CD server. The delivery of the file can be achieved using one of two methods:

- Inclusion within the image
- Injected at runtime as a ConfigMap

The injection method is preferred, as the values contained within the configuration file may differ per environment, which avoids having to build a new plugin image for each variation. This approach also aligns with the principles of the twelve-factor app (*https://12factor.net*), which emphasizes externalizing configurations within the operating environment—and in Kubernetes, this implies storage as a ConfigMap or Secret.

A ConfigMap containing the embedded `ConfigManagementPlugin` resource can be found in the *kustomize-helm-plugin.yml* file within the *ch11/configmanagementplugins* directory of the repository accompanying this book and also shown here:

```
apiVersion: v1
kind: ConfigMap
metadata:
  name: kustomize-helm-plugin
  namespace: argocd
data:
  plugin.yaml: |
    apiVersion: argoproj.io/v1alpha1
    kind: ConfigManagementPlugin
    metadata:
      name: kustomize-helm
    spec:
      generate:
        command: ["/bin/sh", "-c"]
        args: ["kustomize build --enable-helm"]
```

Now, apply the ConfigMap to the `argocd` namespace using the following command from within the project repository directory:

```
$ kubectl apply -f ch11/configmanagementplugins/kustomize-helm-plugin.yml
```

Next, the plugin sidecar must be added to the deployment of the Repository Server. The sidecar is represented by the following configuration:

```
containers:
  - name: kustomize-helm
    securityContext:
      runAsNonRoot: true
      runAsUser: 999 # User ID for the Argo CD service account
    image: registry.k8s.io/kustomize/kustomize:v4.5.7
    imagePullPolicy: IfNotPresent # Only pull image if it's not there
    command: [/var/run/argocd/argocd-cmp-server]
    volumeMounts:
      - mountPath: /var/run/argocd
        name: var-files
      - mountPath: /home/argocd/cmp-server/plugins
        name: plugins
      - mountPath: /home/argocd/cmp-server/config/plugin.yaml
        subPath: plugin.yaml
        name: kustomize-helm-plugin
      - mountPath: /tmp
        name: cmp-tmp
volumes:
  - name: kustomize-helm-plugin
    configMap:
```

```
      name: kustomize-helm-plugin
  - emptyDir: {}
    name: cmp-tmp
```

While the definition of a config management plugin sidecar can vary between each implementation, particularly as it relates to the associated image, there are certainly properties where their values must align to a certain set of rules, as noted here:

- The sidecar must run as user `999` in order for the sidecar to access the files from the Application.
- The `plugin.yaml` file must be located in the */home/argocd/cmp-server/config* directory.
- The Repository Server `Deployment` includes a series of volumes that should be mounted into the sidecar, including `/var/run/argocd`, which contains the `argocd-cmp-server` binary and `/home/argocd/cmp-server/plugins`.

A patch file called *argocd-repo-server-kustomize-helm-plugin-patch.yaml* containing the sidecar definition is also included in the *ch11/configmanagementplugins* directory of the repository accompanying this book.

Patch the repo-server `Deployment` by executing the following command:

```
kubectl -n argocd patch deployments/argo-cd-argocd-repo-server \
--patch-file ch11/configmanagementplugins/argocd-repo-server-kustomize-helm-plugin-patch.yaml
```

With the patch applied, confirm that the updated repo-server `Deployment` now includes the *kustomize-helm-plugin* sidecar for a total of two running containers in the pod:

```
$ kubectl get pods -n argocd -l=app.kubernetes.io/component=repo-server

NAME                                          READY   STATUS    RESTARTS   AGE
argo-cd-argocd-repo-server-9d947b457-pxs8l    2/2     Running   0          121m
```

Included in the *ch11/configmanagementplugins* directory are an additional set of assets that will be used to demonstrate the use of the Helm inflator (to extract the raw Kubernetes manifests) capability of Kustomize with an Argo CD config management plugin. First, the `charts` directory contains a simple Helm chart called *kustomize-helm* which produces a ConfigMap when rendered. And, as with any Kustomize application, there is also a Kustomization (`kustomization.yaml`) file present, which invokes the Helm inflator using a set of properties prefixed with *helm*:

```
apiVersion: kustomize.config.k8s.io/v1beta1
kind: Kustomization

helmCharts:
  - name: kustomize-helm
    version: 0.1.0
    releaseName: kustomize-helm
```

```
helmGlobals:
  chartHome: charts
```

The `helmCharts` property within the Kustomization file includes the majority of the configurations associated with the Helm inflator, such as the name of the chart and the version. Since the desired Helm chart is not in a location relative to the Kustomization file, the `chartHome` property within the `helmGlobals` property specifies where Helm charts should be sourced from. If a Helm chart is not available locally, it can originate from either a remote repository or an OCI registry.

To have Argo CD deploy the Kustomize-based application within the Kubernetes cluster, create an Argo CD Application called *kustomize-helm* that is defined in a file called `kustomize-helm-app.yaml` within the *ch11/configmanagementplugins* directory:

```
kubectl apply -f ch11/configmanagementplugins/kustomize-helm-app.yaml
```

Using either the Argo CD CLI or the UI, check on the status of the newly created Application.

Notice that the kustomize-helm Application is reporting an error with a message similar to the following:

```
Failed to load target state: failed to generate manifest for source 1 of 1: rpc error: ...
```

The error message indicates that it is unable to render the Kustomize application, as even though the Helm inflator capability is being used, it is not being enabled by including the `--enable-helm` flag.

Recall the two ways that an Argo CD config management plugin can be triggered: either through dynamic activation or specified explicitly within the Application itself. Since neither option was used, the error being displayed is expected as the Helm inflator feature in Kustomize is not enabled by default in Argo CD.

To enable the config management plugin that we configured previously, update the kustomize-helm `Application` to specify the name of the plugin within the `.spec.source` property using kubectl, the Argo CD CLI, or the Argo CD UI:

```
spec:
  source:
    plugin:
      name: kustomize-helm
```

Once the configuration of the Application has been updated, the previously seen error will be resolved and the Application will synchronize successfully, as shown in Figure 11-1.

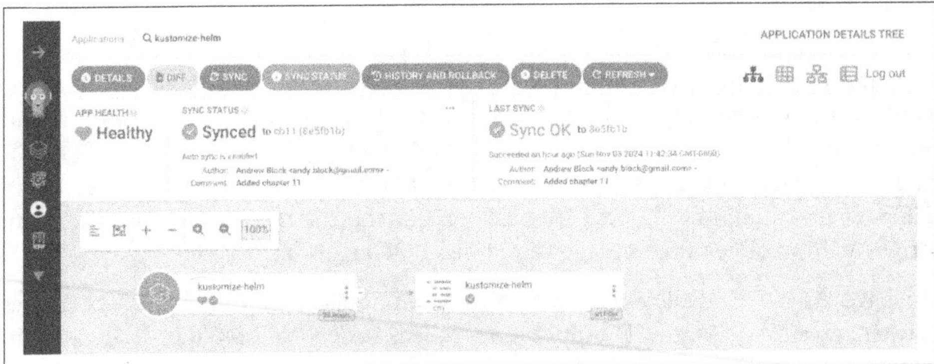


*Figure 11-1. The kustomize-helm application in the Argo CD UI*

If you investigate the contents of the kustomize-helm `ConfigMap` that was created from the Application, two properties are present:

```
apiVersion: v1
kind: ConfigMap
metadata:
  labels:
    app.kubernetes.io/instance: kustomize-helm
    app.kubernetes.io/managed-by: Helm
    app.kubernetes.io/name: kustomize-helm
    argocd.argoproj.io/instance: kustomize-helm
    helm.sh/chart: kustomize-helm-0.1.0
  name: kustomize-helm
  namespace: kustomize-helm
data:
  baseValue: Base Value
  specialValue: Added by Kustomize
```

The `baseValue` property is included by default from the kustomize-helm Helm chart. However, the `specialValue` property was added dynamically as a patch by Kustomize, as defined in the *kustomization.yaml*:

```
patches:
- patch: |-
    apiVersion: v1
    kind: ConfigMap
    metadata:
      name: kustomize-helm
    data:
      specialValue: "Added by Kustomize"
```

The combination of Helm and Kustomize, which is enabled as an opt-in capacity, illustrates the benefits that are provided from a config management plugin.

## Customizing Plugin Execution

The execution of config management plugins can be customized at an `Application` level to curate their operation. They provide the end user both the ability to specify additional configurations at an Application level and also awareness that certain options might be available to them. Two approaches of configuration are available:

- Environment variables
- Parameters

Both of these methods are then exposed to plugins, and it is the responsibility of the plugin author to handle the inputs accordingly.

## Environment Variables

Environment variables are the primary method from which config management plugins glean information about the operating environment and can originate from a variety of system and user-defined sources. Much of the same information is also made available and utilized by the standard build tools, like Helm and Kustomize, and include the following:

- Operating system-level environment variables from within the plugin sidecar
- Build environment variables, including `ARGOCD_APP_NAME`, `ARGOCD_APP_NAMESPACE`, and `KUBE_VERSION`; full list found within the Argo CD documentation (*https://oreil.ly/6D6aK*)

In addition to the system-defined environment variables, end users can explicitly specify their own set of environment variables within the `env` property of the `.spec.source.plugin` field:

```
spec:
  source:
    plugin:
      env:
        - name: FOO
          value: bar
```

User-defined environment variables are prefixed with `ARGOCD_ENV_`. So, the value of the user-defined environment variable here would be accessible within the plugin in the environment variable `ARGOCD_ENV_FOO`.

## Parameters

Another method for customizing the execution of a config management plugin is through the use of parameters. Parameters are also defined in the `.spec.source.plugin` field of an `Application` in the `parameters` property, and they have several advantages when compared to environment variables:

- Support multiple data types aside from strings (string, array, or map are the supported data types)
- "Announced" within the Parameters tab of the Application within the UI
- "Announced" parameters either statically or dynamically defined within the `ConfigManagementPlugin` manifest

Parameters are also exposed to plugins as environment variables and available in two formats:

- Individually with the prefix `PARAM_`. A parameter with the name `example-param` would be exposed as the environment variable `PARAM_EXAMPLE_PARAM`.
- A single `ARGOCD_APP_PARAMETERS` environment variable containing the content of the Application `.spec.source.plugin` field in JSON format.

Complex parameter types, such as arrays or maps, have a slightly different environment variable name format. For arrays, the environment variable is suffixed with the index (`PARAM_NAME_X`, where `X` is the index) of the parameter while maps are suffixed with the key associated with the parameter (foo.bar becomes `PARAM_NAME_FOO_BAR`).

Aside from supporting more complex data types, another strength of plugin parameters is that they can be "announced" within the Argo CD UI, giving end users the awareness of specific parameters as well as the ability for parameters to be defined. The following schema defines how parameters can be exposed (announced):

```
# Name of the parameter
name: string-param
# Description of the parameter
title: "Description goes here"
# Tooltip shown when the user hovers over the field in the user interface
tooltip: "A helpful tip"
# Indicator for whether a parameter is required
required: false
# Indicator for how the user interface should present the entry field (defaults to "string")
itemType: ""
# Data type for non-string values (map or array)
collectionType: ""
# Optional default value
string: default-string-value
```

Parameters that are consistent (static) for each execution of a particular plugin are announced in the `.spec.parameters.static` property of the `ConfigManagementPlugin`.

To illustrate how parameters are presented in the Argo CD UI, define a parameter called *my-static-param* within the *kustomize-helm-plugin* `ConfigMap` containing the `ConfigManagementPlugin` as shown here:

```
spec:
  parameters:
    static:
      - name: my-static-param
        title: Example static parameter
```

Once applied, restart the repo-server pod to enable Argo CD to pick up on changes:

```
kubectl delete pod -n argocd -l=app.kubernetes.io/name=argocd-repo-server
```

With the repo-server restarted, navigate to the Argo CD UI and select the *kustomize-helm* Application. Click on the Details button and then navigate to the Parameters tab, which will display any of the configured parameters, as seen in Figure 11-2.

SUMMARY PARAMETERS MANIFEST EVENTS

PLUGIN

NAME kustomize-helm

ENV

Example static parameter Value

*Figure 11-2. Parameter exposed in the Argo CD UI*

Notice that the *my-static-param* parameter with the title "Example static parameter," as configured in the *kustomize-helm-plugin* `ConfigMap`, is now available on the page as a field to specify.

It is important to note that even though parameters are exposed to the UI, they do not become defined as environment variables for use by config management plugins until their values are specified either in the UI or declaratively in the Application manifest.

Alternatively, instead of explicitly specifying parameters within the `ConfigManagementPlugin`, they can be sourced dynamically from the content within the Application source code. The use of dynamic parameters offloads responsibility for defining plugin parameters that are exposed within the Argo CD UI from the Argo CD administrator as well as enabling parameters to be defined based on the content source associated with each Application. Dynamic parameters are defined within the `.spec.parameters.dynamic` property of the `ConfigManagementPlugin` which specifies a command that should be executed within the Application source, which generates a structure representing the structure of static parameters in JSON format.

## User Interface Customization

One of the primary reasons why Argo CD has gained such popularity in the Kubernetes community is due to its rich UI. Simplifying the steps that a user needs to take to become productive, as well as presenting an easy-to-understand visualization of the current state of GitOps-based deployments and operations, accelerates adoption and management concerns. In order to enable further productivity with the UI, Argo CD provides several injection points for end users to customize the look and feel, as well as to extend the baseline feature set. This section will highlight several of the available methods.

### Banner Notifications

Proactive communication is one of the methods that can be used to enhance the overall experience for end users. One way that Argo CD supports this goal is through the use of banner notifications. When enabled, these messages, defined at a global level by Argo CD administrators, allow for important information to be presented to end users, such as upcoming maintenance periods or new features that are available on the platform. This feature is enabled by setting the `ui.bannercontent` property of the *argocd-cm* `ConfigMap` with the desired content. Additional options, such as the location of where the banner should appear, are set by specifying the `ui.bannerposition` to be either top or bottom, as well as whether the banner should be permanently displayed using the `ui.bannerpermanent` property. Finally, the text provided in the `ui.bannercontent` property can also include a hyperlink to another location, such as a maintenance page, when notifying users of upcoming changes to the environment. This option is set by specifying the `ui.bannerurl` property.

Figure 11-3 illustrates how a banner notification appears within the Argo CD UI.

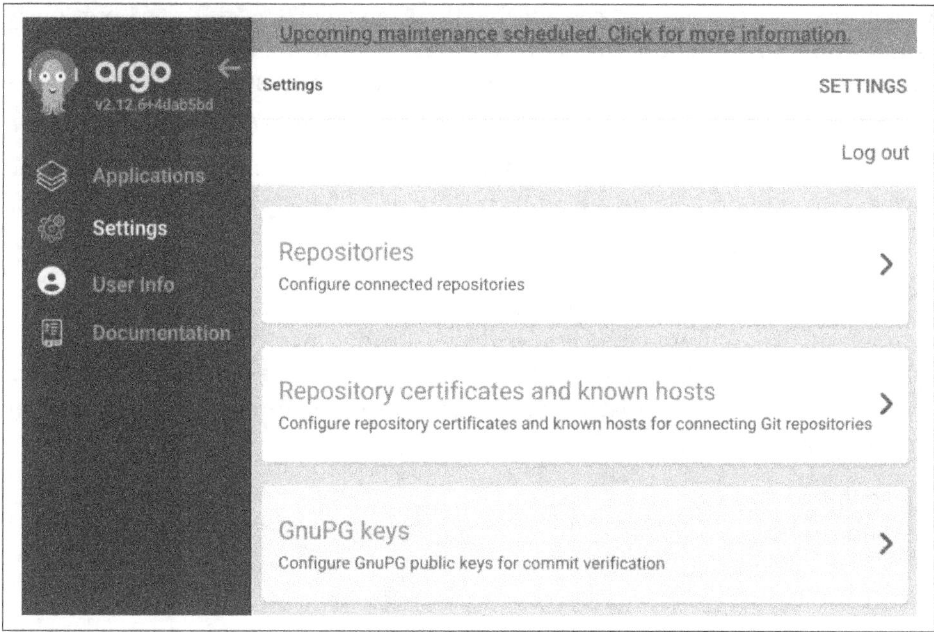


*Figure 11-3. Notification banner displayed in the Argo CD UI*

## Custom Styles

Integral to any user experience is how content is presented, and in modern web applications, the look and feel is driven primarily by Cascading Style Sheets (CSS). These resources are included as part of the argo-ui project (*https://github.com/argoproj/argo-ui*), and the Argo CD UI leverages many of these elements when presenting content to the end user.

As Argo CD usage continues to expand to different environments and in enterprise organizations, there may be a desire to customize how some of the elements are presented. The Argo CD UI supports including custom CSS content in order to supplement the baseline set of content provided by the argo-ui project. Examples of common customizations include replacing the Argo CD logo with a custom logo or setting the background of certain components to represent the operating environment (e.g., development, staging, production) that Argo CD is managing.

Custom stylesheets can be applied either by specifying the location of resources from a remote URL or from a location within the `argocd-server` container using the `ui.cssurl` property of the argocd-cm `ConfigMap`. For example, to reference an externally hosted CSS file from a remote resource, set the `ui.cssurl` property using the following format:

```
ui.cssurl: "https://www.example.com/my-styles.css"
```

One of the common uses for customizing the Argo CD UI, as described previously, is to change background elements to represent the environment that Argo CD is managing. This small enhancement gives end users an extra level of assurance, particularly when multiple Argo CD instances have been deployed.

The `argocd-server` deployment that was installed using the Argo CD Helm chart includes an optional volume mount leveraging a ConfigMap called `argocd-styles-cm` containing custom CSS styles to the location `/shared/app/custom` within the container. This ConfigMap is not included in the set of resources when Argo CD is deployed, and since the volume is marked as *optional*, the container can start without any issue. If an alternate installation method was chosen and the volume for setting up mounting custom styles to the Argo CD server container was not configured, a `volume` and associated `volumeMount` can be applied to the `argocd-server` Deployment:

```
apiVersion: apps/v1
kind: Deployment
metadata:
  name: argocd-server
  ...
spec:
  template:
    ...
    spec:
      containers:
      - command:
        ...
        volumeMounts:
        ...
        - mountPath: /shared/app/custom
          name: styles
      ...
      volumes:
      ...
      - configMap:
          name: argocd-styles-cm
        name: styles
```

To implement the use case for changing the background element of the Argo CD UI, we can embed the custom CSS content within the `argocd-styles-cm` ConfigMap to achieve the desired goal.

The following CSS properties can be used to update the top bar of the Argo CD UI to be the color red, potentially indicating that the Argo CD instance represents a production environment:

```
div.columns.small-9.top-bar__left-side {
    background: #fefefe;
}
div.columns.top-bar__left-side,
div.top-bar__title.text-truncate.top-bar__right-side {
    background: #EE0000;
    color: #fff;
```

```
}
.top-bar__breadcrumbs {
    color: #fff !important;
}
.top-bar__title {
    color: #fff !important;
}
```

The `argocd-styles-cm.yaml` file within the *ch11/ui* directory of the project repository contains the updated ConfigMap with the CSS classes previously illustrated already included.

Apply the changes to the ConfigMap by running the following command from within the project directory:

```
kubectl apply -f ch11/ui/argocd-styles-cm.yaml
```

Restart the `argocd-server` pod so that the changes to the ConfigMap can be picked up:

```
kubectl delete pod -n argocd -l=app.kubernetes.io/component=server
```

Once the pod is running and ready, reload the UI. Notice that the toolbar is now red, confirming that the changes specified are being used, as shown in Figure 11-4.

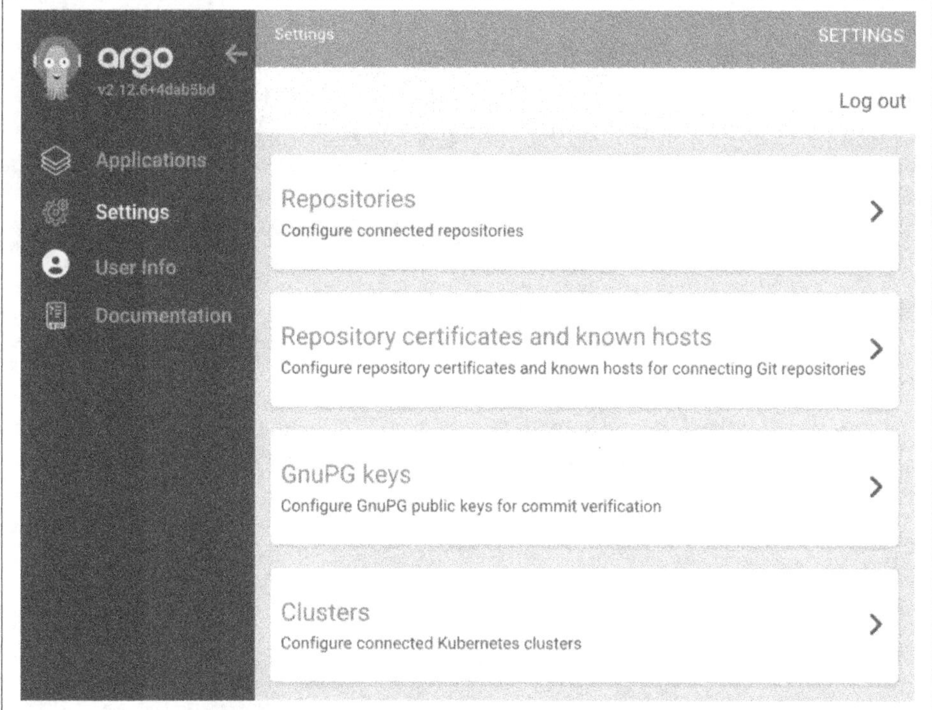


*Figure 11-4. Custom toolbar color applied within the Argo CD UI*

While modifying the toolbar is just a minor change, it illustrates the potential options available for customizing the style of the Argo CD UI.

## UI Extensions

Not only can the look and feel of the Argo CD UI be customized, but entirely new elements can be added through the use of UI extensions. Since the Argo CD UI is React (*https://react.dev*) based, extensions are delivered as React components within JavaScript files matching the pattern `extensions*.js` from within the `/tmp/extensions` directory of the `argocd-server` pod.

Three types of UI extensions are available:

*Resource tab extensions*
: Provides an additional tab within the sliding panel on the Argo CD Application details page

*System-level extensions*
: Adds new items to the sidebar that displays a new page with content when selected

*Application status panel extensions*
: Adds new items to the status panel of an Application

Extensions are registered using the exposed extensions API global variable. Each extension type provides its own registration method along with a series of method parameters. For example, to register a system-level extension, the following method is used:

```
registerSystemLevelExtension(component: ExtensionComponent,
    title: string, options: {icon?: string})
```

With a basic understanding of Argo CD UI extensions, including the types that can be defined, let's walk through the steps it takes to create and implement a system-level extension.

A system-level extension, once again, exposes a link on the sidebar to a dedicated page with content. The following is the JavaScript that is needed to create a minimal extension:

```
((window) => {
  const component = () => {
    return React.createElement(
      "div",
      { style: { padding: "10px" } },
      "Argo CD Up and Running"
    );
  };
  window.extensionsAPI.registerSystemLevelExtension(
    component,
    "Argo CD Book",
```

```
        "/argocd-book",
        "fa-book"
    );
})(window);
```

When added to Argo CD, the UI will contain a new link called *Argo CD Book* with a book icon (using a book icon from the content library *https://fontawesome.com*) that presents a page (component) with a simple line of text. Notice how the extension is registered to Argo using the `registerSystemLevelExtension` method of the `extensionsAPI`.

There are two methods that UI extensions are typically delivered to the `argocd-server` pod:

- Mounted as a volume
- Loaded dynamically using the Argo CD Extension Installer Project (*https://oreil.ly/1VJgx*)

In our case, we will use the first strategy and inject the extension within a ConfigMap as a volume. The ConfigMap containing the extension can be found in a file called `ui-extensions.yaml` within the *ch11/ui* directory of the project repository.

Create the ConfigMap by running the following command from the project repository directory:

```
kubectl apply -f ch11/ui/ui-extensions.yaml
```

Next, update the `argocd-server` deployment with the contents of the `argo-cd-server-ui-extensions.yaml` file within the *ch11/ui* directory that will include the *ui-extensions* ConfigMap that will be mounted within the */tmp/extensions* directory of the container by executing the following command:

```
kubectl apply -f ch11/ui/argo-cd-argocd-server.yaml --server-side=true
```

Wait until the server pod has restarted and becomes ready. Navigate to the UI and verify that the new link exposed by the extension is present on the sidebar, as shown in Figure 11-5.

Clicking on the Argo CD Book link will present the minimal amount of content that was provided in the extension, but can easily be expanded upon as desired.

While this walk-through provided a glimpse into the power provided by Argo CD UI extensions, more fully featured extensions are available. One such example from the Argo Labs project is the ArgoCD Extension Metrics (*https://oreil.ly/qXlZy*), which exposes Prometheus metrics on the Resources tab of the UI. It is projects, like Argo CD Extension Metrics, that illustrate just how extensible Argo CD UI has become.

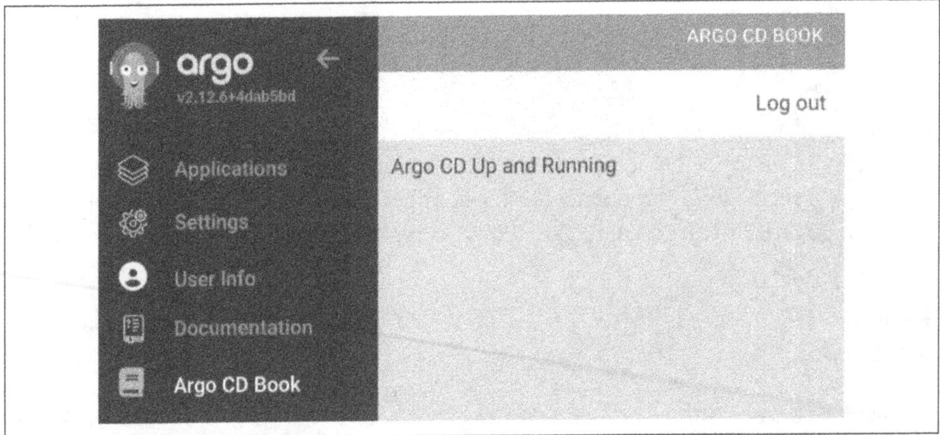


*Figure 11-5. System-level extension within the Argo CD UI*

## Summary

In this chapter, we covered some of the ways that the base capabilities provided by Argo CD can be extended by end users. We first explored how config management plugins enable complete control for how manifests are rendered by Argo CD, including how they are configured using a config management plugin and implemented as a sidecar to the Argo CD Repository Server. Then, we looked at the Argo CD UI and how the look and feel can be customized through the use of banner notifications and custom CSS styles. Finally, we saw how UI extensions allow end users to add elements, including custom components, at the resource, system, or application status level, to extend the baseline set of capabilities that the Argo CD UI provides.

## CHAPTER 12

# Integrating CI with Argo CD

Continuous integration/continuous delivery (CI/CD) have long been foundational practices for efficiently delivering applications to various environments. Over the years, these methodologies have shaped the development landscape, giving rise to a wide array of tools and frameworks, with Jenkins being a notable example. However, as CI/CD practices have evolved, they have often become conflated, leading many users to merge CI/CD into a single, indistinguishable process.

This produces an issue with GitOps and, by extension, Argo CD.

CI is a synchronous process with a finite runtime, typically triggered by events like commits to a repository or branch, making it ideal for builds, tests, and related pipelines. In contrast, GitOps (which focuses on CD) operates asynchronously. Tools like Argo CD remain independent of CI activities, focusing solely on the declared source of truth (e.g., Git or Helm) and acting only when changes to the desired state are detected.

In this chapter, we will focus on how to best integrate Argo CD with a CI system to effectively make use of the strength of each process.

## Reconciliation Response Time

Argo CD adheres to OpenGitOps' third principle, "Pulled automatically," by leveraging a reconciliation loop to continuously monitor and synchronize with the source of truth (in this chapter, Git will be the focus). This approach operates independently of event-driven mechanisms, such as webhook-triggered deployments. By default, Argo CD relies exclusively on the reconciliation loop to detect changes in the source of truth.

However, webhooks provide a mechanism for "on-demand" synchronization, enabling changes to be applied immediately without waiting for the next reconciliation cycle. To support this use case, Argo CD allows webhooks to work alongside the reconciliation loop, offering seamless integration with Git workflows and enabling prompt synchronization when necessary.

## Modifying Reconciliation

By default, Argo CD's reconciliation loop that is used to check for updates within the source is set to 180 seconds (3 minutes). This value can be adjusted by modifying the `argocd-cm` ConfigMap in the `argocd` namespace. You can add (or update if it's already there) the `timeout.reconciliation` section of the `data` field. For example, the following configuration sets the reconciliation to run every 2 minutes:

```
apiVersion: v1
kind: ConfigMap
metadata:
  name: argocd-cm
  namespace: argocd
data:
  timeout.reconciliation: 120s
```

Once you update/add this field, you will need to restart the `argocd-repo-server` Deployment and the `argocd-application-controller` StatefulSet in order to pick up the new setting. Run the following two commands to restart these components:

```
$ kubectl rollout restart sts -n argocd \
-l app.kubernetes.io/component=application-controller

$ kubectl rollout restart deployment -n argocd \
-l app.kubernetes.io/component=repo-server
```

Reducing the reconciliation timeout interval allows changes to be detected and applied more quickly. However, this comes with potential trade-offs, including increased system load, which may impact the overall performance of your Argo CD implementation. Additionally, shorter intervals may lead to rate limiting from your Git provider, particularly when using hosted services, like GitHub or GitLab. Setting the reconciliation timeout to 0s effectively disables reconciliation.

In general, retaining the default reconciliation interval of 3 minutes is considered best practice and is our recommended approach. Rather than reducing the reconciliation timeout, we suggest configuring webhooks for on-demand synchronization and to enable better integration with CI systems. This allows the webhook-triggered updates to complement the default reconciliation process, providing a balanced and efficient workflow.

## Setting Up Webhooks

Setting up webhooks requires configuration both on the Argo CD side and on the Git provider side. It is considered best practice to first set up a webhook secret, then move on to other required configurations. Argo CD accepts unauthenticated webhook events since the only action it performs is an on-demand refresh of the Application (which potentially leads to reconciliation). However, the potential exists for a distributed denial-of-service (DDoS) attack. This is especially true if your Argo CD installation is public.

For more information about DDoS attacks, the article from Cloudflare (*https://oreil.ly/gNLPR*) is a great read.

Set the webhook secret by patching the `argocd-secret` Secret in the `argocd` namespace. This can be accomplished by patching the resource. Inspect the `ch12/manifests/argocd-secret.yaml` file:

```
apiVersion: v1
kind: Secret
metadata:
  name: argocd-secret
  namespace: argocd
type: Opaque
stringData:
  webhook.gogs.secret: supersecret
```

Apply this manifest by patching the existing `argocd-secret` resource:

```
kubectl patch secret argocd-secret -n argocd \
--patch-file ch12/manifests/argocd-secret.yaml
```

After applying the manifest, the changes should take effect immediately.

Next, we'll migrate a repository that we'll use to test the webhook. Some of these steps were completed as part of the installation of Gitea in Chapter 9. Using Gitea to migrate a repository is beyond the scope of this book, so a script can be run to handle the migration for you:

```
bash ch12/scripts/migrate_repo.sh
```

Once the script runs successfully, you should be able to see the simple-go repository (*https://git.upandrunning.local/upandrunning/simple-go*). It should appear similar to Figure 12-1.

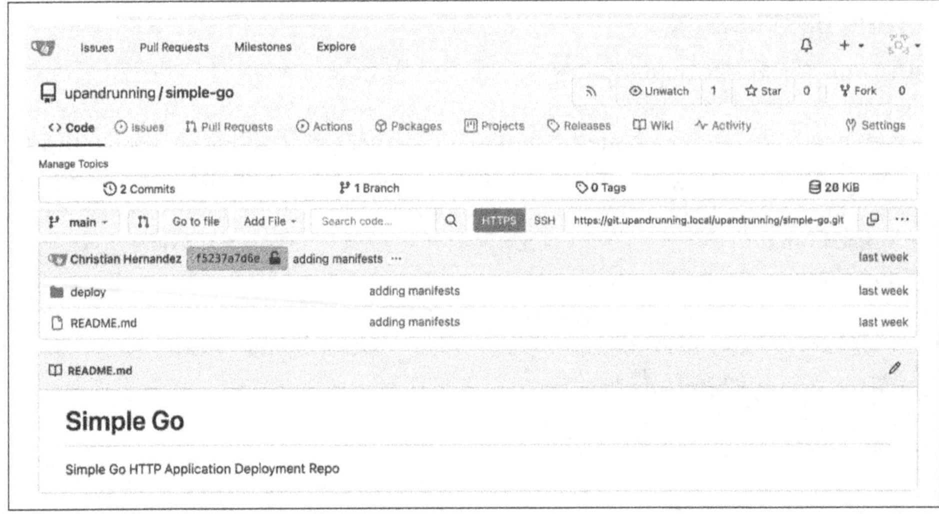


*Figure 12-1. Simple-go on Gitea*

Deploy the manifests contained in the simple-go repository by applying the Argo CD Application manifest for this chapter. Inspecting the `ch12/applications/simple-go.yaml` file, you will see the reference to the Gitea repository:

```
apiVersion: argoproj.io/v1alpha1
kind: Application
metadata:
  name: simple-go
  namespace: argocd
spec:
  project: default
  source:
    repoURL: https://git.upandrunning.local/upandrunning/simple-go
    targetRevision: main
    path: deploy/overlays/default
  destination:
    namespace: webhooks
    name: in-cluster
  syncPolicy:
    automated:
      prune: true
      selfHeal: true
    syncOptions:
    - CreateNamespace=true
```

Apply this manifest by running:

```
kubectl apply -f ch12/applications/simple-go.yaml
```

Once added, the Application should appear similar to Figure 12-2.

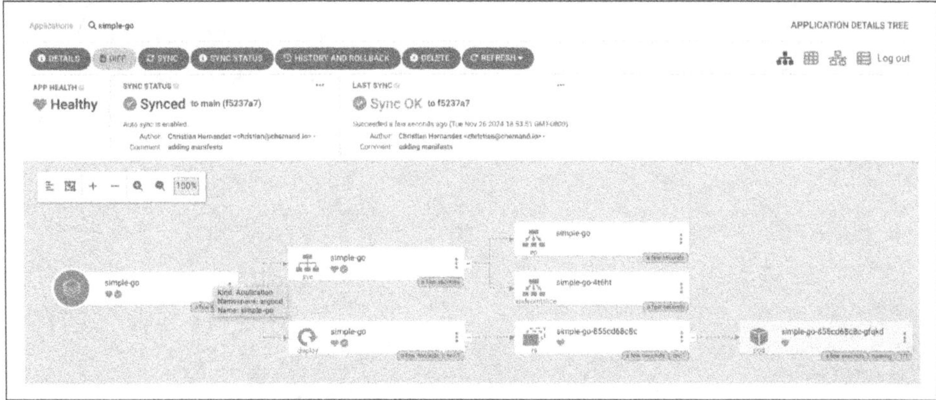


*Figure 12-2. Simple-go Application deployed*

If you were to make a change in the repository, the change wouldn't be applied until the 3-minute reconciliation loop runs. To shorten this timeframe, we will add a webhook to perform an on-demand reconciliation as soon as a change is made. Navigate to the simple-go repository (*https://git.upandrunning.local/upandrunning/simple-go*) and configure the webhook by completing the following steps:

1. Click Settings in the upper right corner.
2. Click Webhooks on the left navigation bar.
3. Click Add Webhook on the righthand side and select Gitea.

Fill out the following in the form:

- In the Target URL, enter *https://argocd.upandrunning.local/api/webhook*.
- Leave HTTP Method as POST.
- Leave POST Content Type as "application/json."
- In the Secret field, enter **supersecret**.
- Make sure to leave Trigger On as Push Events.
- Leave the "Branch filter" as "*."
- Leave Authorization Header blank.
- Make sure Active is checkmarked.

Once complete, the form should appear similar to Figure 12-3.

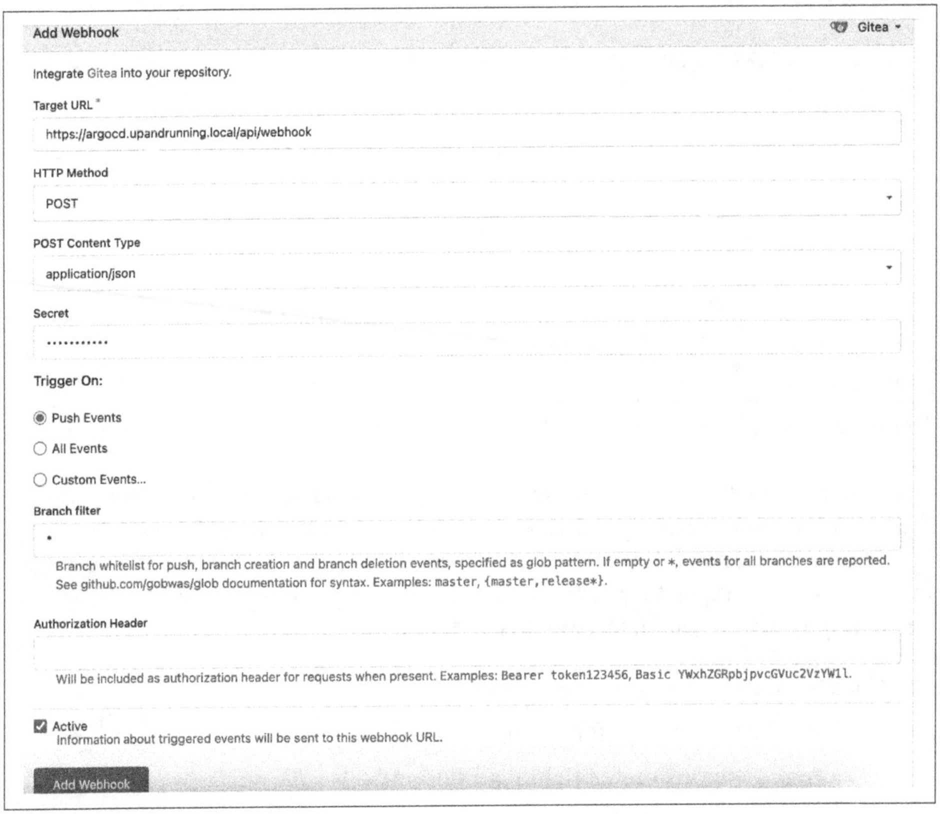

*Figure 12-3. Webhook setup*

Click on the Add Webhook button, and the page listing the configured webhooks should be presented. You can test this webhook by making a change in the repository, which will trigger a reconciliation request to Argo CD. Test this by navigating to the webhook repository (*https://git.upandrunning.local/upandrunning/simple-go/src/branch/main/deploy/base/deploy.yaml*) and click the pencil icon to make an edit to the Deployment.

Change the value of the `spec.replicas` field from 1 to 2. Then, scroll down and click on the Commit Changes button. Visiting your Argo CD web UI, you will see the change immediately reflected without having to wait for the reconciliation loop. The configured webhook now will trigger the reconciliation any time there's a change to the repository.

Navigate to the simple-go repository webhook settings page (*https://git.upandrunning.local/upandrunning/simple-go/settings/hooks*), and you will see a green dot next to the webhook you just created, indicating that the webhook was successfully submitted. The status within the webhooks page should appear similar to Figure 12-4.

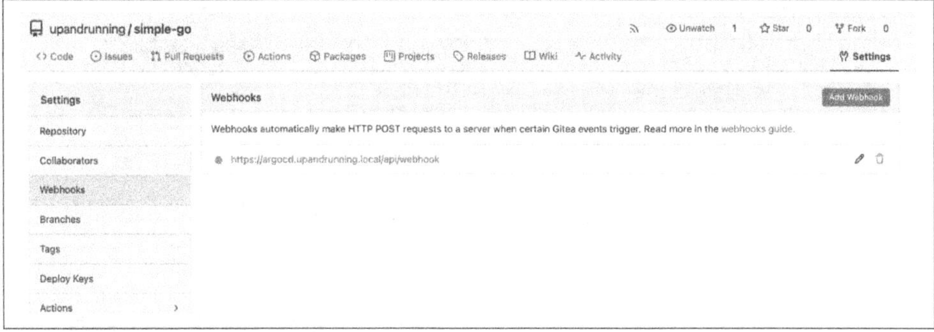


*Figure 12-4. Successful webhook*

Webhooks are an important part of a CI/CD workflow using Argo CD because they enable automated, real-time synchronization between a Git repository and Kubernetes clusters. By triggering updates whenever changes occur in Git, webhooks eliminate the need to wait for the reconciliation loop and ensure immediate deployment of new configurations.

# CI/CD Integration via Tekton

Similar to an application that is managed by Argo CD, the lifecycle of Argo CD Applications and their associated manifests can take advantage of CI methodologies as well. Triggering synchronization activities within Argo CD via webhooks are a great way to reduce the time that it takes to realize changes within Kubernetes clusters. However, by leveraging this approach, it bypasses being able to leverage some of the benefits that are inherent to CI, including the ability to perform static analysis of the code base and to facilitate more thorough testing scenarios.

A variety of CI tools and systems are available for use and range from those that are a software as a service (SaaS) solution to those that are self-managed. Similar to the approach taken with source code management (SCM) and the use of the Gitea instance that was deployed previously, a self-managed solution will be used.

Tekton (*https://tekton.dev*) is a cloud native, Kubernetes-based system for building CI/CD actions and offers platform engineers and developers the ability to build robust solutions. Several subprojects are available with Tekton, and its modular design allows consumers the ability to enable only the components they need. Table 12-1 provides an overview of the Tekton subprojects and their purpose.

*Table 12-1. Tekton projects*

| Project | Description |
|---|---|
| Tekton Pipelines | A set of Kubernetes CRDs for constructing CI/CD pipelines |
| Tekton Triggers | Instantiate pipelines based on events |
| Tekton Chains | Tools to generate, store, and sign provenance for artifacts that are built with Tekton Pipelines |
| Tekton Operator | Kubernetes-based operator to manage the lifecycle of Tekton projects |

## Building a Tekton Pipeline

*Pipelines* provide the foundation for Tekton, as it includes, as its name suggests, the tools necessary for building CI/CD pipelines. We can use it to build a pipeline that not only implements CI methodologies, but also illustrates how Argo CD can be integrated within CI systems.

In addition to triggering the synchronization of Argo CD Applications, which emulates the webhook invocation that was used previously, we will also add a step that performs syntactical analysis of the manifests that will be produced to ensure that the manifests not only produce valid YAML-formatted content, but also conform to recommended practices.

So, in the end, our pipeline will consist of the following actions:

- Clone the Argo CD manifests from the Gitea instance.
- Verify the manifests meet conformance requirements.
- Synchronize the Argo CD Application.

Before focusing on the pipeline, the first step is to install Tekton Pipelines to the `kind` cluster. The installation consists of applying a single manifest file containing all of the necessary resources. Execute the following command to install Tekton Pipelines to the `kind` instance:

```
kubectl apply -f https://storage.googleapis.com/tekton-releases/pipeline/latest/release.yaml
```

A new namespace called `tekton-pipelines` contains all of the namespaced scoped assets associated with Tekton Pipelines:

```
NAME                                          READY   STATUS    RESTARTS   AGE
tekton-events-controller-869dfbbb89-4p9sm     1/1     Running   0          9m45s
tekton-pipelines-controller-84f497b9dd-2q62v  1/1     Running   0          9m45s
tekton-pipelines-webhook-6449f66676-9vjzj     1/1     Running   0          9m44s
```

Since Tekton is a Kubernetes-based CI/CD platform, each of the components is implemented as a Custom Resource Definition (CRD). Table 12-2 describes the key CRDs associated with Tekton Pipelines.

*Table 12-2. Tekton Pipelines entities*

| Entity | Description |
|---|---|
| `Task` | A series of steps that launches a specific activity. Input parameters can be provided to customize the execution, and outputs are produced containing results. |
| `TaskRun` | Instantiation of a `Task` containing input, output, and execution parameters. |
| `Pipeline` | A series of `Tasks` that accomplishes a desired goal. |
| `PipelineRun` | Instantiation of a `Pipeline` containing input, output, and execution parameters. |

As our pipeline consists of three distinct activities, each will have an associated `Task` that defines the actions involved. The first `Task` clones the repository from Git and includes a set of input parameters, such as the URL and branch, that should be retrieved. The second `Task`, which verifies the manifests themselves, is where our pipeline provides real business value.

Kustomize is used within Argo CD as the tool to process the manifests stored within the Git repository. Only after the manifests have been rendered by Kustomize can they be verified. Linting is one such approach for performing static code analysis and can be used as a method for verifying the manifests that would be produced by Argo CD. yamllint (*https://oreil.ly/HsvSr*) is one of the more popular YAML linting tools and includes not only a wide range of features, but also the ability to customize the execution to meet individual needs. The linting `Task` contains two total steps: render the manifests provided to a target directory using Kustomize and then execute yamllint against the rendered manifests.

The final task in our Pipeline uses the Argo CD CLI to synchronize an individual Application within the Argo CD instance.

Each of these tasks as well as the remainder of the components needed to construct our pipeline are located in the *ch12/tekton/pipelines* directory of the project repository.

Navigate to the project repository and add each of the `Tasks` to the `webhooks` namespace:

```
kubectl apply -n webhooks -f ch12/tekton/pipelines/git-clone-task.yaml
kubectl apply -n webhooks -f ch12/tekton/pipelines/kustomize-lint-task.yaml
kubectl apply -n webhooks -f ch12/tekton/pipelines/argocd-app-sync-task.yaml
```

A `TaskRun` is one such way any of these `Tasks` could be executed. However, we will instead create a `Pipeline` called *lint-sync-argocd* that coordinates the invocation between each of these tasks to produce the desired business goal. The `Pipeline` is included within the project repository and is located at `ch12/tekton/pipelines/pipeline.yaml`.

Upon inspecting the pipeline from the `pipeline.yaml` manifest, you will see not only how tasks are referenced, but also how input parameters can be provided. The following are some of the primary components of a Tekton Pipeline:

`params`
: Parameters to customize the execution of a `Pipeline` or `Task`

`workspaces`
: Allocates a `Volume` to a `Pipeline` or `Task`; commonly used to share content between multiple tasks

`taskRef`
: Reference to an existing `Task` that should be executed by the `Pipeline`

`runAfter`
: Coordinates when a specific `Task` is executed only after the completion of another `Task`

Add the `Pipeline` to the `webhooks` namespace by executing the following command:

```
kubectl apply -n webhooks -f ch12/tekton/pipelines/pipeline.yaml
```

Now that the `Tasks` and `Pipeline` have been added to the `webhooks` namespace, we are almost ready to run our Pipeline. A few more steps still need to be completed, as they are requirements of the individual `Tasks`.

Recall from when the yamllint tool was introduced previously that the execution can be customized, depending on the desired use. Any customization to the default execution can be made using a configuration file. This approach mirrors how many other utilities are configured. By inspecting the `kustomize-lint` task, you will see a reference to a ConfigMap within the `volumes` section:

```
volumes:
- name: shared
  emptyDir: {}
- name: yamllint-config
  configMap:
    name: '$(params.yamllint-configmap)'
```

Variables starting with `params` reference a *parameter* that was previously defined within the `Task`. For the *yamllint-configmap* within the kustomize lint `Task`, the default value is `yamllint-config`. However, like any parameter, this value can be overridden as needed.

A ConfigMap manifest has been provided in the `ch12/tekton/pipelines/yamllint-configmap.yaml` file and includes an embedded `yamllint.yaml` file that customizes the execution of yamllint. The default yamllint configuration needs to be modified to comply with the content that is produced by the invocation of Kustomize against the manifests. In particular, we need to disable the check performed to verify that three dashes are included at the beginning of each manifest (known as the document start) as well as some of the rules associated with how content is indented:

```
rules:
  document-start: disable
  indentation:
    indent-sequences: false
```

Add the ConfigMap to the `webhooks` namespace by executing the following command:

```
kubectl apply -n webhooks -f ch12/tekton/pipelines/yamllint-configmap.yaml
```

The final preparatory step prior to triggering the Pipeline is to provide the *argocd-task-sync-and-wait* task with the location of the Argo CD server and the credentials that should be used to facilitate the connection. By inspecting the task, you can see that the address of the Argo CD server instance is stored as a ConfigMap and the credentials are stored as a Secret:

```
  stepTemplate:
    envFrom:
      - configMapRef:
          name: argocd-env-configmap  # used for server address
      - secretRef:
          name: argocd-env-secret  # used for auth (username/password or auth token)
  steps:
    - name: sync-app
      image: quay.io/argoproj/argocd:$(params.argocd-version)
      script: |
        if [ -z "$ARGOCD_AUTH_TOKEN" ]; then
          yes | argocd login "$ARGOCD_SERVER" --username="$ARGOCD_USERNAME" \
          --password="$ARGOCD_PASSWORD";
        fi
        argocd app sync "$(params.application-name)" \
            --revision "$(params.revision)" $(params.flags)
        argocd app wait "$(params.application-name)" --health $(params.flags)
```

The `stepTemplate` declaration exposes the properties of both the ConfigMap and Secret as environment variables into any of the steps included in the Task.

Create a ConfigMap named `argocd-env-configmap` within the `webhooks` namespace with the location of the Argo CD server in a property called `ARGOCD_SERVER` using the following command:

```
kubectl create configmap argocd-env-configmap \
--from-literal="ARGOCD_SERVER=argocd.upandrunning.local" \
-n webhooks --dry-run=client \
-o yaml | kubectl apply -f-
```

Next, credentials must be provided so that commands can be executed against the Argo CD server using the Argo CD CLI from within the task. While we highlighted how Argo CD handles users and RBAC in Chapter 9, one of the concepts that was not covered at that time, which does provide an optimal solution for this use case, is *project roles*.

Instead of creating and managing a full-fledged user for use by our Pipeline, a project role can be used to perform a restricted set of actions within a project using the CLI or API. Access to resources is granted using the same syntax as the standard Argo CD configuration. So, for this use case, we will want to create a project role that has access to synchronize and retrieve the state of `Application` resources.

Using the Argo CD CLI, since the *simple-go* Application is present within the default project, create a new project role called *tekton* using the `argocd proj role` subcommand by specifying the name of the project that the project role should be created within and the name of the role:

```
argocd proj role create default tekton
```

With the project role created, assign policies so that it can retrieve and synchronize Application resources using the following commands:

```
argocd proj role add-policy default tekton \
  --action get --permission allow --object "*"
argocd proj role add-policy default tekton \
  --action sync --permission allow --object "*"
```

Since project roles are included within the AppProject custom resource, the configurations can be expressed declaratively. For the *tekton* project role created previously, the following represents how it is defined within the AppProject:

```
apiVersion: argoproj.io/v1alpha1
kind: AppProject
metadata:
  name: default
  namespace: argocd
spec:
  roles:
  - name: tekton
    policies:
    - p, proj:default:tekton, applications, get, default/*, allow
    - p, proj:default:tekton, applications, sync, default/*, allow
...
```

By default, applications are the resource for which project role policies are applied. However, other resources, like repositories, clusters, logs, and projects, can also be used. It is also important to note that the target of a specific policy must follow the `proj:<project-name>:<role-name>` format; otherwise, the policy will not take effect.

To use a project role, and in our case, within a Tekton pipeline, a JWT token must be created. The `argocd proj role create-token` command is used to generate a JWT token to a project role. By default, the token has no expiration. However, an expiration should be added by specifying the `-e` flag with the length of time the token should become invalidated (such as `12h`).

Create a JWT token for the token project role and set the resulting value in the PROJECT_ROLE_JWT_TOKEN variable:

```
PROJECT_ROLE_JWT_TOKEN=$(argocd proj role create-token default tekton --token-only)
```

Finally, create a secret called *argocd-env-secret* in the webhooks namespace, which will be used by the *argocd-task-sync-and-wait* task by executing the following command:

```
kubectl create secret generic argocd-env-secret \
  --from-literal=ARGOCD_AUTH_TOKEN=$PROJECT_ROLE_JWT_TOKEN \
  --namespace webhooks --dry-run=client -o yaml | kubectl apply -f -
```

Now that all of the components of the *lint-sync-argocd* Pipeline, including the Tasks that the Pipeline will invoke and the associated ConfigMaps and Secrets that are used within the Tasks have been added, the next step is to run the Pipeline. A Tekton Pipeline can be started by either creating a PipelineRun custom resource or by using the Tekton CLI (tkn).

The tkn CLI, similar to the Kubernetes (kubectl) and Argo CD (argocd) CLIs, helps simplify the interaction and user experience working with Tekton. It can be obtained from multiple sources, including as a Kubernetes plugin, and is supported on multiple platforms, including Linux, Windows, and macOS. Download and install the plugin from the Tekton website (*https://oreil.ly/d_i10*) and follow the installation steps for the associated platform.

Once the tkn CLI has been installed, the tkn pipeline start subcommand can be used to start the *lint-sync-argocd* Pipeline. This command is helpful for building a Tekton PipelineRun resource. However, if a PipelineRun manifest is already available, kubectl can be used instead to start an instance of a Pipeline.

The *ch12/tekton/pipelines* directory includes a PipelineRun manifest in the pipelinerun.yaml file. Start the *lint-sync-argocd* Pipeline by adding the PipelineRun manifest to the webhooks namespace by executing the following command:

```
kubectl create -n webhooks -f ch12/tekton/pipelines/pipelinerun.yaml
```

Once a PipelineRun has been created, list the status using the tkn pipelinerun list command in the webhooks namespace:

```
tkn pipelinerun list -n webhooks

NAME                     STARTED         DURATION   STATUS
lint-sync-argocd-2ktht   7 seconds ago   ---        Running
```

The best method for tracking the state of a PipelineRun as it progresses is by viewing the execution logs using the tkn pipelinerun logs subcommand. Monitor the status of the PipelineRun created previously by executing the following command:

```
tkn pipelinerun -n webhooks logs -L
```

The -L flag will display the content of the most recent PipelineRun, while the -f flag follows the progress up to completion.

Once the output completes, verify that the PipelineRun completed successfully:

```
NAME                    STARTED         DURATION   STATUS
lint-sync-argocd-2ktht  2 minutes ago   24s        Succeeded
```

You can also verify that the Argo CD Application has synced successfully by viewing the status using either the Argo CD CLI or the web interface, as shown in Figure 12-5.

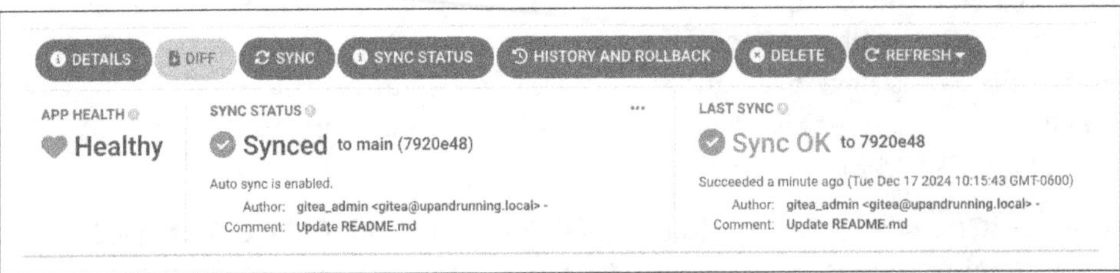


*Figure 12-5. Argo CD Application status after synchronization from the Tekton Pipeline*

The execution of the Tekton Pipeline provides the capability to automate the verification of the manifests Argo CD will process, including the synchronization of the Argo CD Application. The missing piece, as it currently stands, is for Gitea to trigger a Tekton Pipeline to begin whenever a change to the repository occurs. This topic will be covered in the following section.

## Triggering Tekton Pipelines

Tekton Pipelines provides the constructs for building CI/CD pipelines, but it does not include the capacity to automatically start a pipeline. This is where another Tekton subproject, Tekton Triggers, can fill the void. Tekton Triggers enables the automated triggering of Tekton Pipelines based on a variety of event sources and conditions. One of the ways that a Pipeline can be activated is from a webhook event whenever a change to a repository occurs. By enabling this feature, not only will it emulate how the Gitea instance is currently triggering the synchronization of the Argo CD Application in an automated fashion, but it can also provide the additional enhancements that we have built into the Tekton Pipeline.

Since Tekton Triggers is a separate Tekton subproject, it is not included when Tekton Pipelines was installed previously. However, it can be installed to the kind cluster by adding the base set of resources along with a set of supported interceptors, which provide additional logic for specific types of events:

```
kubectl apply -f \
https://storage.googleapis.com/tekton-releases/triggers/latest/release.yaml
kubectl apply -f \
https://storage.googleapis.com/tekton-releases/triggers/latest/interceptors.yaml
```

Now that Tekton Triggers has been installed, let's review the installed set of components. Similar to Tekton Pipelines, Tekton Triggers also contain a number of CRDs that are used to expose and manage how Pipelines are triggered. Table 12-3 describes the entities associated with Tekton Triggers.

*Table 12-3. Tekton Triggers entities*

| Entity | Description |
|---|---|
| `EventListener` | Application listening for Events |
| `Trigger` | Specifies what will occur when an Event is received; contains a `TriggerTemplate` and `TriggerBinding` and, optionally, an `Interceptor` |
| `TriggerTemplate` | The blueprint for a `TaskRun` or `PipelineRun` |
| `TriggerBinding` | Fields in the Event payload that are injected into a `TriggerTemplate`, which can in turn populate the `TaskRun` or `PipelineRun` resource |
| `Interceptor` | "Catchall" event processor to perform additional payload filtering, verification |

The relationship between each of these entities and how a webhook invocation results in the creation of a `PipelineRun` is depicted in Figure 12-6.

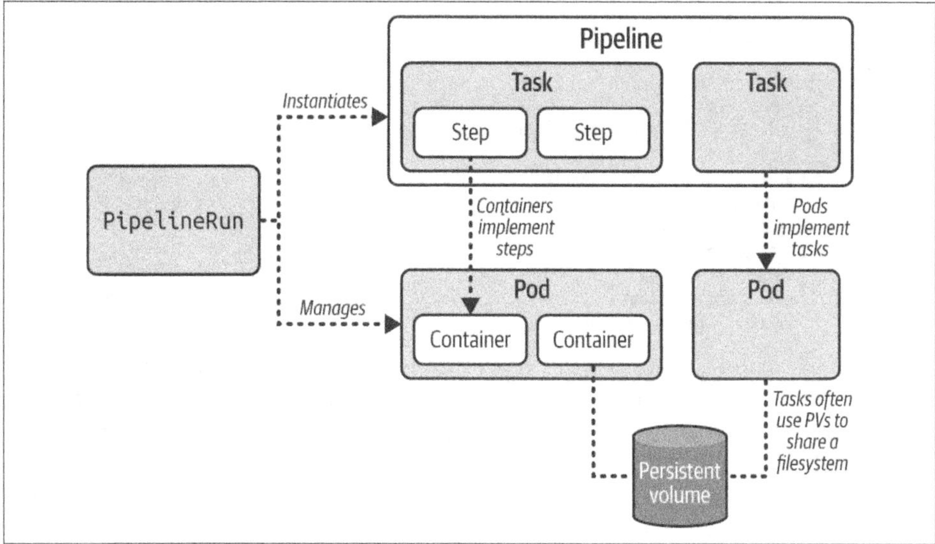


*Figure 12-6. Tekton `PipelineRun`*

The first step when transitioning from a standalone `PipelineRun` resource to Tekton Triggers is how the `PipelineRun` will be instantiated. A `TriggerBinding` resource provides the construct for creating a `PipelineRun` whenever an event is produced. Locate the `tekton-triggers-argocd-triggertemplate.yaml` file within the *ch12/tekton/triggers* directory and notice how the existing `PipelineRun` has been included within the `resourcetemplates` property:

```yaml
apiVersion: triggers.tekton.dev/v1beta1
kind: TriggerTemplate
metadata:
  name: tekton-triggers-argocd
spec:
  params:
    - description: Git revision
      name: revision
  resourcetemplates:
    - apiVersion: tekton.dev/v1beta1
      kind: PipelineRun
      metadata:
        generateName: lint-sync-argocd-
      spec:
        pipelineRef:
          name: lint-sync-argocd
        podTemplate:
          securityContext:
            fsGroup: 65532
        workspaces:
        - name: shared-data
          volumeClaimTemplate:
            spec:
              accessModes:
              - ReadWriteOnce
              resources:
                requests:
                  storage: 1Gi
        params:
        - name: repo-url
          value:  https://git.upandrunning.local/upandrunning/simple-go.git
        - name: argocd-revision
          value: $(tt.params.revision)
        - name: manifests-dir
          value: deploy/overlays/default
        - name: app-name
          value: simple-go
        - name: argocd-flags
          value: --insecure --grpc-web
```

One of the key constants that you will see throughout this implementation of Tekton Triggers is the ability to pass along information from the Gitea webhook invocation to the Tekton Pipeline. In particular, we will reference the specific Git revision that triggered the webhook invocation, which enables Argo CD to synchronize a specific commit so that there is an assurance the only content that has undergone the Tekton Pipeline is applied to the cluster.

By reviewing the `TriggerTemplate`, you will see that the `.spec.params` section contains a parameter called `revision`. This parameter is then used within the blueprint for the `PipelineRun` resource through the `$(tt.params.revision)` property.

The glue between the content provided by the Gitea webhook and how it is fed to the `TriggerTemplate` is a `TriggerBinding`:

```
apiVersion: triggers.tekton.dev/v1beta1
kind: TriggerBinding
metadata:
  name: tekton-triggers-argocd
spec:
  params:
  - name: revision
    value: $(body.after)
```

By inspecting the content of the `tekton-triggers-argocd-triggerbinding.yaml` within the *ch12/tekton/triggers* directory, notice how the name within the `.spec.params` property includes a reference to the name of the parameter from the `TriggerTemplate`. The *value* can originate from either the webhook body or header. In this case, the `after` property within the body contains the specific revision.

Finally, an `EventListener` is used to not only expose an endpoint for triggering Tekton Pipeline, but it also brings together the `TriggerTemplate` and `TriggerBinding`. An `EventListener` essentially starts a pod that has the responsibility of capturing the input, extracting the relevant fields, and creating an associated `PipelineRun` resource.

Since the pod associated with the `EventListener` performs invocations against the Kubernetes API, appropriate RBAC permissions must be assigned. To do so, a `ServiceAccount` and a `RoleBinding` must also be created and associated with the `EventListener`. Inspect the contents of the `EventListener` in the file located at `ch12/tekton/triggers/tekton-triggers-argocd-el.yaml` of the project repository, where you will see how each of these concepts is brought together. In addition, an `Ingress` is also included to demonstrate how an `EventListener` can be exposed to services running outside the cluster. Even though the Gitea instance that triggers the webhook is running within the cluster, it is important to illustrate how to expose CI/CD capabilities for other services to use.

Execute the following commands to apply the remaining Tekton Triggers–related resources to the `webhooks` namespace:

```
kubectl apply -n webhooks \
  ch12/tekton/triggers/tekton-triggers-argocd-el-clusterrolebinding.yaml
kubectl apply -n webhooks ch12/tekton/triggers/tekton-triggers-argocd-el-serviceaccount.yaml
kubectl apply -n webhooks ch12/tekton/triggers/tekton-triggers-argocd-triggerbinding.yaml
kubectl apply -n webhooks ch12/tekton/triggers/tekton-triggers-argocd-triggertemplate.yaml
kubectl apply -n webhooks ch12/tekton/triggers/tekton-triggers-argocd-el.yaml
kubectl apply -n webhooks ch12/tekton/triggers/tekton-triggers-argocd-ingress.yaml
```

The last step is to modify how the Argo CD Application synchronizes content. Currently, as soon as modifications are detected or triggered, content from the `main` branch of the Git repository is applied to the Kubernetes cluster. To ensure that changes are only applied via the Tekton Pipeline and at a specific revision, update the

Argo CD Application to remove the automated `syncPolicy` and the `targetRevision` properties using the following command:

```
kubectl patch application simple-go -n argocd --type=json \
-p="[{'op': 'remove', 'path': '/spec/source/targetRevision'},
 {'op': 'remove', 'path': '/spec/syncPolicy/automated'}]"
```

Now, update the URL of the webhook configured within the simple-go repository by navigating to the repository (*https://git.upandrunning.local/upandrunning/simple-go*) and then completing the following steps:

1. Click the Settings button.
2. Click the Webhooks button on the navigation bar.
3. Click the pencil icon next to the already configured webhook currently pointing at Argo CD.
4. Update the Target URL with *https://tekton-triggers-argocd.upandrunning.local/webhook*.
5. Click the Update Settings button to apply the changes.

Either make a change to the repository using the steps provided previously or click the Test Delivery button within the Webhook Update page. Regardless of the option chosen, as soon as either a new commit is pushed to the repository or a test delivery is triggered, verify that a new `PipelineRun` has started by executing the following command:

```
tkn pipelinerun list -n webhooks
```

The manifests contained within the repository will once again undergo linting, and the Argo CD Application will be synchronized. However, one very important difference occurred compared to the prior synchronizations. Instead of synchronizing the state of a target branch, an individual revision was used associated with the webhook. This can be confirmed by reviewing the current status of the Argo CD Application:

```
argocd app get argocd/simple-go

Name:               argocd/simple-go
Project:            default
Server:             in-cluster
Namespace:          webhooks
URL:                https://argocd.example.com/applications/simple-go
Repo:               https://git.upandrunning.local/upandrunning/simple-go
Target:
Path:               deploy/overlays/default
SyncWindow:         Sync Allowed
Sync Policy:        <none>
Sync Status:        Synced to  (7920e48)
Health Status:      Healthy
```

Notice that the `Sync Status` value contains the specific revision instead of just the branch name. This confirms that not only did the webhook trigger the Tekton Pipeline, but the revision was also extracted properly from the payload and passed all the way to the Argo CD Application.

# Summary

In this chapter, we illustrated how to apply continuous integration concepts with Argo CD. We first enabled Argo CD to accept triggering Application synchronizations through webhook innovations. Then, we set up a new repository within our Gitea instance along with adding a webhook to target automatically synchronizing an Argo CD Application whenever a new change occurred. Afterward, we introduced Tekton as a Kubernetes-based platform for implementing CI patterns. We explored how to not only configure a CI pipeline using Tekton Pipelines to perform multiple actions, including the linting of manifests and synchronization of an Argo CD Application, but also how to automatically trigger the pipeline when a change occurred within the Git repository using Tekton Triggers. By demonstrating how to implement CI practices with Argo CD, changes can be applied more rapidly with the necessary safeguards in place to release more confidently.

CHAPTER 13

# Operationalizing Argo CD

As Argo CD becomes the interface for all your Kubernetes clusters, it quickly becomes an important piece to your organization. Integrating monitoring capabilities with Argo CD can provide insights into deployment status and health, enabling teams to swiftly detect and resolve issues beyond just Argo CD Application triage. Coupled together with notifications, these features ensure that the stakeholders in your organization are immediately informed of any changes or problems with your infrastructure or applications, allowing for prompt response and mitigating downtime. High availability is another important aspect, as it ensures that the Argo CD service remains resilient and accessible. Scalability is also important and related to the topic of high availability, allowing Argo CD to manage the increasing number of applications and clusters seamlessly as the organization grows.

Operationalizing Argo CD not only enhances deployment reliability and efficiency, but also supports the organization's ability to scale and adapt to evolving demands, ensuring sustained delivery of business value. In this chapter, we'll dive into these important factors and go over different methods that will help you to operationalize Argo CD.

## Monitoring

Using the Argo CD UI for application issue triage and observability offers advantages in managing and troubleshooting Kubernetes workload deployments. The web interface of Argo CD provides real-time visibility into the state of your Argo CD Applications, enabling quick identification of discrepancies between the desired and actual states. This visual representation simplifies the detection of issues, such as configuration drifts or failed deployments, allowing for faster root cause analysis. Also, the UI facilitates easy navigation through application histories, manifest changes, and deployment logs, streamlining the debugging process.

The original intent of the Argo CD UI is to abstract Kubernetes primitives and bubble up information that developers care about. Argo CD UI can tell you when something goes wrong and give you the tools to help you triage; however, it doesn't give you the "how" or "why" something failed. Moreover, Argo CD UI only gives you information about itself. It doesn't know any information about other Argo CD instances. This is why tools like Prometheus and Grafana are needed for a complete picture.

Monitoring with Prometheus and Grafana on a Kubernetes system is crucial for ensuring the health, performance, and reliability of not only applications, but also infrastructure components as well. Prometheus, an open source monitoring and alerting toolkit, excels at collecting and storing time-series data, which is essential for tracking metrics all across your organization's environment. It enables real-time monitoring of application performance, resource usage, and cluster health. Grafana complements Prometheus by providing powerful visualization capabilities, allowing operators to create intuitive dashboards and alerts. Together, they enable proactive issue detection, efficient troubleshooting, and informed decision-making, thereby enhancing system stability and optimizing resource utilization. This combination with Argo CD can provide more visibility into your workload deployments.

## Installing Prometheus Stack

The Prometheus Stack consists of Prometheus, which is used to collect metrics, and Grafana, which is used to visualize those metrics. Installing the Prometheus Stack is pretty straightforward using Helm. In the accompanying Git repository, we've included a Helm values file to use to install this stack. We are using the basic installation, but applying some basic additional configurations. If you inspect the `ch13/helm/values/prometheus-values.yaml` file, observe that as part of the installation, we are installing the recommended Grafana dashboard from the Argo CD Project repository:

```
grafana:
  # snippet for brevity
  dashboards:
    default:
      argocd:
        url: https://raw.githubusercontent.com/argoproj/argo-cd/ \
        master/examples/dashboard.json
```

Using this baseline configuration is enough to not only get you started with monitoring Argo CD, but it is also enough for you to see the value right away. You'll be able to gain valuable insights, including how much memory Argo CD is taking up or how long syncs are lasting. To install the Prometheus Stack, follow these steps:

1. Add the Prometheus repository using Helm:

   ```
   $ helm repo add \
   prometheus-community https://prometheus-community.github.io/helm-charts
   ```

2. Update the Helm repo data to get the most recent content:

```
$ helm repo update
```

3. Install the Prometheus Stack (which includes Grafana), using the provided values in the accompanying Git repo:

```
$ helm upgrade -i kube-prometheus-stack -n monitoring --create-namespace \
--values ch13/helm/values/prometheus-values.yaml \
prometheus-community/kube-prometheus-stack
```

After installing the chart, you should see Pods running in the `monitoring` namespace, similar to the following:

```
$ kubectl get pods -n monitoring
NAME                                                       READY   STATUS    RESTARTS   AGE
alertmanager-kube-prometheus-stack-alertmanager-0          2/2     Running   0          34s
kube-prometheus-stack-grafana-5c77f67c66-zvnnr             3/3     Running   0          41s
kube-prometheus-stack-kube-state-metrics-c854dc876-zt7bs   1/1     Running   0          41s
kube-prometheus-stack-operator-5c68cddf55-khf97            1/1     Running   0          41s
kube-prometheus-stack-prometheus-node-exporter-lzqpb       1/1     Running   0          41s
prometheus-kube-prometheus-stack-prometheus-0              2/2     Running   0          34s
```

Now that the Prometheus Stack is up and running, you can configure Argo CD to enable Prometheus to scrape the metrics provided by Argo CD.

## Configuring Argo CD for Prometheus

Next, you will need to set up Argo CD to expose the metrics endpoints. This can be accomplished by using the provided *ch13/helm/values/argocd-metrics-values.yaml* values file. In the file, you will notice that each component, Application, ApplicationSet, repo server, and API server controller has a similar setup configuration:

```
# snipped for brevity
  metrics:
    enabled: true
    serviceMonitor:
      enabled: true
      additionalLabels:
        release: kube-prometheus-stack
```

It's important to note that the `*<controllerName>*.metrics.serviceMonitor.additionalLables.release` section needs to be set to the release name of your Prometheus Stack Helm install. In our case, we named the release `kube-prometheus-stack`.

You can retrieve the name by running `helm ls -n monitoring`.

To set up Argo CD for Prometheus, you can use Helm directly. Update the Argo CD installation using the provided values file in the accompanying Git repository:

```
$ helm upgrade -i argo-cd -n argocd --create-namespace \
--reuse-values --values ch13/helm/values/argocd-metrics-values.yaml argo/argo-cd
```

Using `--reuse-values` will ensure you don't overwrite the values you've already used when installing and modifying your Argo CD installation.

The upgrade not only sets up Argo CD monitoring endpoints, but also sets up the `ServiceMonitor` needed to let Prometheus know where these endpoints are. You can see which `ServiceMonitors` got applied by running the following command:

```
$ kubectl get ServiceMonitor -n argocd
NAME                                 AGE
argocd-application-controller        86m
argocd-applicationset-controller     86m
argocd-repo-server                   86m
argocd-server                        86m
```

You can inspect these ServiceMonitors if you wish. For example, inspect the `argocd-server` by running `kubectl get ServiceMonitor/argocd-server -n argocd -o yaml` and you should see a result similar to the following:

```
apiVersion: monitoring.coreos.com/v1
kind: ServiceMonitor
metadata:
  labels:
    release: kube-prometheus-stack
  name: argocd-server
  namespace: argocd
spec:
  endpoints:
    - interval: 30s
      path: /metrics
      port: http-metrics
  namespaceSelector:
    matchNames:
      - argocd
  selector:
    matchLabels:
      app.kubernetes.io/component: server
      app.kubernetes.io/instance: argocd
      app.kubernetes.io/name: argocd-server-metrics
```

Here, the `endpoints`, `namespaceSelector`, and `selector` that Prometheus uses for metric scraping have been configured for you by the Helm release we completed. For more information about Prometheus, please see the official documentation (*https://prometheus.io/docs*).

## Accessing Grafana

As previously mentioned, Grafana was installed as part of the Prometheus Stack installation. Grafana is also integrated with Prometheus to visualize the metrics being collected. You can view the Grafana UI by running the following port-forwarding command in a terminal window:

```
$ kubectl port-forward -n monitoring svc/kube-prometheus-stack-grafana 8080:80
```

Most likely, you'll want to add an Ingress instead of using port forwarding. Consult the Prometheus Helm chart for more information on how to enable Ingress.

Once the connection has been established, you can visit http://localhost:8080 in a web browser and log in with "admin" as the username and "prom-operator" as the password. Once authenticated, you will be presented with the following page, as seen in Figure 13-1.

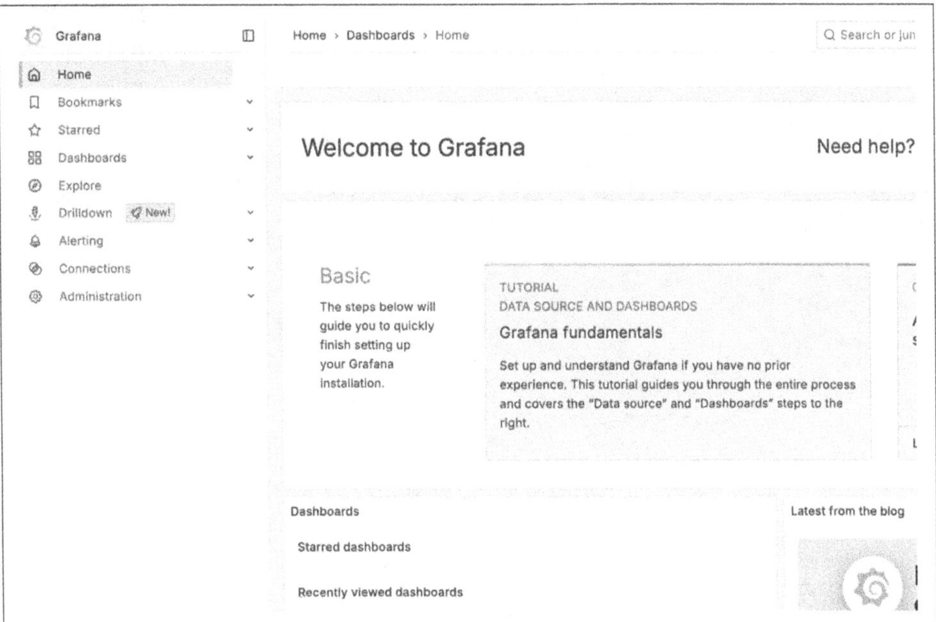


*Figure 13-1. Grafana overview page*

From here, you can click on Dashboards, which will take you to the *dashboard* overview page, as seen in Figure 13-2.

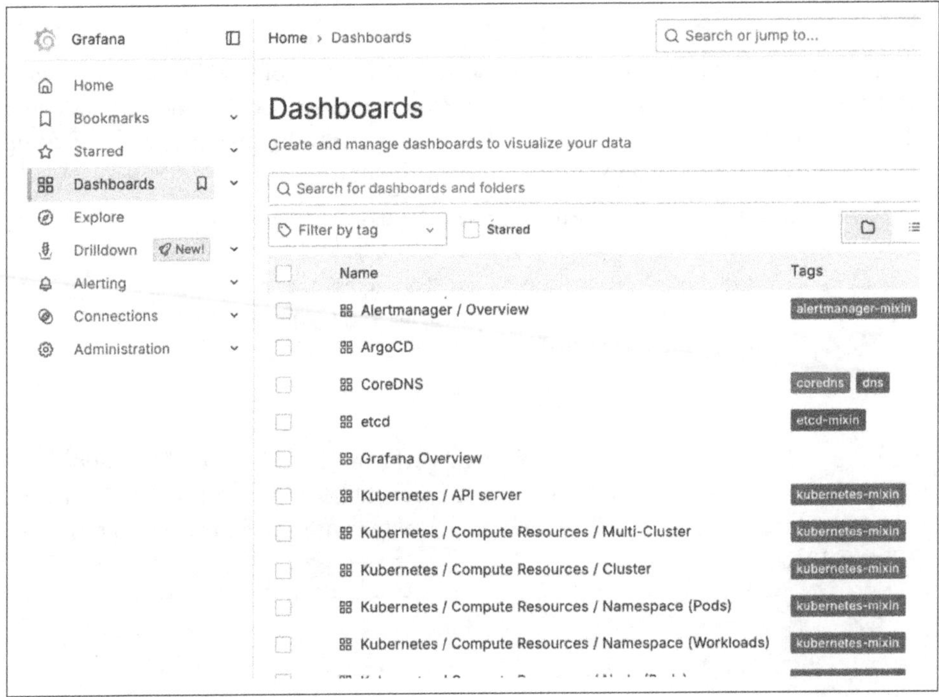


*Figure 13-2. Dashboard overview*

From here, select ArgoCD to be taken to the Argo CD metrics dashboard. The dashboard will appear similar to the depiction in Figure 13-3.

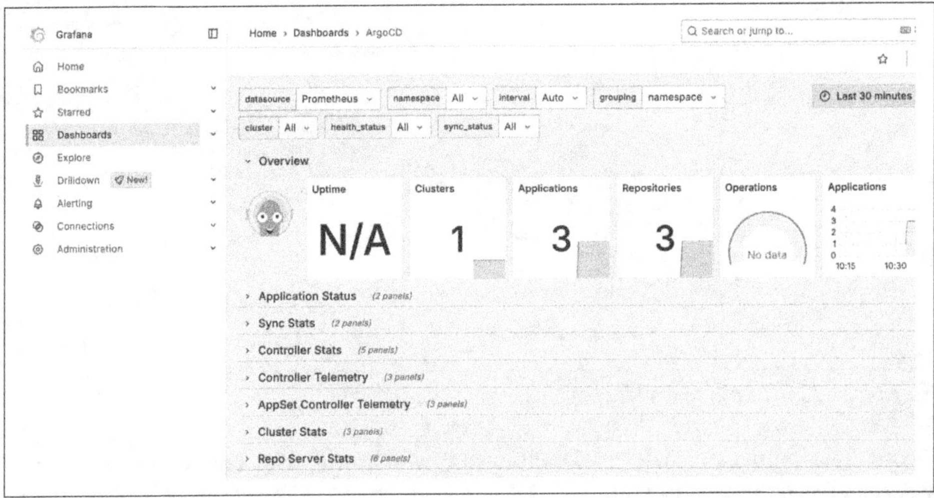


*Figure 13-3. Argo CD metrics page*

Feel free to explore the available metrics. You will see things that aren't normally visible in the Argo CD UI; for example, system-based metrics like Memory Usage, CPU Usage, and Goroutines (*https://oreil.ly/uUOtp*). These metrics go beyond just Argo CD Application–specific metrics and also include the platform performance; as a whole.

## Notifications

Argo CD Notifications is an essential extension for Argo CD. The premise of Argo CD Notifications is that it continuously monitors Argo CD Application events, including (but not limited to) successful syncs, failed syncs, when an Application is deployed, or when an Application enters a degraded stage. It also provides a flexible mechanism to notify users about important changes in the Application state. Leveraging a system of triggers and templates, it allows users to configure when notifications should be sent and customize the notification content to provide any relevant information.

Argo CD Notifications includes a catalog of useful pre-built notification *triggers* and *templates*, enabling teams to quickly set up notifications without the need to create new notifications from scratch. These triggers and templates are stored in the `argocd-notifications-cm` ConfigMap in the `argocd` namespace.

For example, the following template will send information about the sync status of an Argo CD Application:

```
apiVersion: v1
kind: ConfigMap
metadata:
  name: argocd-notifications-cm
data:
  template.my-custom-template-slack-template: |
    message: |
      Application {{.app.metadata.name}} sync is {{.app.status.sync.status}}.
      Application details: {{.context.argocdUrl}}/applications/{{.app.metadata.name}}.
```

While templates are used to generate the notification content, triggers define the condition of when the notification needs to be sent. The definition includes items like name, condition, and notification template reference. For example, the following trigger sends a notification when an Argo CD Application sync was successful:

```
apiVersion: v1
kind: ConfigMap
metadata:
  name: argocd-notifications-cm
data:
  trigger.on-sync-succeeded: |
    - description: Application syncing has succeeded
      send:
      - app-sync-succeeded
      when: app.status.operationState.phase in ['Succeeded']
```

Note that it defines which template to use when sending the notification. In the previous example, the `app-sync-succeeded` template will be used.

Another component of Argo CD Notifications is the *Notification Services*. These services include the receiving end of the notification process—Slack, email, GitHub, and the catchall webhook, as it can invoke arbitrary endpoints. Depending on your organization, you may elect to only send notifications that are critical (like using the email service to send an alert to PagerDuty) or just informational, like sending a notification to a Slack channel.

In this section, we will be setting up Mattermost, an open source chat platform, to receive notifications from Argo CD.

## Installing Mattermost

We will be using Helm to install Mattermost, as well as several of its dependencies. In order to install the Mattermost Helm chart, you will need to add the repository and update the content. Run the following command to add the repository:

```
$ helm repo add mattermost https://helm.mattermost.com
```

Next, run the following to update the repository definitions:

```
$ helm repo update
```

Once complete, you can use the Helm chart and values provided in the accompanying Git repository to install the Mattermost Operator and the required PostgreSQL database:

```
$ helm upgrade -i --dependency-update mattermost-operator \
-n mattermost-operator --create-namespace ch13/helm/charts/mattermost/
```

The Helm chart installs the Mattermost Operator and database, but not Mattermost itself. To install Mattermost, you will need to apply the Mattermost custom resource to instantiate the instance. The custom resource is included within the Git repo. Execute the following command to apply the configuration:

```
$ kubectl apply -f ch13/manifests/mattermost.yaml
```

After a few moments, the Mattermost stack should be running in the `mattermost-operator` namespace along with its dependencies:

```
$ kubectl get pods -n mattermost-operator
NAME                                   READY   STATUS    RESTARTS   AGE
mattermost-b948dc97c-2khkk             1/1     Running   0          116s
mattermost-operator-679d85f859-wsrft   1/1     Running   0          13m
mattermost-operator-postgresql-0       1/1     Running   0          13m
minio-868f8c994b-2cljs                 1/1     Running   0          116s
```

## Configuring Mattermost

Now that Mattermost and its dependencies are up and running, you will need to perform the initial configuration of the stack in order for it to receive notifications from Argo CD. Visit *https://mattermost.upandrunning.local* and you should see a page similar to Figure 13-4.

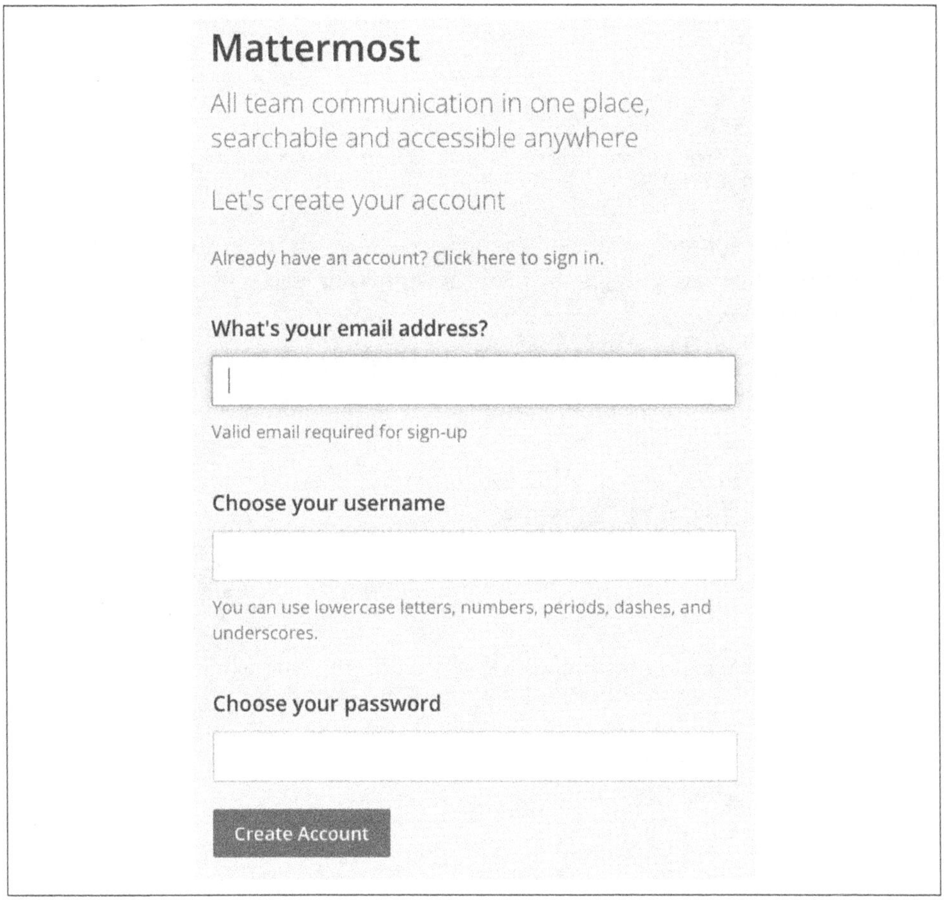

*Figure 13-4. Mattermost setup*

Here, you can enter an email address, a username, and a password. Once complete, click on Create Account. This will take you to the next page, where you can join a team. Since this is a new installation, there will not be any team to join, as depicted in Figure 13-5.

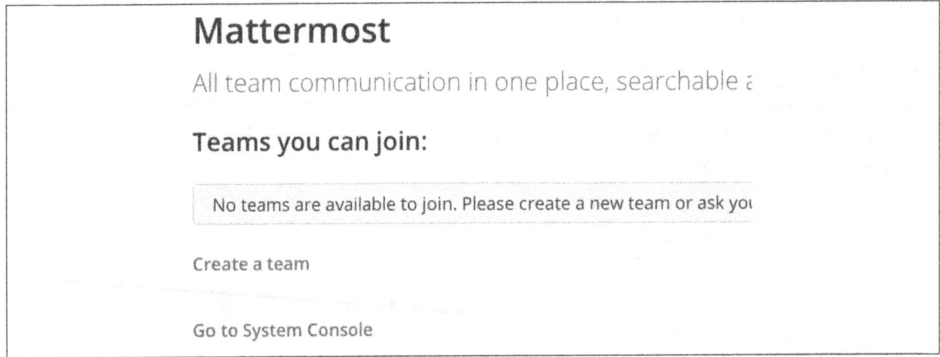


*Figure 13-5. Join a team page*

Since no team has been previously created, create a new team by clicking on the "Create a team" line and entering the name **devops**, as in Figure 13-6.

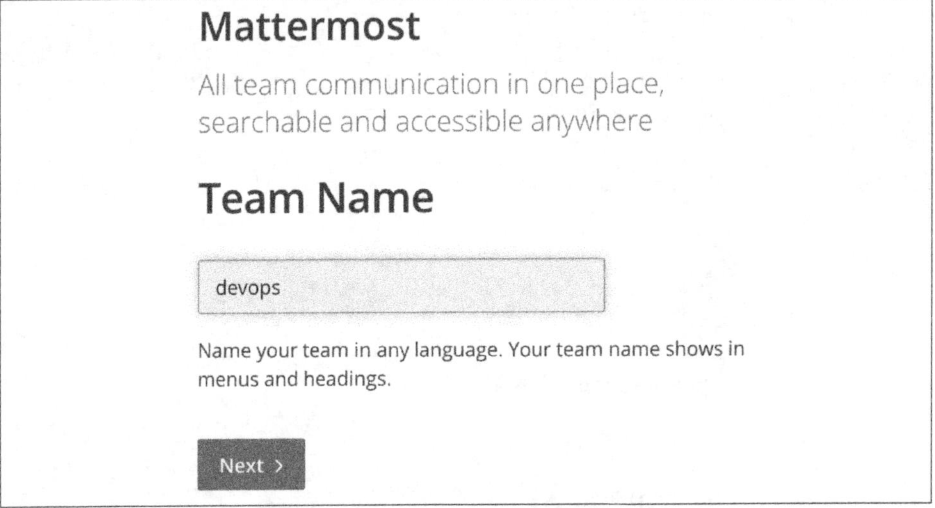


*Figure 13-6. Create DevOps team*

After clicking Next, a confirmation page will be displayed. Verify the team URL name, as it should appear similar to Figure 13-7.

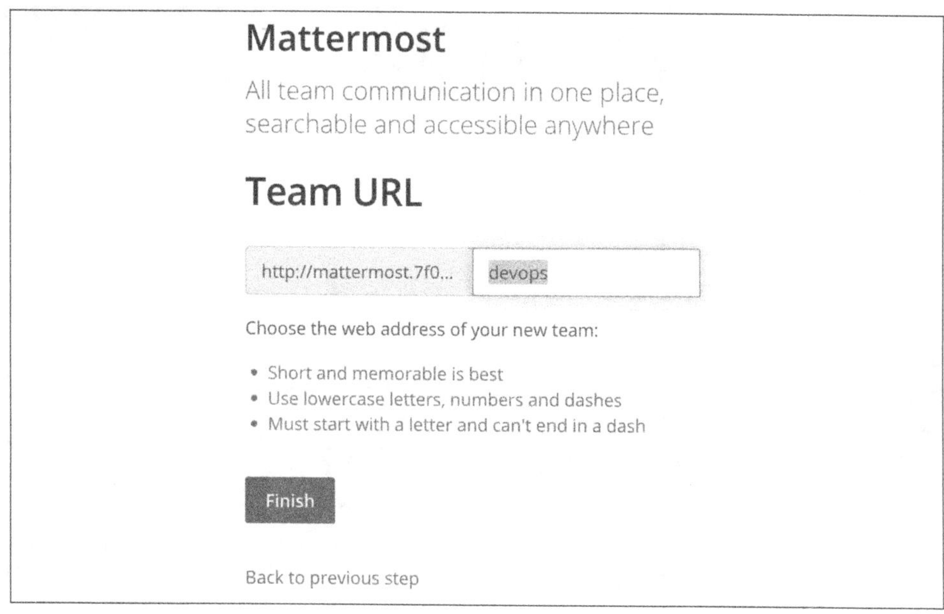


*Figure 13-7. Team confirmation page*

Now, on the following page, click on the three-line hamburger menu and select System Console, as shown in Figure 13-8.

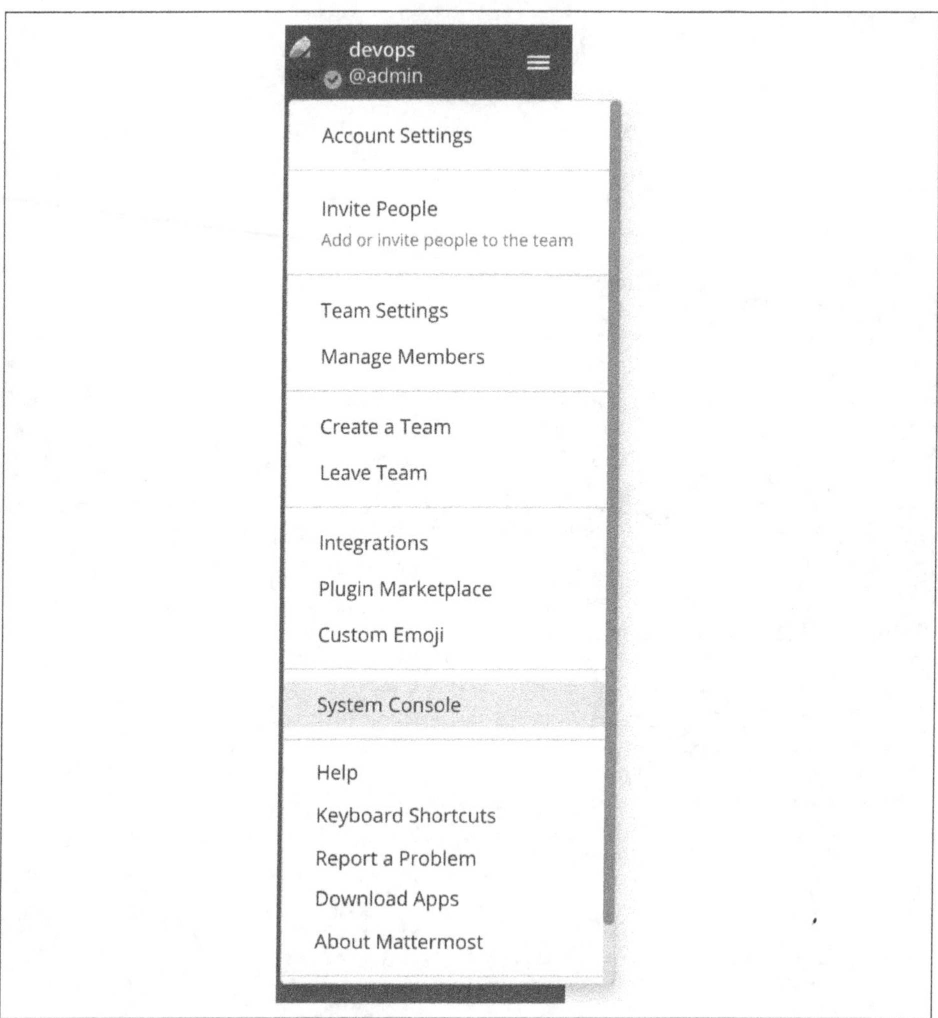


*Figure 13-8. Selecting System Console*

On the System Console page, scroll down on the left navigation bar and select Bot Accounts under Integrations, as shown in Figure 13-9.

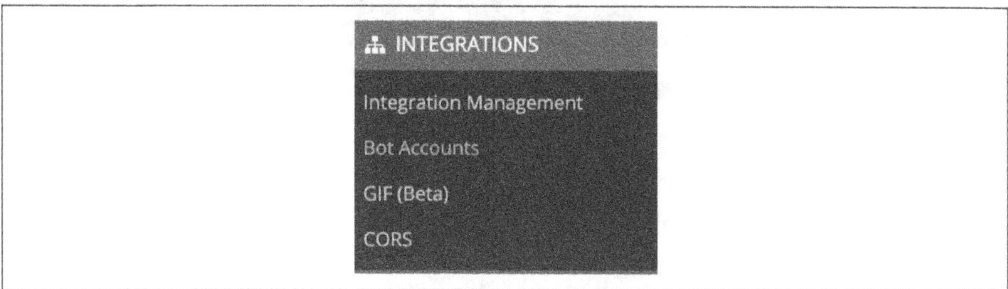


*Figure 13-9. Integration Bot Account settings*

In the Bot Accounts configuration page, select "true" next to the Enable Bot Account Creation setting, as shown in Figure 13-10.

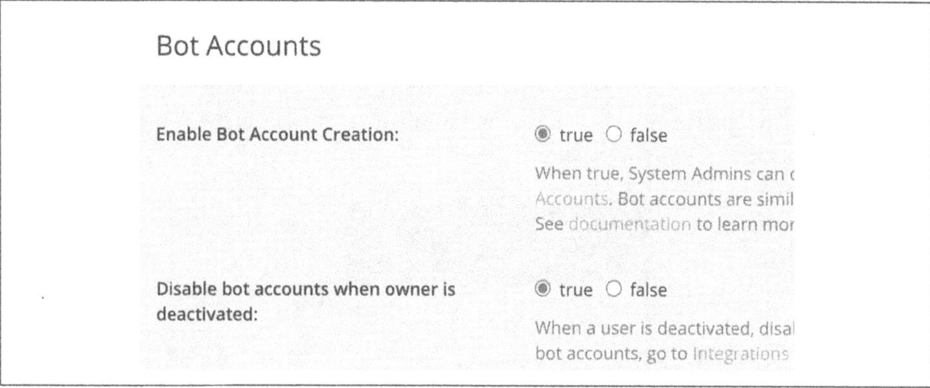


*Figure 13-10. Enable Bot Account Creation*

Click Save and then click on the hamburger menu button on the top left and select "Switch to devops," as shown in Figure 13-11.

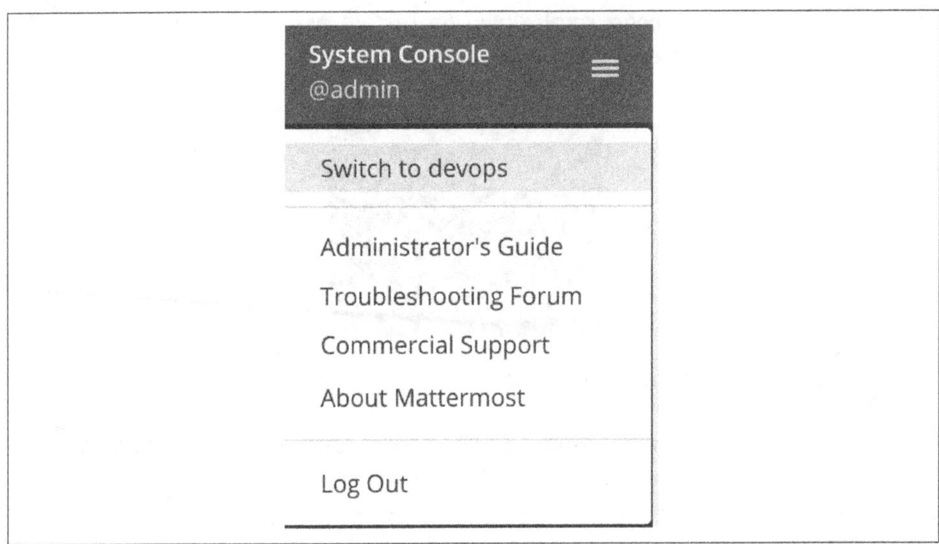


*Figure 13-11. Switching to DevOps*

Back in the DevOps team page, select the hamburger menu on the top left again and select Integrations, as shown in Figure 13-12.

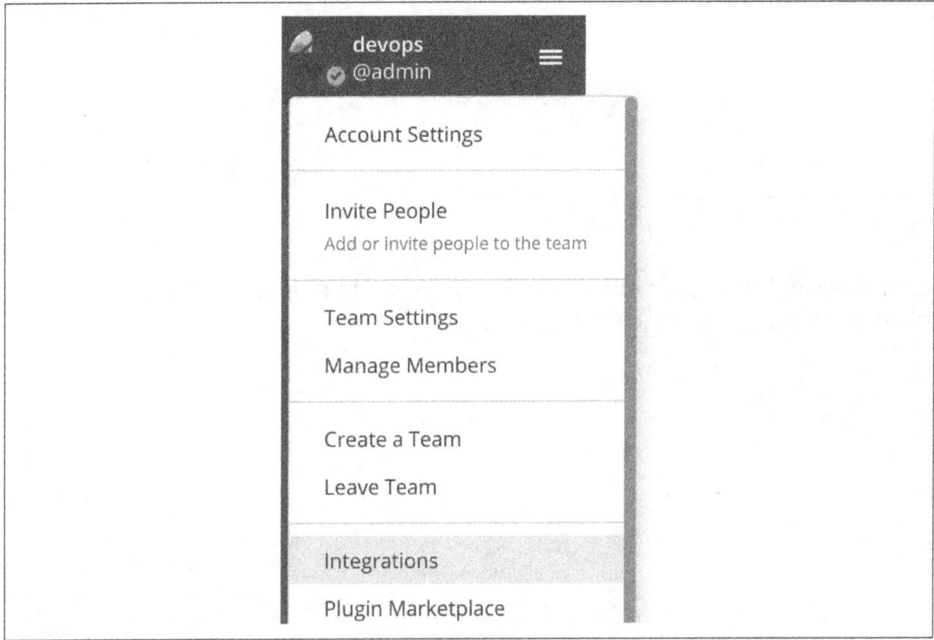


*Figure 13-12. Selecting Integrations*

On the left navigation menu, click on Bot Accounts, and then click on the Add Bot Account button. This will take you to the Add Bot Account page. Here, enter "argocd-notifications" as the username for the bot account, leaving the rest as the defaults, and click on Create Bot Account at the bottom of the page. Once the bot account has been created, the resulting page will display your bot's token, as shown in Figure 13-13.

Bot Accounts > Add

Setup Successful

Your bot account **argocd-notifications** has been created successfully. Please use the following further details).

**Token**: tm4j8djeybyw7pq1mfzi3zzaue

Make sure to add this bot account to teams and channels you want it to interact in. See docum

*Figure 13-13. Token page*

Your token *will* be different.

Make note of this token, as you won't be able to see it again (you can always re-create the token if needed). Click on the Done button on the bottom right to complete the bot account creation process.

Next, on the top left, click on "Back to Mattermost." There, you will now need to invite the bot to your team. To complete this task, click on the hamburger menu on the top left again and select Invite People. On the "Invite Members to devops" page, add the *@argocd-notifications* bot account, as shown in Figure 13-14.

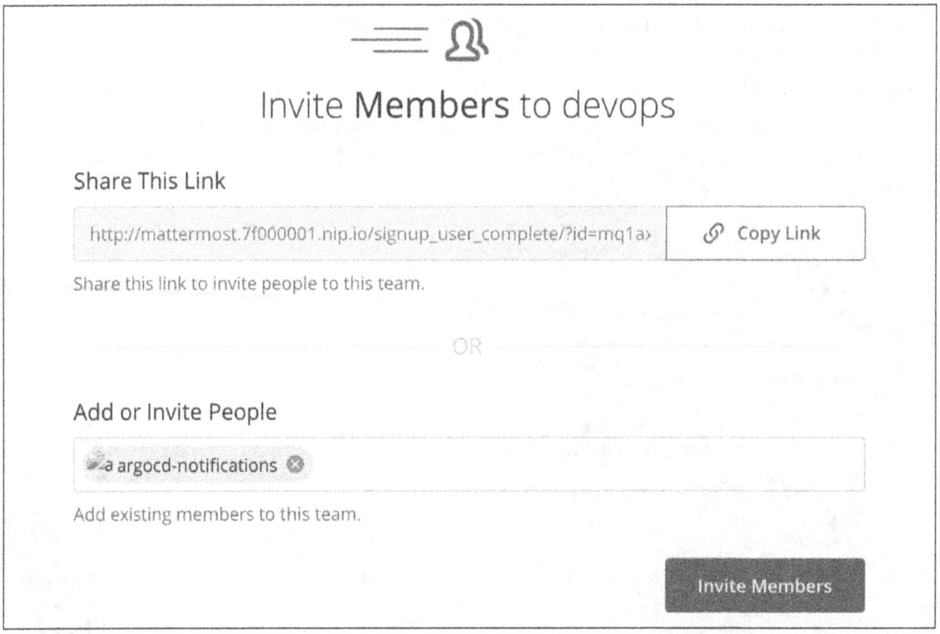

*Figure 13-14. Inviting argocd-notifications*

Click on Invite Members; on the following page, click on the Done button to return to the DevOps team page. Add a channel by clicking the "+" symbol next to the PUBLIC CHANNELS navigation on the lefthand side of the page. This will bring up the New Channel dialog box. Enter **appstatus** in the Name field, as shown in Figure 13-15.

New Channel ×

Type

Public - Anyone can join this channel

Private - Only invited members can join this channel

Name

appstatus

URL: /appstatus (Edit)

Purpose *(optional)*

E.g.: "A channel to file bugs and improvements"

Describe how this channel should be used.

Header *(optional)*

E.g.: "[Link Title](http://example.com)"

Set text that will appear in the header of the channel beside the channel name. For example, include frequently used links by typing [Link Title] (http://example.com).

Cancel Create Channel

*Figure 13-15. Setting up appstatus channel*

Leaving the remaining fields at their default values, click on Create Channel. Once the channel has been created, you will return to the DevOps team page. Here, select the newly created "appstatus" channel by clicking on it on the left navigation bar. Then, in the chat input field, type **/invite @argocd-notifications**, as shown in Figure 13-16.

You might need to click on Skip Tutorial or go through the tutorial before you can invite the bot to the "appstatus" channel you just created.

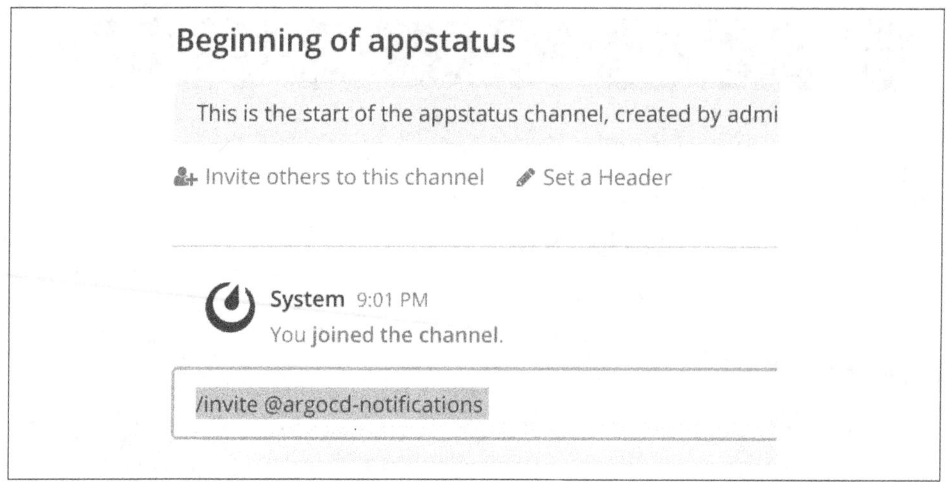


*Figure 13-16. Invite argocd-notifications bot*

Press Enter, and your bot should be added to the channel now. Next, on the top left where it displays "appstatus," you'll see a down arrow. Click on it and select View Info, as shown in Figure 13-17.

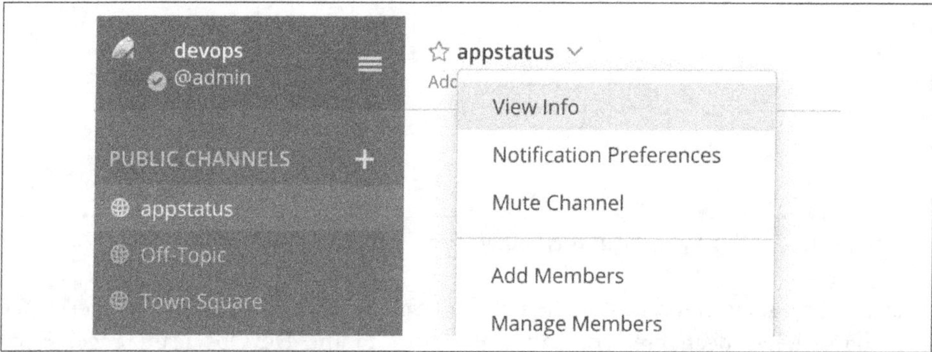


*Figure 13-17. View Info selection*

On the "About appstatus" page, make note of the channel ID, as it will be needed later on. A depiction will appear similar to Figure 13-18.

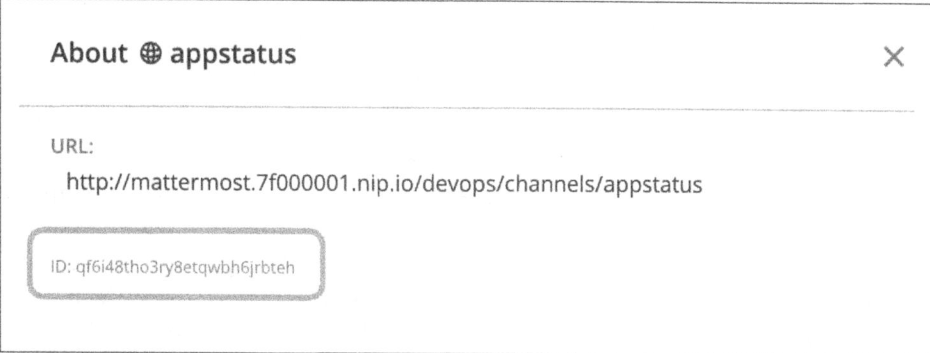


*Figure 13-18. About appstatus ID dialog*

Note that we've outlined the ID in a red square, as it's hard to see on the pop-up. Also note that your ID *will* be different based on your environment. Go ahead and close this pop-up by clicking on the X in the upper right corner.

Now that you have set up Mattermost and you have made note of your Token ID and your Channel ID, you can move on to integrating Argo CD Notifications.

## Setting Up Argo CD Notifications

We will be using Helm to upgrade the configuration of Argo CD to send notifications. We will use the chart to add an Argo CD Notifications template and a trigger as well. We will also use the Helm chart to tell Argo CD about the Mattermost token that was created in the previous section.

By inspecting the template we will be using found in the *ch13/helm/values/argocd-notification-values.yaml* file, you will see the following (code has been cut off for space reasons):

```
notifications:
  templates:
    template.app-sync-succeeded: |
      message: |
        Application {{.app.metadata.name}} has been successfully synced at ...
        Sync operation details are available at: {{.context.argocdUrl}}...
      mattermost:
        attachments: "[{\n  \"title\": \"{{ .app.metadata.name}}\",\n  \"title_link\"...
```

This is the template that will be used when sending a message to the Mattermost channel we configured in the previous section. Take note here where we define the name of service under the `message` section, which is set to `mattermost`. The trigger for this template can be seen in the same *ch13/helm/values/argocd-notification-values.yaml* file:

```
notifications:
  triggers:
    trigger.on-sync-succeeded: |
      - description: Application syncing has succeeded
        send:
        - app-sync-succeeded
        when: app.status.operationState.phase in ['Succeeded']
```

Here, the trigger is configured to send the `app-sync-succeeded` template (with the relevant data) when an Application has successfully performed a sync. Using the token from the previous step where you created the *argocd-notifications* bot account, set up the Argo CD Notification integration with Mattermost using the Helm *ch13/helm/values/argocd-notification-values.yaml* values file provided, replacing ***`<token>`*** with your Mattermost bot token:

```
$ helm upgrade -i argocd -n argocd --create-namespace \
--reuse-values --values ch13/helm/values/argocd-notification-values.yaml \
--set notifications.secret.items.mattermost-token=<token> argo/argo-cd
```

You can verify that the configuration has been set properly by running `kubectl get cm argocd-notifications-cm -n argocd -o yaml` and `kubectl get secret argocd-notifications-secret -n argocd -o yaml`. The output should show the configuration update we provided in the Helm values file.

The next step is to set up a subscription on an Argo CD Application, which is how Argo CD knows when to set a notification. A *subscription* on an Argo CD Application can be defined using the `notifications.argoproj.io/subscribe.<trigger>.<service>: <recipient>` annotation on the Application object where `<trigger>` is the `on-sync-succeeded` trigger we added, `<service>` is `mattermost` (which is configured in the template), and `<recipient>` is the channel ID you copied from the previous section.

To demonstrate the use of Argo CD Notifications, we will first deploy a sample Application included for this chapter and wait for it to sync:

```
$ argocd app create --file ch13/argocd/simple-go.yaml
$ argocd app sync argocd/ch13-simplego
```

Now that the Argo CD Application is applied and synced, we will subscribe it to the notification engine by providing the proper annotation, replacing ***`<channel-id>`*** with the channel ID you copied in the previous section:

```
$ kubectl annotate application ch13-simplego -n argocd \
notifications.argoproj.io/subscribe.on-sync-succeeded.mattermost=<channel-id>
```

Next, sync the Argo CD Application:

```
$ argocd app sync argocd/ch13-simplego
```

By executing this command, a notification will be sent to the "appstatus" channel on your Mattermost installation. The received notification should look similar to Figure 13-19.

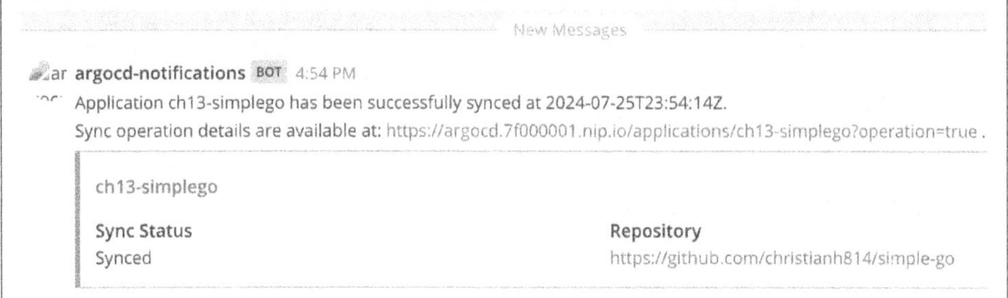


*Figure 13-19. Notification sent*

You can send notifications to multiple channels by listing them in the annotation separated by semicolons. For example, `channel-id1;channel=id2`.

As demonstrated by this use case, integrating Argo CD Notifications into your deployment process enhances observability, reliability, and responsiveness, ensuring that teams are promptly informed about the state of their applications and deployments, allowing them to swiftly address any issues and maintain the desired state of their applications.

# High Availability

Argo CD operates in a stateless architecture, ensuring robustness and reliability. All data used for Argo CD is persisted as Kubernetes objects, which are subsequently stored in Kubernetes' etcd datastore. Redis is utilized within Argo CD solely as a transient cache, meaning it serves to temporarily store data to improve performance. Should Redis be lost or experience failure, it poses no risk to the continuity of service, as the cache can be seamlessly rebuilt without any data loss or service disruption when the cache system returns online. This design choice puts the responsibility of high availability onto Kubernetes to reschedule Pods and other workloads to different nodes. This means that if Argo CD is running on a highly available Kubernetes installation, Argo CD will be highly available.

Still, more resiliency can still be achieved, even in a relatively robust environment. To that end, Argo CD does provide a mechanism for running Argo CD in a highly available configuration. This mechanism can be accomplished using the Argo CD Helm chart. There are two primary ways of deploying Argo CD in high availability (HA) mode: using autoscaling of pods or setting a fixed number of pods.

If you're using the `kind` cluster, the following won't work. You will need a multinode (minimum of three) Kubernetes cluster. You can view how to create a multiple-node cluster in the kind documentation page (*https://oreil.ly/ok4ro*).

To use HA mode, the following Helm values can be used:

```
redis-ha:
  enabled: true

controller:
  replicas: 1 # We will scale this controller in a different section

server:
  replicas: 2

repoServer:
  replicas: 2

applicationSet:
  replicas: 2
```

To use HA mode with autoscaling, the following Helm values can be used:

```
redis-ha:
  enabled: true

controller:
  replicas: 1

server:
  autoscaling:
    enabled: true
    minReplicas: 2

repoServer:
  autoscaling:
    enabled: true
    minReplicas: 2

applicationSet:
  replicas: 2
```

The `controller.replicas` section is set to 1 because setting it to anything higher will enable sharding. Sharding will be covered in the next section.

Once you have set those values, you can use Helm to upgrade an existing release to use the HA configuration. For example:

```
$ helm upgrade -i argocd -n argocd --reuse-values \
--values your-values-argocd-ha.yaml argo/argo-cd
```

Running Argo CD in an HA configuration assumes you are running at *least* three worker nodes in your Kubernetes environment. The reason for this is that Argo CD deploys Redis using a StatefulSet with `podAntiAffinity` rules that is configured to not schedule two of the same Redis pods on the same node. The reason that three is needed is that it's the minimum number of replicas required for Redis to reach quorum. For more information about the configuration needed to achieve HA with Redis, you can read its documentation (*https://oreil.ly/NImCm*).

It's recommended to set affinity rules as well for the controllers you are scaling to take advantage of the additional nodes.

# Scalability

Scalability is another important topic that goes hand in hand with high availability. While high availability helps with scalability, that is not the main focus. Further configuration must be completed in order to achieve scalability, beyond just setting up high availability. While how you scale will depend on a number of factors, the two most common things to take into account are scaling up and scaling out (sharding).

## Scaling Up

The quickest way to get the most out of your Argo CD installation is to add more resources to each component. Each component is configured with sensible defaults with respect to resource limits and requests. These defaults are satisfactory for most cases for the majority of workloads. As your organization grows, and your Argo CD implementation gets busier and busier, you may find the need to adjust these limits. Table 13-1 summarizes each Argo CD component, what they are used for, and some of the considerations when scaling up your installation.

*Table 13-1. Argo CD components summary*

| Controller | When to scale |
|---|---|
| Redis | When your installation is sending a lot of requests to Kubernetes; also when you have a lot of repositories or large repositories |
| Application controller | When you have many Applications, where it might take some time to get the statuses of all Applications |
| API server | A busy system in a multi-tenant setup where UI and CLI are becoming slow |
| Repo server | When you have many repos and/or when you have a large mono-repo (a single repository with most or all K8S resources) |
| ApplicationSet controller | When you have many ApplicationSets or when you have ApplicationSets that generate many Applications |

You can use the Argo CD Helm chart to set the resources for each component. The following is an example set of values that can be used as a baseline. Keep in mind that your settings will be different, depending on a number of factors, like your specific implementation, environment, and Kubernetes cluster settings:

```
redis:
  resources:
    limits:
      cpu: 200m
      memory: 128Mi
    requests:
      cpu: 100m
      memory: 64Mi

controller:
  resources:
    limits:
      cpu: 500m
      memory: 512Mi
    requests:
      cpu: 250m
      memory: 256Mi

server:
  resources:
    limits:
      cpu: 100m
      memory: 128Mi
    requests:
      cpu: 50m
      memory: 64Mi

repoServer:
  resources:
    limits:
      cpu: 50m
      memory: 128Mi
    requests:
      cpu: 10m
      memory: 64Mi

applicationSet:
  resources:
    limits:
      cpu: 100m
      memory: 128Mi
    requests:
      cpu: 100m
      memory: 128Mi
```

Once you set your desired settings, you can use Helm to upgrade your Argo CD installation with the values in the following command:

```
$ helm upgrade -i argo-cd -n argocd --reuse-values \
--values  sample-argo-cd-resources-values.yaml argo/argo-cd
```

It's recommended to monitor your Argo CD consumption (using Prometheus and Grafana, for example) and adjust these accordingly once you have some historical data.

## Sharding

In the previous section on high availability, it was noted that the number of Application controller replicas was set to 1. This is because scaling the Application controller not only gives you high availability, but it also enables sharding for the Argo CD installation. In this section, we will introduce sharding and how it can be enabled in your Argo CD installation.

Sharding occurs at the Application controller level and focuses solely on the managed clusters that you have added to Argo CD during a sync operation. When your Argo CD installation is set up for sharding, each managed cluster will use one of the shards to perform the duties of the Application controller (syncing state is one example). How Argo CD decides which managed cluster uses which shard depends on which algorithm is being used. As of this writing, there are two algorithms available, `legacy` and `round-robin`:

`legacy`
: This is the default algorithm and uses a unique identifier (UID)-based distribution of sync operations (which is nonuniform). This means that you may not get an even distribution of shards to managed clusters.

`round-robin`
: This algorithm uses an equal distribution across all shards. As of this writing, this method of sharding is considered "alpha."

We are going to be using the `legacy` algorithm for this section, since `round-robin` is still in its first phase of development at the time of this writing. Also, practically speaking, `round-robin` is a good use case for when you're adding/removing managed clusters frequently. Generally speaking, `legacy` is recommended and will work for most use cases.

The Argo CD Application controller runs in a StatefulSet and can be viewed by executing the following command:

```
$ kubectl get statefulset -n argocd
NAME                            READY   AGE
argocd-application-controller   1/1     66m
```

View the pods associated with this StatefulSet:

```
$ kubectl get pods -n argocd  -l app.kubernetes.io/component=application-controller
NAME                              READY   STATUS    RESTARTS   AGE
argocd-application-controller-0   1/1     Running   0          66m
```

The 0 not only denotes the ID of this Pod for the StatefulSet, but it's also used by Argo CD to identify shards. Currently, since there's only one Application controller pod, all Argo CD Application operations are being handled by this one resource. And, if you recall, we added a cluster in Chapter 7, so you can see which shard is being used for these operations:

```
$ argocd admin cluster stats -n argocd
SERVER                          SHARD  CONNECTION  NAMESPACES COUNT  APPS COUNT ...
https://192.168.4.134:60183     0                  1                 0          ...
https://kubernetes.default.svc  0                  4                 0          ...
```

The IP of your cluster, and list above, may be different.

To add additional shards, you scale up the replicas and mirror that configuration with the `ARGOCD_CONTROLLER_REPLICAS` environment variable in the Application controller StatefulSet. This can be accomplished easily with the Helm chart. Taking a look at the values found in the *ch13/helm/values/argocd-sharding-values.yaml* file in the accompanying Git repository, you should see the following:

```
controller:
  replicas: 2
```

That's it! Using Helm with the provided values file, you can enable sharding with the following command:

```
$ helm upgrade -i argocd -n argocd --reuse-values \
--values ch13/helm/values/argocd-sharding-values.yaml argo/argo-cd
```

This should have scaled the StatefulSet to two replicas:

```
$ kubectl get sts -n argocd
NAME                            READY   AGE
argocd-application-controller   2/2     129m
```

Checking the pods, you should have a pod with a 0 and another with a 1:

```
$ kubectl get pods -n argocd -l app.kubernetes.io/component=application-controller
NAME                              READY   STATUS    RESTARTS   AGE
argocd-application-controller-0   1/1     Running   0          3m5s
argocd-application-controller-1   1/1     Running   0          3m15s
```

This corresponds to shard 0 and shard 1, respectively. Taking a look at the clusters and shards, you will notice that both clusters are still being managed by shard 0:

```
$ argocd admin cluster stats -n argocd
SERVER                          SHARD  CONNECTION  NAMESPACES COUNT  APPS COUNT ...
https://192.168.4.134:60183     0                  1                 0          ...
https://kubernetes.default.svc  0                  4                 0          ...
```

Since we are using the `legacy` algorithm, the algorithm chooses the shard based on a hash of the UID, which is then assigned based on the modulo of that hash. As your implementation grows more and more as you add clusters, you will notice that this method creates an "imbalance," and "hot spots" (where one shard is doing more work than the others) can occur. To remedy this, it's recommended to assign shards to clusters.

In Chapter 7, you learned that cluster definitions are stored as Kubernetes Secrets. In order to assign a shard to a cluster, you update the cluster secret with the shard ID by adding the `data.shard` field in the secret with the corresponding shard ID.

Taking a look at the cluster that was added, we'll need the name:

```
$ kubectl get secrets -n argocd -l argocd.argoproj.io/secret-type=cluster
NAME      TYPE      DATA   AGE
remote    Opaque    3      154m
```

Add the `data.shard` field in the secret by patching the Secret using `stringData` and the value of 1:

```
$ kubectl patch secret remote -n argocd --patch '{"stringData":{"shard":"1"}}'
```

You can verify this by again listing which shard is managing which cluster. You will see that shard 1 is now managing the cluster:

```
$ argocd admin cluster stats -n argocd
SERVER                           SHARD  CONNECTION  NAMESPACES COUNT  APPS COUNT  ...
https://192.168.4.134:60183      1                  1                 0           ...
https://kubernetes.default.svc   0                  4                 0           ...
```

The default behavior is that the defined shard will be used for Argo CD Application operations unless the shard pod goes away. The default timeout for checking the shard health is 10 seconds. Each controller replica is trying to "claim" the shard (by updating the field in a config map), "holds" it for 10 seconds, and must renew before the hold expires. So, if one replica dies, then another replica will pick up a shard at least 10 seconds later. To change the default 10-second timeout, you can change the value of `controller.heartbeatTime` to your desired timeout in your values file.

It's recommended that you treat shard-to-cluster ratios in a 1:1 relationship on very busy systems. Another method is to have two to three shards handling all your preprod environments and have dedicated shards for each cluster in your prod environment. In the end, you will have to use data collected from monitoring Argo CD to determine which direction you ultimately head toward.

## Summary

Operationalizing Argo CD in an enterprise environment is crucial for ensuring robust and efficient deployments within a Kubernetes ecosystem. Integrating monitoring capabilities with tools, like Prometheus and Grafana, provides insights into deployment status and health, enabling swift detection and resolution of issues. This integration offers a comprehensive view beyond Argo CD's native interface, allowing for proactive issue detection, efficient troubleshooting, and informed decision-making. Coupled with notifications, stakeholders are immediately informed of changes or problems, ensuring prompt responses and mitigating downtime. High availability and scalability further enhance Argo CD's reliability and capacity to manage increasing applications and clusters as the adoption grows.

# CHAPTER 14
# Future Considerations

Throughout this book, we have focused on the general operationalization of Argo CD, including deploying, configuring, and managing the application. While we touched on several different technologies and practices, the ecosystem surrounding Argo CD is much broader, and other considerations will need to be taken into account as you progress through your Argo CD journey. This ecosystem is still evolving, and many patterns are emerging, so it is important to know how to engage with the community and investigate new practices, patterns, and common approaches.

This chapter will provide the context and resources you need to get the most out of your Argo CD implementation—both now and in the future.

## GitOps Is Still Evolving

While operationalizing Argo CD is an important topic, it is imperative to recognize that Argo CD was built with GitOps at its core. This alignment necessitates that any effort to operationalize Argo CD should inherently incorporate GitOps best practices and strategic pattern planning to maximize the efficiency and effectiveness of any Argo CD implementation. To achieve optimal results, it is essential to consider the broader implications of GitOps to better integrate it with DevOps. This will contribute significantly to the robustness of your Argo CD implementation.

While the GitOps principles (*https://opengitops.dev*) have reached v1.0, patterns and implementations are still evolving; best practices are emerging as adoption grows for not only Argo CD, but GitOps in general. Whether you are new to Argo CD and GitOps or are already running it in production, it's always good to see what patterns organizations are using to make the most of their approaches. In this section, we will be highlighting some of the emerging patterns and best practices, including what to consider when structuring your GitOps directory, rendered manifest patterns, and

GitOps workflows. Understanding these can take your Argo CD and GitOps journey to the next level.

## GitOps Directory Structure Considerations

One of the initial hurdles organizations must face when adopting GitOps is deciding how to best organize their Git directory structure. Since Git has become the interface for how an organization interacts with important application deployments and infrastructure management concerns, it is imperative that these fundamental design concerns are addressed upfront. With this in mind, there isn't, unfortunately, a one-size-fits-all solution or universally accepted repository layout. The central theme around the structure of a GitOps directory has a lot to do with Conway's law, which states (adapted from the original wording):

> Any organization that designs a system (defined broadly) will produce a design whose structure is a copy of the organization's communication structure.
>
> —Melvin E. Conway

In short, how your organization and/or team is structured will dictate how your directory structure is implemented, and not the other way around. Organizational boundaries and separation of responsibilities will also have a large influence on your GitOps directory structure implementation.

Keeping Conway's law in mind, if you find your directory structure isn't working for you, you either need to change your directory structure or change your communication/interaction structure in your organization (the former is typically much easier). Even though there is no generic GitOps directory structure that works for all, there are some general guidelines that you can follow to make the most of your implementation.

### The DRY approach

When structuring directories, you want to follow the same programming principles as you do in the infrastructure-as-code realm of GitOps. You should avoid applying redundant actions and instead make use of the practice of DRY, which stands for "Don't repeat yourself." Since the focus of this book has been centered on Argo CD and Kubernetes, you can think of the "Y" in *DRY* as standing for *YAML*.

It's possible that storing everything in Git can lead to the same YAML being repeated because similar workloads are deployed across multiple environments. However, you can avoid repeating a lot of the same YAML by using configuration management tools. This will keep your repository clean and easy to understand and avoids any unnecessary duplication of manifests.

There are many to choose from, but we recommend using Kustomize and/or Helm since Argo CD has native support for these two tools. They will help you to keep the base configuration of your deployment and then store the deltas as patched overlays (in the case of Kustomize) or different values files (in the case of Helm). Since Argo CD has support for config management plugins (as covered in Chapter 11), the configuration management tool you use does not matter as long as you follow the DRY principle.

### Parameterize where you can

While Kustomize is a popular choice, and is also supported natively with Argo CD, it is important to note that there are certain situations where patching manifests with Kustomize does not make sense. Although patching YAML is easy when you already know the values beforehand, there are occasions when you will not know the desired value that should be specified. In many cases, this is due to details related to the destination of the manifests.

An example of this situation can be found with the host field in an Ingress object, which specifies the fully qualified domain name (FQDN) that can be used to access an application available within the cluster. The challenge comes to a head when you're deploying across a fleet of Kubernetes clusters with varying FQDNs that you may not know until deployment time.

This is where parameterizing your configurations provides the greatest benefit and where Helm truly shines. It is also the primary reason why Helm was chosen as the tool of choice in this book. Helm allows you to parameterize certain fields and abstracts away a lot of nuances of Kubernetes manifests, which is attractive if you're running a multi-tenant system where developers just want to focus on getting their applications deployed. In reality, you will most likely use a combination of Kustomize and Helm.

Utilizing the best of both tools, you should be able to limit the amount of manifest duplication in your GitOps deployments.

### How many repositories are needed?

The most common best practice is to separate your deployment manifests away from the same repository that the source code of your application lives in. There are many resources on this topic, but generally speaking, this principle exists because application and GitOps configurations typically have different lifecycles and are (in many instances) managed completely differently by different teams. So, as a general practice, it is recommended that each be kept separate in their own management process and structure.

But how many repositories are the right amount?

Some organizations store everything in what we call a *monolithic repo* (monorepo). A *monorepo* is where all Kubernetes manifests reside in a single repository for an organization. This is usually where organizations start, and there is typically a heavy emphasis on Kustomize in these repositories. The advantage of using a monorepo is that all the resources are managed centrally, and there is a single point of governance and management interface. However, there is a drawback, which is that Argo CD struggles, with respect to performance, with large monorepos. This is a known limit within Argo CD, which ultimately leads many organizations to favor polyrepos, which will be covered next. Those that do leverage a monorepo architecture for their GitOps manifests have to trade simplicity with a need to scale and tune the performance of Argo CD in order to achieve operational stability. Scaling and tuning Argo CD was covered in Chapter 13.

Polyrepos, as the name indicates, is the use of more than one repository to manage GitOps application deployment(s). Beyond that, they have a singular or siloed responsibility, and components from them can work with other repositories across the ecosystem. The most common starting point for organizations adopting GitOps with Argo CD is to have a control plane repository and an application deployment repository. A control plane repository stores resources needed to manage Argo CD itself. These include assets like (but not limited to) Argo CD AppProjects, Applications, Argo CD–specific Secrets, and ConfigMaps. In addition, the control plane repository is also used to store other supporting tools needed for organizational policies and governance—for example, manifests related to tools, like Kyverno, Istio, and External Secrets (to name a few). This repository is typically managed by a platform engineering or DevOps team, whereas the application deployment repository, in contrast, is used to store the actual application manifests used by Kubernetes. Those normally contain resources such as Deployments, Secrets, ConfigMaps, Ingress, and other related manifests. While most organizations start at two repositories, your case might be different and, in most cases, will include more than two. The number of repositories will increase depending on the separation of concerns and/or organizational boundaries that might exist. The main drawback for using this pattern is that it creates a large number of Git repositories, each having their own release process that needs to be coordinated. Still, the use of polyrepos is a popular approach, and it's the method used by Intuit (the creators of the Argo Project).

### Directory structure resources

As mentioned before, your Git repository structure will depend heavily on how your organization runs, is governed, and how it communicates with disparate teams. The repositories created will be a reflection of that fact. Another thing to take into consideration is how your current deployment + CI/CD workflow is implemented. This all makes logical sense when you start thinking about who has access to what resource. Developers will not need to modify platform configurations, and operators, who work on platforms, normally won't make changes in the source code of development teams.

Since aspiring to a single, general template GitOps repository structure is not feasible, and the answer will eventually result in "it depends," there are an assortment of examples that you can use to influence your approach. These also include several getting-started structures that provide a good foundation to build from:

*Christian Hernandez's (Akuity and coauthor of this book) GitOps 1:1 Repo (https://oreil.ly/-b9mt)*
: This repository outlines a 1:1, or repository to cluster, layout. This example can be expanded to be used as a monorepo or as a basis for a polyrepo.

*Gerald Nunn's (Red Hat) GitOps Standards (https://oreil.ly/_NRX-)*
: This repository illustrates the use of Gerald's GitOps standards, which is designed from his experiences working with his clients. It provides an example repository layout that includes how to handle multiple clusters using a monorepo design architecture.

*Johannes Schnatterer (Cloudogu GmbH), "GitOps Repository Structures and Patterns" (https://oreil.ly/sJZAn)*
: This blog describes the pros and cons of implementing a repo per team versus a repo for application approach and other important, related considerations with examples.

*The GitOps Bridge Project (https://oreil.ly/kl8id)*
: This project aims to unify infrastructure management with GitOps application deployment practices by providing a generic framework for building cloud infrastructure and using cloud metadata to enhance the GitOps controller (like Argo CD).

*Flux, "Ways of Structuring Your Repositories" (https://oreil.ly/aDoHN)*
: Although this article is focused solely on Argo CD, Flux CD has wide adoption and thus, a number of best practices of its own. Many of these can be used generally, regardless of which tool is being used, so it's worth taking a look at through the lens of Argo CD.

With these examples, you'll get a better sense of a good starting-off point for setting up your GitOps repositories.

## Rendered Manifests Pattern

Earlier in this section, we covered how to use the DRY method for managing Kubernetes manifests in a GitOps repository. This included suggestions around using configuration management tools to aid in keeping your manifests DRY. While the choice of configuration management tools has minimal impact on the implementation of GitOps, there exists a challenge with having that abstraction.

Argo CD (and other GitOps tools) typically reference these abstractions, which keep your manifests DRY, directly in order to determine the desired state of your system. As a result, any modification made via your configuration management tool (like Kustomize or Helm) gets altered by Argo CD itself, making the actual impact on the manifests deployed across environments ambiguous. Within the realm of Argo CD, the tool mutates the desired state manifests prior to applying them onto the destination cluster during deployment time. This process is depicted in Figure 14-1.

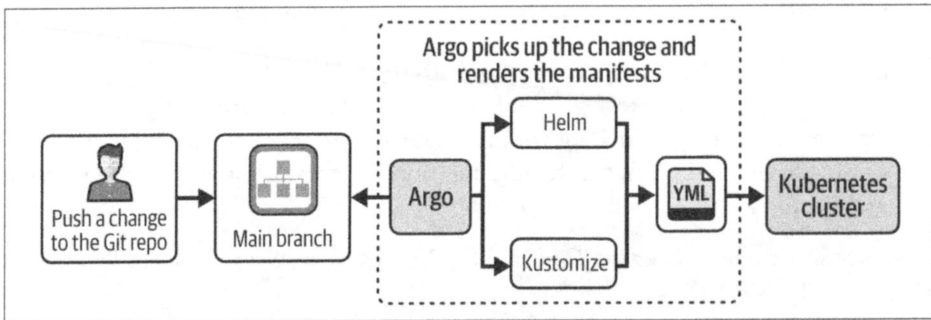


*Figure 14-1. Argo CD rendering at deployment time*

While this is a completely valid approach, some organizations found challenges in having the source of truth being mutated by Argo CD before being applied to the destination cluster. The primary challenge is diffing and knowing the impact of a change before the manifests are deployed onto the destination. Take, for example, modifying a Helm configuration (like an umbrella chart) for Prometheus:

```
$ diff new-Chart.yaml Chart.yaml
8c8
<   version: 58.6.1
---
>   version: 61.9.0
```

Seeing this, you instinctively know that this is a major version change that most likely has large implications. But, seeing this difference (diff), either in the command line or in a pull request, does not show the full extent that this change will cause. In contrast, the full diff illustrates the *major* changes that this one line change can cause. The diff is so large, that we had to create a Gist (*https://oreil.ly/2Y-t4*) to show it all.

Because of this challenge, a pattern arose in the GitOps community called the *rendered manifests pattern* (sometimes called *hydrated manifests*). The most important tenet of the rendered manifest pattern is that the desired state, which in most cases is stored in Git, should contain no ambiguity from what will be applied by Argo CD. It should be thought of similarly to a container image, where it's immutable and applied as is.

These rendered manifests are to be stored into environment-specific branches. As updates are introduced in these branches, the diff in the manifests between commits will be completely transparent. Changes are visible, and they are clear along with effects that will be made on each environment. Figure 14-2 depicts the entire process.

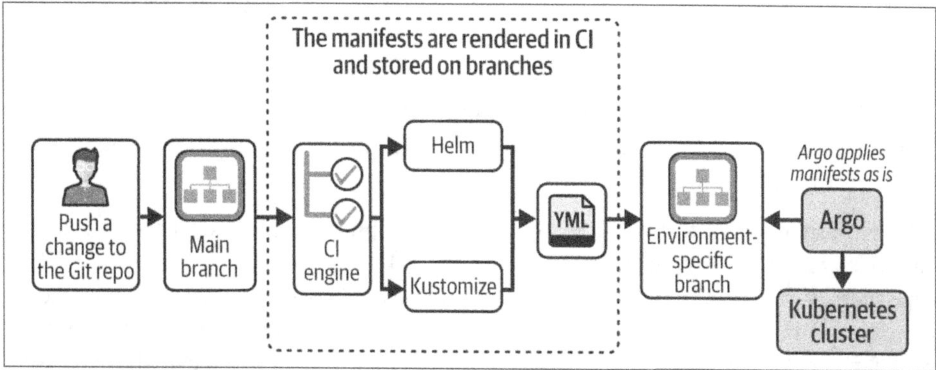


*Figure 14-2. Rendered manifests workflow*

The rendered manifests pattern offers several key advantages, including enhanced visibility into the desired state by eliminating the obfuscation typically introduced by configuration management tools. It also reduces risk by establishing a truly immutable desired state and greatly improves the performance of Argo CD by removing the need for Argo CD to perform the rendering. Additionally, this pattern allows for the setting of deployment and protection policies tailored to specific environments since they will be stored in specific branches. However, there are two notable drawbacks: shifting manifest rendering to the CI engine introduces additional complexity, and this approach is less effective with tools that render plain-text secrets, such as sealed secrets.

There are tools that can help remove the complexity of introducing the rendered manifests pattern into your CI system, and we'll review them later in this chapter. It's worth mentioning that many GitOps practitioners mistake the rendered manifests pattern with GitOps workflows (which will be covered in the next section). It's important to note that the rendered manifests pattern is a method to create a *deployment* bundle in the branch. Branches are used as a vehicle to store the resulting deployment bundle and do not require merging between one another.

## GitOps Workflow Best Practices

Git workflows (also called *Git Flows*) have long been integral to application development and have become the de facto industry standard for both development and deployment processes. With the rise of GitOps and the growing popularity of infrastructure as code, Git now serves not only as the source of truth but also as the primary interface for managing environments. These workflows are well-known in development, and operational teams are increasingly adopting similar practices as well.

Naturally, many organizations are inclined to implement Git Flow, given its long-standing role as the default process. However, there are important distinctions between managing application code and managing a GitOps repository.

### Separation of concerns

One of the key challenges organizations encounter is how to manage the code that powers their application separately from the manifests that deploy them. The solution is quite simple: keep them separate.

While many organizations utilize Git Flow for application development, a growing number of DevOps engineers are adopting trunk-based development for their GitOps repositories. These are two fundamentally different workflows, which can lead to complications. For example, a simple update, like adjusting the replica count of a deployment—where the underlying code remains unchanged—can unnecessarily trigger a rebuild and retesting of a codebase that is already in production. Additionally, the approval process for environment changes differs from that for code changes and should not impede the continuous integration process for developers.

This is a key reason for maintaining separation. Trunk-based development is significantly better aligned with GitOps workflows and repositories. Therefore, it is advisable to adopt trunk-based development for GitOps, irrespective of the development process used for the application itself.

### Merging strategy

When implementing GitOps, it's essential to move away from traditional Git Flow practices, especially for managing environment-specific configurations. While Git Flow is well-suited for application development, its approach favoring long-lived branches and merging changes between branches doesn't align with the needs of a GitOps workflow.

One of the critical shifts organizations must make is to avoid using long-lived branches to manage environments. In a GitOps context, you are handling the promotion of manifests, not source code. Environment-specific configurations—like Secrets and ConfigMaps—are often unique and shouldn't be merged across environments. Using Git Flow for this purpose can lead to significant complications, such as the need to cherry-pick changes, which can become cumbersome and error-prone. Instead, adopting trunk-based development, combined with tools like Kustomize and Helm, allows for a more streamlined and efficient GitOps workflow.

Keeping rendered manifests in mind, it's important to note that this approach enables you to still maintain a single source of truth on the main branch, with environment-specific configurations managed through automated workflows. Although tendered manifests may utilize branches, these are not used for promotion between environments. Instead, they act as release artifacts, generated automatically from the main branch and not directly modified by contributors.

In essence, while the rendered manifests pattern may superficially resemble Git Flow, it fundamentally differs in practice. By embracing trunk-based development and leveraging templating tools, you can simplify your GitOps processes and avoid the pitfalls of traditional Git Flow in an infrastructure context.

# Interacting with the Community

The landscape surrounding GitOps and Argo CD is continually evolving, with new methods and practices emerging regularly. While this book aims to cover the fundamental approaches necessary for implementing these technologies, it cannot predict future developments. Therefore, it is crucial to stay informed about ongoing community activities and actively participate in these groups in order to maximize the effectiveness of your implementation.

## Slack

The Argo Project is part of the larger Cloud Native Computing Foundation (CNCF), and as such, the best place to get involved in the project, ask questions, or share any information is the CNCF Slack workspace. This Slack workspace is open to the general public and is the recommended way to get started with contributions and interactions. You can obtain an invitation by visiting the CNCF website (*https://slack.cncf.io*).

Once you have access to the Slack workspace, the following Argo Project-specific channels are listed on the Argo Project website (*https://oreil.ly/cqR9t*).

While the CNCF projects reside in the CNCF Slack workspace, the Kubernetes community (and any related toolsets) can be found by requesting access at *https://slack.k8s.io*. The channels that are related to Argo CD and GitOps in general are:

- #kustomize
- #helm-users and #helm-dev
- #gitops
- #kind

If you are interested in attending Argo Project meetings where you can engage with engineers and solicit feedback, you can find meeting times and information on how to join by visiting the Argo Project meeting calendar (*https://bit.ly/argoproj-calendar*).

## GitHub

The Argo Project was donated as a suite of cloud native DevOps tools and can therefore be thought of as more of an ecosystem. To that end, the best place on GitHub to become familiar with this ecosystem is the Argo Project GitHub organization (*https://github.com/argoproj*).

The source code repository for Argo CD can be found in the Argo Project organization, and it contains all of the contributions, issues, and requests for enhancements.

The Argo Project CNCF status is officially in a "graduated" state. Graduated projects and tools are considered, by the CNCF, to be stable and are used successfully in production environments. This designation is significant because any of the toolsets in the Argo Project are also considered graduated (currently, these include Argo Workflows, Argo CD, Argo Rollouts, and Argo Events). The ecosystem of the Argo Project goes beyond the four graduated tools; therefore, the Argo Project Labs organization was created and can be found by visiting the associated GitHub organization (*https://github.com/argoproj-labs*).

The Argo Project labs organization is managed by the Argo Project maintainers, and not part of the CNCF Argo umbrella projects. New repositories in this organization need to be sponsored and created by one of the Argo project maintainers. Although not holding any *official* standing in the CNCF, tools in the Argo Project labs organization aren't necessarily "unsupported." The goal of the organization is to have a place to collaborate with the community to quickly run experiments, proof of concepts (POCs), and possibly new features to be later incorporated in one of the Argo Projects.

# Next Steps

Outside of Argo CD and GitOps, there are other considerations to take into account when implementing these tools and practices in your CI/CD and IaC workflows. We've touched on a few throughout this book; still, there are other considerations that are important for the full success of your implementation.

## Progressive Delivery

Progressive delivery refers to the controlled and incremental release of product updates, aimed at minimizing the risks associated with deployments. This approach typically leverages automation and metric analysis to facilitate the programmatic promotion or rollback of updates based on observed performance. While delving into the finer details of progressive delivery is outside the scope of this book, it's important to highlight the solutions available for Argo CD users.

Often viewed as an advancement of continuous delivery, progressive delivery builds upon the velocity achieved in CI/CD by enhancing the deployment process. It achieves this by initially limiting the exposure of the new version to a select group of users. Through continuous observation and analysis, the new version is gradually introduced to a broader audience, with ongoing verification to ensure correct behavior at each stage.

There are two common strategies for implementing progressive delivery, and all variations can be seen as a subset of the two. The first strategy uses blue-green deployments, which involve deploying both the new version in addition to the existing version of an application. This allows tests to be conducted on the new version in a controlled manner. The second strategy involves canary deployments, which introduce the new version of an application to a small subset of users while the majority of users continue to use the existing version. This approach allows for monitoring the new version to collect data. Once validated, the new version is progressively rolled out to the entire user base, replacing the old version.

Argo CD doesn't perform progressive delivery of any kind and relies on the end user to use another tool or process to perform a progressive delivery. This was briefly touched on in Chapter 1, Introduction to Argo CD. The Argo Project has a complementary tool called Argo Rollouts, which focuses on providing a common interface to perform progressive delivery. It can be used as a standalone or integrated directly with Argo CD. Argo Rollouts features methods for declaratively performing progressive delivery, independent of your traffic provider (Istio, NGINX, Traefik, etc.).

While Argo Rollouts is not required to achieve progressive delivery, it is a recommended tool for users looking for a progressive delivery solution that complements Argo CD and that can still be used with existing traffic managers. For more information, visit the Argo Rollouts website (*https://oreil.ly/A_Sz0*).

## GitOps Promotions

Initially, GitOps promotions (performing updates when a new version is introduced) are seemingly inconsequential, but they can provide a lot of value. Most workflows consist of using CI to generate new manifests, writing those changes into a feature branch, and creating a PR to the branch that is being tracked by Argo CD. Eventually, as adoption of GitOps grows and as microservices continue to gain in popularity, there comes an issue with orchestrating independent services with their own GitOps workflow into an application stack release. This leads many to fall back to using CI scripts to try and orchestrate a release on these systems and workflow in order to perform a release using GitOps principles. While going further into the challenges of GitOps promotions is beyond the scope of this book, it's important to know what solutions are available to help you in your GitOps promotion implementation.

The Argo Project labs organization has a tool called the Argo CD Image Updater. The aim is to aid administrators in GitOps promotion by detecting image updates and committing those changes back to a GitOps Git repository automatically. This tool focuses on detecting image updates only and can be seen as a spot feature. More information can be found by visiting Argo CD Image Updater (*https://oreil.ly/qBcCh*).

A more holistic proposal for Argo CD GitOps promotions can be found in the Argo CD repository, which focuses on detecting Git commits as well. You can track the progress of this proposal by visiting its GitHub page (*https://oreil.ly/xq7L4*).

Kargo is an open source project started by the original creators of the Argo Project, who are now at Akuity (*https://akuity.io*), and takes a more holistic approach to GitOps promotions by focusing on tracking updates from various GitOps-related repositories, like Git, Helm, and Image repositories. A user can track one or more related supported repositories and orchestrate related Git commits based on rulesets (which are set by the user). Kargo aims to help, generically, orchestrate and promote applications in a GitOps-friendly way. You can find out more by visiting the Kargo website (*https://kargo.akuity.io*).

Telefonistka is an open source tool developed by Wayfair engineers to enable safe and controlled GitOps promotions across multiple environments. It ensures consistent deployments by securely managing environment promotions through automation. By establishing predefined directory structures, Telefonistka detects changes in your Git repository and automatically creates pull requests to the relevant tracked branches. Once the user approves these changes, synchronization occurs with the GitOps controller of choice, minimizing deployment risks. You can find out more information by visiting the Telefonistka GitHub repository (*https://oreil.ly/d0nd4*).

## Summary

This chapter has explored the deployment, configuration, and management of Argo CD, emphasizing the importance of integrating GitOps best practices to optimize implementation. As GitOps is still evolving, new patterns and practices are continually emerging, necessitating community engagement and exploration of these advancements. Key areas include GitOps directory structures, where organizational design influences repository layout; the DRY principle for avoiding YAML duplication; and parameterization of configurations, with tools like Kustomize and Helm. This chapter also discussed repository management strategies, distinguishing between monorepo and polyrepo approaches, and highlighted the rendered manifests pattern for clearer, immutable deployment states. Additionally, it contrasted GitOps workflows with traditional Git Flow, recommending trunk-based development for GitOps repositories. To stay updated with the latest practices and tools, community involvement through channels like CNCF Slack and GitHub is encouraged. Finally, the chapter touched on progressive delivery strategies and tools for GitOps promotions, such as Argo Rollouts and Kargo, to enhance deployment processes.

And with that, you've made it! There was a lot of information and implementation details that went into writing this book, and the fact that you've made it to the end makes us very grateful. We'd like to thank you for taking the time to read this book, and we are happy that you decided to take us on your journey in implementing GitOps with Argo CD. While we strived to make this book work 80% of the time for most organizations; there is no way to account for every single situation. Therefore, we recommend using this book as a reference guide and less as an end-to-end implementation.

One final note: it's worth reiterating that the Argo and GitOps communities are your best resources to not only gain feedback, find validated patterns, and get advice, but also they are a place where we urge you to share your successes and implementation strategies. You may find that certain patterns work fantastically for you while others do not. Or you may find some solutions/patterns that work well for you that aren't talked about too often. In sharing your journey, you can help those that may be just starting theirs.

With that, we'll leave you with a quote:

> I often compare open source to science. To where science took this whole notion of developing ideas in the open and improving on other peoples' ideas and making it into what science is today and the incredible advances that we have had.
>
> —Linus Torvalds, creator for the Linux Kernel

# Index

## Symbols



## A

## B



## C

## D

## E

## F



## G

## H

## I

## J



## K

## L



## M

## P

## R



## S

## T

## U

## W



## Y

## About the Authors

**Andrew Block** is a distinguished architect at Red Hat who works with organizations throughout the world to design and implement solutions leveraging cloud native and emerging technologies. He specializes in embracing security at every phase of the software development lifecycle and delivering software in a repeatable and consistent manner. Andrew has authored several publications related to the cloud native ecosystem including *Managing Kubernetes Resources Using Helm* and *Kubernetes Secrets Management* in order to share his knowledge with others. He holds several roles in the open source community and is a core maintainer of Helm, a package manager for Kubernetes.

**Christian Hernandez** is a well-rounded technologist with experience in infrastructure engineering, systems administration, enterprise architecture, tech support, advocacy, and product management. Passionate about open source and containerizing the world one application at a time, he is currently a maintainer of the OpenGitOps project, a member of the Argo Project, and the head of community at Akuity. He focuses on GitOps practices, DevOps, Kubernetes, and Containers.

## Colophon

The animal on the cover of *Argo CD: Up and Running* is a starry night octopus (*Callistoctopus luteus*). This animal's skin is reddish-brown and adorned with small white iridescent spots that give the species its evocative common name. It is found in warm tropical and subtropical oceans in the Indo-Pacific region, including near the countries of Indonesia, Australia, and the Philippines.

The starry night octopus has long, slender arms that are often up to three times the length of its body. It is nocturnal and lives near coral reefs or rubble-strewn areas, which provide plenty of crevices in which to hide as well as ample prey. This octopus primarily eats small crustaceans, mollusks, and fish—it is an exceptional hunter with high intelligence, problem-solving skills, and the ability to camouflage itself.

This octopus species is still relatively understudied by scientists, though it is believed to be mostly solitary and have a lifespan of only a few years (which is common for octopi). Despite its striking "star-studded" appearance, it is not often seen by divers or marine biologists due to its nocturnal lifestyle and highly effective camouflage.

Many of the animals on O'Reilly covers are endangered; all of them are important to the world.

The cover illustration is by Karen Montgomery, based on an antique engraving from *Oceanworld*. The cover fonts are Gilroy Semibold and Guardian Sans. The text font is Adobe Minion Pro; the heading font is Adobe Myriad Condensed; and the code font is Dalton Maag's Ubuntu Mono.

O'REILLY®

Learn from experts.
Become one yourself.

60,000+ titles | Live events with experts | Role-based courses
Interactive learning | Certification preparation

**Try the O'Reilly learning platform free for 10 days.**

©2025 O'Reilly Media, Inc. O'Reilly is a registered trademark of O'Reilly Media, Inc. 718900_7x9.1875

www.ingramcontent.com/pod-product-compliance
Lightning Source LLC
Jackson TN
JSHW050305220625
86473JS00002BA/4

* 9 7 8 1 0 9 8 1 4 2 0 0 1 *